THE
MEON HILL
MURDER
1945

THE MEON HILL MURDER 1945

UNSOLVED CRIME IN WITCH COUNTRY

M. J. TROW

PEN & SWORD
TRUE CRIME

First published in Great Britain in 2023 by
Pen & Sword True Crime
An imprint of
Pen & Sword Books Ltd
Yorkshire - Philadelphia

Copyright © M.J. Trow, 2023

ISBN 978 1 39906 660 0

Typeset in INDIA by IMPEC eSolutions
Printed and bound in England by CPI (UK) Ltd.

Pen & Sword Books Ltd. incorporates the Imprints of Pen & Sword
Archaeology, Atlas, Aviation, Battleground, Discovery, Family History, History,
Maritime, Military, Naval, Politics, Railways, Select, Transport, True Crime,
Fiction, Frontline Books, Leo Cooper, Praetorian Press, Seaforth Publishing,
Wharncliffe and White Owl.

For a complete list of Pen & Sword titles please contact

PEN & SWORD BOOKS LIMITED
47 Church Street, Barnsley, South Yorkshire, S70 2AS, England
E-mail: enquiries@pen-and-sword.co.uk
Website: www.pen-and-sword.co.uk

or

PEN AND SWORD BOOKS
1950 Lawrence Rd, Havertown, PA 19083, USA
E-mail: uspen-and-sword@casematepublishers.com
Website: www.penandswordbooks.com

Contents

Acknowledgements

Telling the story of the death of Charles Walton has been a project I had had in mind for years and so when Heather Williams of Pen and Sword gave me the green light I was delighted – so my thanks go to her, first of all.

Thank you to my editor, Gaynor Haliday, for her usual sensitive and thoughtful work on this book.

I spent a day in the National Archives and could not have been made more welcome by the staff, so thanks to them, too numerous to mention. Also to the staff of the Warwick Record Office. Warwickshire Police put me on the right track when I approached them on the case, so my thanks also go to them and their excellent and clear website and especially to Lucie Harris of the Freedom of Information Unit.

Most of the research for this book has taken place online and although my technological skills are of a higher level than most people expect – I have been a self-confessed dinosaur since the first gleam of an idea in Tim Berners-Lee's eye – I still needed help and so for that, I thank my wife, Carol. She has had a hand in all the books I have ever written, from typing to co-authoring but in this book, she has been more than usually invaluable. Not only was she born and brought up in a village not unlike Lower Quinton and only just over 20 miles away, but as a small child she accompanied her grandfather as he hedged and ditched his way around the fields beyond the village. 'Laying' hedges is a dying art and so I was blessed to have someone close at hand to show me how it was done; I think she was as startled as I was to find that she can still do it after more years than it is polite to enumerate here. The icing on the cake was her knowledge of the Warwickshire dialect, allowing me to have an insight into what villagers really meant when they gave their statements. So, as always, thanks to her, but even more so than usual.

M.J. Trow
Vectis and The Land of the Prince Bishops

Introduction

Q: Where Am I?
A: In the Village.

R eaders of a certain age will remember Patrick McGoohan's *The Prisoner*, a dystopian thriller series on television between 1966 and 1968. The premise was that McGoohan was a rogue secret service agent who knew too much. Rather than kill him, the powers that be decided that he should be kept in 'the Village' for ever – hence the series' title. We never found out McGoohan's character's name; he was simply Number Six and his interrogator (a different actor for each episode) was Number Two. Number Six's quest was not only to escape from the Village, but to discover the identity of the mysterious Number One, who had presumably imprisoned him in the first place.

The series was filmed in the Italianate fantasy of Portmeirion in North Wales, the dreamchild of the architect Clough Williams-Ellis, which he began in 1925 and which took fifty years to complete. The village had an eeriness in *The Prisoner* which almost made it a star in its own right. Everything was surreal, from giant chess pieces to penny-farthing bicycles. Nobody was what they seemed. And, of course, there was no escape from the place. Anyone trying to cross the estuary of the River Dwyryd, south-east of Porthmadog, was destined to be brought back (and suffocated) by a huge balloon called Rover!

Long before the series, various luminaries had visited the village and stayed in its hotel. George Bernard Shaw and H.G. Wells enjoyed their time there, as did Noel Coward, who wrote his 'supernatural' comedy *Blithe Spirit* during his stay.

The village that is the focus of this book could not be more different from Williams-Ellis's flight of fantasy, yet any village as old as Lower

Quinton and especially one associated with the supernatural because of the events that happened there in the winter of 1945 has an atmosphere all its own. Many writers on the murder of Charles Walton have dismissed this as hokum, designed to sell books and encourage visits to websites, but that is to misunderstand village life as it used to be. To understand it fully, as with everything else, is to have lived it. My wife was born and brought up in a Warwickshire village just like Lower Quinton and I spent eleven years of my life there. Such villages have lives of their own. And, like Portmeirion, some people in those villages are not what they seem.

As Chief Inspector Robert Fabian of Scotland Yard wrote in 1950, 'The natives of Upper and Lower Quinton and the surrounding district are of a secretive disposition and they do not take easily to strangers.'

The first mention we have of Lower and Upper Quinton (the places are half a mile apart) is in William I's Domesday Book of 1086–7. The Book is actually an incomplete record of the Norman king's new realm for the purposes of taxation. His commissioners travelled the length and breadth of the country, over scattered, unmade roads, across marshes and through forests, asking locals about the place most of them had lived in all their lives. For that reason, quizzed by outsiders they did not trust, in a language they did not understand, many people assumed that this was the Day of Judgement (Doom's Day) as prophesied in the Bible. Intriguingly, a field and ditch in the vicinity of Lower Quinton are still called Doomsday. Both villages were then called Quenintune and they were in the county (the new Norman terminology which replaced the Saxon shire) of Gloucestershire. Not until 1935, when Charles Walton had reached retirement age, would they become part of Warwickshire. According to Robert Atkyns, an eighteenth-century topographer and antiquarian, the origin of the name was 'Quean', a Saxon term for a woman, so Quenintune was the women's manor.[1] Antiquarians were not

---

[1] Robert Atkyns, *The Ancient and Present state of Glostershire*, 1712.

historians in the modern sense, but mere information gatherers; their wild speculations on such things as name derivations are best ignored.

The Quintons in 1086 were in the Celfledeton Hundred in the demesne of the Norman knight Hugh de Grandmesnil. In Upper Quinton, where the body of Charles Walton would be found 859 years later, there were two hides (a land measurement equivalent to 247 acres) which, before the conquest of 1066, used to belong to a Saxon thegn. On the demesne (the land which de Grandmesnil worked personally) there were two ploughs (pulled by oxen in those days), five villans and one bordar (all peasants) with three ploughs. There were four serfs (slaves) and one female serf. Land that had been worth £7 a year was now only worth £4, a sign of a flaky Medieval economy made flakier by the upheaval of the Norman conquest. In Lower Quinton, de Grandmesnil's estates were rented by someone called Roger – this was a time before established surnames. Previously, TRE (*Tempus Regni Edwardi* – in the time of King Edward the Confessor) Baldwin had rented it. There were twelve hides here with three ploughs in demesne, seventeen villans and two bordars, with nine ploughs. There were six serfs and its value had not deteriorated as far – once worth £7, it was now worth £6.

De Grandmesnil held other estates in the area from the king. Under the law, the whole of England belonged to William and he rented out portions of it in exchange for military aid (knight service) and advice. This was the feudal system, reliant not on a cash economy, but land. It would survive, more or less intact, for 500 years.

Like any other Medieval settlement, the Quintons followed a certain pattern. The church of St Swithin was probably eleventh-century but it was seriously altered in the twelfth and fourteenth centuries and by the Victorians, who did their best to install a heating system that did not destroy the integrity of the Medieval building. The great and good of the Quintons were buried inside the church (their alabaster and brass tombs are still there). The size and grandeur of the church gives an indication of the status of the village in the Middle Ages. The south arcade is all that remains of the Norman church, but the nave is in the early English style. The imposing spire, visible for miles around, is fifteenth century. The pulpit survived Victorian renovation and was the one used twice by John Wesley, the Methodist leader, before the Anglican church banned him. In October 1743, Wesley wrote in his journal that he 'preached in Mr Taylor's church to a thin, dull congregation'.

Two of the more spectacular tombs are those of Sir William Clopton and his wife. Oddly, they are separate and in very different style. William's is of stone, showing the knight in the plate armour and jupon of the 1370s. He owned estates all over Warwickshire and was regarded as a kind and charitable lord. His wife, Joanna, has an altar tomb with an incised memorial brass on top. She died in 1430, having taken the vows of a nun in widowhood (a common occurrence). The Latin inscription around her effigy tells us that she was 'generous to hapless children and unstinting to strangers ... For merits as great as these, grant that she may enter thy blessed realms and that the urn of death may not weigh heavily on her ...' The enamel of her heraldry has been replaced and I was delighted to find that (unusually) the church still allows brass-rubbing of the tomb, a guilty secret of my youth!

As with hundreds of other Medieval country churchyards, stand in any of them and you are standing on at least seven layers of bodies, the lesser mortals crushed by the weight of centuries and the need to lay people to rest in consecrated ground. One grave that is not marked is that of Charles Walton; neither is that of his wife. His headstone was removed years ago, either at the request of his family or of the Church of England itself to deter ghouls. Our 'finding' of Walton's grave in the photograph in this book is conjecture. The odd unmarked space lies between other gravestones from the 1940s, so logically, this is where it should have been.[2]

---

2   Intriguingly, there is no gravestone for farmer Alfred Potter, for whom Charles Walton worked, even though he was a sidesman and, like his wife, a regular churchgoer.

Beyond the church, the other great Medieval building was the manor house, although all traces of the Medieval version have now disappeared. An impressive Georgian house stands on the site. By the fourteenth century, when a cash economy was replacing the feudal system, the manor of Lower Quinton belonged to Magdalen College, Oxford. Both English universities, Oxford and Cambridge, owned land all over the country and drew rents from it. Before that, in the reign of Henry III in the thirteenth century, Quinton had been given to a nunnery at Polesworth.

The manor house, at any period in its history, would have employed a relatively large number of locals as in-house staff, groundskeepers and labourers. Others, in what was a very rural area, would have worked the land. Intriguingly, there is the vaguest shadow of some of them from research carried out into Poll Tax returns for the year of the Peasants' Revolt, 1381. Richard Large was an archer from Mune (Meon Hill) who together with his wife Isabella, paid 12d (1 shilling) a year in tax. To put this into context, five years earlier, Edward of Woodstock, the Black Prince who commanded the king's army, paid himself £1 a day. Despite the arrival of twentieth-century technology, Charles Walton was carrying out his hedging work at Upper Quinton on the day he died, just as his forebears had done for centuries. He was even using the same tools as they did; and those became the weapons that killed him. Enclosure of open fields, first for sheep farming under the Tudors, then for arable farming in the eighteenth century as the population grew, created the maze of hedges on which Walton worked.

Charles Walton's father, also Charles, listed in the records, like him, as a labourer, was born in Offchurch, Warwickshire. The village gets no mention in Domesday Book which is probably an oversight because the place is named for Offa, the eighth-century king of Mercia when Saxon England was made up of seven kingdoms. The original church was St Fremund's, named for Offa's son who was himself a murder victim at Long Itchington. The current church – St Gregory's – has a fourteenth-century tower with shot marks reputedly made during the civil war in the 1640s.

Charles senior worked the land until he was too old to carry on and died, aged 79, at Quinton. The murder victim's mother was Emma from nearby Honington and since no occupation is listed for her, we can assume that she was mother, housekeeper and general dogsbody, which was the lot of most women in a village community. She probably kept chickens, perhaps geese and would have joined the whole village, little Charlie included, in getting in the harvest, ''ere the winter storms begin' as the Victorian hymn had it. She died in 1912, aged 65.

Charles Walton junior was born in Upper Quinton in 1870, the year that the Irish Home Rule movement was founded, ultimately leading to the creation of an independent Eire. Dr Thomas Barnardo, appalled by the destitution of London's East End, set up a home for boys at Stepney Causeway. Charles Dickens died, exhausted apparently by fame, and the prime minister, William Gladstone, brought in a Land Act intended to 'pacify Ireland'; it did not work.

When Walton was born, Quinton had a tiny population. Most of the houses were brick versions of their Medieval ancestors' homes – oak timbered, A-framed and thatched, with small windows, no bathrooms and an outside toilet. 'Civilization' did not reach such communities until surprisingly recently. In the year of Walton's birth, William Forster's Elementary Education Act made huge strides in improving schools for all children over 5. That said, 'schooling' was not compulsory until at least 1886, by which time Walton, who would already have been regarded as an adult, was working in the fields. We have no idea how much education the boy actually received. The school in Lower Quinton, now a private house, had painted over its entranceway 'Remember Thy Creator in the Days of Thy Youth'. He left school at the age of 10, which was standard then.

Charles Walton appears as a 10-month-old in the census for 1871. He had three older siblings – Harriet, who was 10; May, 5 and Martha, 3. The existence of these sisters makes nonsense of some of the supernatural legends that have become associated with his murder, as we shall see in a later chapter.

By 1881, Walton is referred to as a 'scholar', which marked his last year at school. Ten years later, now aged 20, he is listed as an agricultural labourer and has two younger brothers, George, 18, and Richard, 15. Harriet appears to have died before 1881 because she is not listed in the census. It is depressing to note that information on Walton's siblings has been redacted in the Warwickshire police archive, despite the fact that all of them must be dead by now.

The next time we hear of Charles Walton is 1897. By now 27, he married Alice Elizabeth Claridge at Offchurch on 30 December. Alice's father was John, also a labourer and she was 21. The marriage certificate lists Walton as a labourer still and Alice as 'spinster', both terms generic and unhelpful in terms of the work they actually did. The fact that the marriage took place in Offchurch means that Charles Walton was resident there – the church requires this in order for anyone planning marriage to be able to have the banns read.

Alice Walton, born in Eathorpe nearby, had been a domestic servant before her marriage, working for the Morrish family in Leamington Priors, on the outskirts of Leamington Spa. This was the lot of many unmarried women before the invention of the typewriter and the telephone in the 1880s opened up more job opportunities.

The link with Quinton came via Joseph Watson, a Leeds soap manufacturer who would become the first Baron Watson in 1922. He owned land in both parishes and this probably explains why the Waltons moved; Charles worked for Watson.

The year of Queen Victoria's Diamond Jubilee fell in 1897, celebrating sixty years of prosperity, power and imperialism. The British Empire was at its zenith, yet to be rocked by two world wars and the Solent was clogged with beflagged warships that kept that Empire together. Foreign dignitaries flocked to London and there were miles of bunting and hundreds of brass bands everywhere. No doubt Offchurch was fluttering with red, white and blue as well. Nottingham and Hull were made cities and the brand-new taxi cabs were in the news in London, the first not to be horse drawn. In September, George Smith was convicted of drink-driving while in charge of a cab and a 9-year-old boy was crushed to death by another one in Hackney; all in all, not a great beginning.

A report compiled by a sergeant in the Warwickshire police with the number 321 (his name, in accordance with the force's policy, has been redacted) was put together in June 1950 by which time the murder was already five years old. From it, emerges the fact that Walton had only one friend, almost certainly George Higgins (the name is redacted in the report) and in his youth had a reputation as both a hard worker and hard drinker. He smoked and chased girls – 'courting' was the phrase in use – but there is no record of his fathering any children 'which was very common in that district in those years'.

In his thirties, Walton went to live with a family elsewhere. All this information has been redacted, but it does set the record straight about the man never having left Quinton. What is interesting in the 1950 report is that it states that Walton married his cousin (also surnamed Walton) in Stratford-upon-Avon in 1913. This is completely at odds with the Offchurch parish records and since the police report gives no sources, I am inclined to believe the Offchurch version. The report makes it clear, however, that married life slowed Walton's lifestyle down a little. He gave up smoking and drank only a limited amount until, as an old man, he usually confined his pub visits to a jaunt on Sundays with his old friend Higgins.

Charles Walton virtually disappears from the record as an adult. He does not, for example, appear in the Census for 1921, by which time he and Alice had been married for nearly a quarter of a century – or eight years, depending on which version you believe – and we can assume they lived in Quinton. A photograph of Walton's cottage in this book was taken in the 1920s. It would be fascinating to know if one of the little girls playing outside was his niece, Edith. She told the police in her statement after her uncle's murder, that he and Alice had moved into the place around 1915. The 1931 Census does not exist – it was destroyed by fire some years later – and in any case would not have been available to us for a decade.

Because the Second World War broke out in September 1939, there was no Census for 1941. Instead, there was a Register taken in 1939, the year the war began. Charles Walton is listed there, although Alice was dead by then.

Because of the accident of his birth date, Walton appears in no military records either. He would have been of military age in the Boer War (1899-1902), which broke out soon after his marriage, but although the army was hugely increased to fight the Boers, it was still done on a voluntary basis. Clearly, Charles Walton saw no reason to obey his country's call, however much flag-waving was involved. By the time conscription was introduced for the first time in British history, in 1916, Walton was 46, five years too old for active service. By the time of the Second World War, of course, he was 69.

Neither, oddly, is there a record of Alice's death. All recent accounts contend that she died in 1927 (the evidence given by Edith at the inquest gives the date as 9 December), by which time she was 51. There is, however, no death certificate in any records that I can find and no marked grave in St Swithin's churchyard.

Is all this simply the bad luck of a researcher, something which constantly plagues people trying to trace their family trees? Or were Mr and Mrs Charles Walton the secretive type (like the rest of Lower Quinton, according to Inspector Fabian), perfectly happy to hide under the radar for whatever reason, avoiding officialdom wherever possible?

When he was still a toddler, Charles Walton had a famous neighbour. He was Joseph Arch, a farm labourer from Barford near Warwick who through determination and self-help became a Methodist preacher and champion of the agricultural worker. The trade union movement was well established by the 1870s but it was an urban organization, geared to mills, factories and mines. Ever since the transportation to Australia of the 'martyrs' of Tolpuddle in Dorset in 1836, rural workers had become the forgotten of the Industrial Revolution. While the rule of the mill-owner was iron-handed enough, that of the squire, be it J.S. Hyatt or Joseph Watson in Quinton, was far more powerful. Men like Walton, without the vote until 1918, had, all their lives, tugged their caps when the squire rode by. Arch went on to become an MP in the 1880s and died in Barford in 1919. Was Charles Walton one of the new breed of men under his influence, with nothing but contempt for the authorities, who represented a 'them and us' mentality which would grow as the twentieth century grew? Is that why he refused to fill in the paperwork? Refused to play the game and follow the rules? That all depends on what kind of man Charles Walton was. The 1950 police report contends that he never quarrelled with anyone but that he called a spade a spade and always spoke his mind. There is an old adage in police circles; if you want to know why a man died, you must first look at how he lived. And in the case of Charles Walton, that is easier said than done.

If that dead man lived in a town, it might be hard to pick him out from his thousands of fellow townsfolk, but when you do, the chances are that you will be able to find out almost everything about him. It may be as simple as buying a round in a pub, or visiting his place of work. In a village, despite the fact that the field is a fraction of the size, then it is unlikely that any stranger, no matter how talented they might be at winkling out information, will be able to find out anything at all. There were 493 villagers in Lower and Upper Quinton in February 1945 and none of them could tell the police a thing.

Because villages look after their own. The boundaries might not be very clearly drawn on any map, but in the minds of the villagers inside those boundaries, they are cast in stone. One example will perhaps clarify what it was – and to an extent, still is – like to live in a village. In a village not far from Lower Quinton, a little bigger, but not by much, a child was born in the year that Charles Walton died. His mother was married, but the baby's father was an African American from the nearby army base – the Americans had joined the war in 1941 and the GIs had been welcomed with literally open arms by many women across the country. In those days, when the Windrush generation was still far in the future, black faces were rare and so the baby was very much a novelty in the village; though of course, eyebrows were raised.

The baby's grandmother – his 'paternal' grandmother, on paper at least – had an answer for any villager who asked why the baby was so dark. 'That's easy,' she would say. 'It's because his father is working down the pit.' Behind her back, this would cause much hilarity, except when an outsider – in a specific case, the district nurse – was crass enough to say that this reasoning was nonsense. If that happened, the village closed ranks and were all agreed that, yes, this was clearly the reason and they had seen the same on many occasions, for generations, in fact. Although decades have passed and grandmother, mother, both fathers and indeed child are long dead, if anyone from outside the village were to broach this subject with a villager of long-standing, the answer would still be the same.

And *that's* what it's like to question a villager, if you haven't yourself lived there since practically Domesday.

One of the best descriptions of rural village life before the age of the car and TripAdvisor, is Laurie Lee's *Cider With Rosie*, originally published in 1959 and dealing with the author's childhood in Slad, Gloucestershire, 37 miles from Lower Quinton. In a chapter called 'Public Death, Private Murder'. Lee relates the story of an event that:

> drew [the village] together in a web of silence and cut us off for a while almost entirely from the outside world … Though it was seldom discussed – and never with strangers – the facts of that night were familiar to us all and common consent buried the thing deep down and raked out the tracks around it.

A man who had left the village years ago suddenly returned and bought drinks at the village pub. He had emigrated to New Zealand and made a fortune. That night, as the ale was downed and the fire glowed, he crowed about his wealth and his success. One by one, his audience left him to go home. But they did not go home. They waited at a lonely crossroads and beat him to death when he emerged from the pub. 'The police came, of course, but discovered nothing,' Lee remembered. 'Their enquiries were met with stares ... The police left at last with the case unsolved; but neither we nor they forgot it.'

Various researchers have tried to find this case, in local and national papers and in the records of the Gloucestershire constabulary. It does not exist. But I do not believe that Laurie Lee made it up entirely. One version of events is that his mother told him this story in 1945. Perhaps it was something she had read in a local paper, an event that had actually happened in another village, not very far away, a village that, in fact, until recently, used to be in Gloucestershire. It was called Lower Quinton. And there was no triumphal return of a prodigal son from overseas; no hidden resentment by locals who despised the victim's wealth. But the village's silence was real enough. The victim's name was Charles Walton.

But Laurie Lee had not quite finished. Ten years after the fictional Slad murder, he writes that an old lady, nearing her end, started rambling about a watch. 'The watch,' she kept mumbling, 'they maun find the watch. Tell the boy to get it hid.' A detective turned up to ask her about it, but 'she just leaned back on the pillow, closed her lips and eyes, folded her hands and died ... No other leads appeared after that and the case was never solved.'

The curious thing about this is that Charles Walton's watch was the only thing *known* to be missing from his body when it was found. And when the watch was discovered, it assumed a significance out of all proportion.

But it was not found until 1960, the year *after* the publication of *Cider With Rosie* ...

Chapter 1

Caveat Lector!
(Reader, beware!)

The statement was taken by DS E.W. Jenkins of the Warwickshire Constabulary on 5 March 1945. Three weeks earlier, 74-year-old hedger Charles Walton, from the village of Lower Quinton, had been found beaten and hacked to death in Hillground, a field near the village.

Jenkins was one of a number of detectives taking statements from the people who were in the area that day, St Valentine's Day and Ash Wednesday, as it was that year. Using the still archaic terminology of police enquiries and law courts, Jenkins wrote down what Mildred Lilian Nicholls 'saith':

I am the wife of Gerald Arthur Nicholls and we have lived at the above address [Valender's Cottage, Upper Quinton] since November 1942. On Wednesday, 14th February, 1945, Miss Gough and myself were washing all morning and during the afternoon my mother, sister Mrs Thomas, Miss Gough and myself went to Stratford-on-Avon. We went by car at about 2.10 p.m. We came back about 6 p.m.

I didn't go out again all evening.

Apart from Miss Gough and Miss Walton, who called during the morning, I did not see anyone about that day. Miss Walton lives at Lower Quinton. She called about a wireless set which my husband was repairing for Ray Vallender [sic] and she later bought it. It was about twelve o'clock when Miss Walton came.

While I was in Stratford during the afternoon, about 4 p.m., I was in either the Chain Library or Lacey's in Wood Street, I saw Mr Goode, who is courting Mr Walton's niece. He did not see me.

Mr Goode also called at our house at about 9 p.m. He said 'I hear you have bad news about Edie.' He then corrected himself and said 'I mean Edie's Uncle.' I did not know what he was talking about and I told him that my husband was at Lower Quinton and had taken a wireless set to Miss Walton's. Edgar Goode then went away.

I later heard that Mr Walton had been found dead in a field.

Both Mildred and DS Jenkins signed this statement in accordance with police procedure.

On the face of it, Mildred Nicholls' statement tells us nothing about the grisly murder that took place a quarter of a mile from her house. From medical evidence already known to the police, Charles Walton had been attacked and killed between one and two in the afternoon. The timing of this and the vicious nature of the attack effectively ruled Mildred out as a possible suspect. She was in other people's company during the hour in question and Charles Walton was probably already dead by the time she and the others left for Stratford.

Even so, there are a number of oddities about this statement. The Miss Gough referred to was 33-year-old Feronia Gough, a spinster who worked as a cleaner at a number of local houses. Her statement was made on the same day as Mildred's and was taken by another officer. As we shall see, Feronia's cottage was the nearest to the murder scene. Edith Walton had indeed called at lunchtime with enquiries about the radio and she did indeed buy it for £7.

The ladies' return from Stratford 'about 6 p.m.' coincided with the time that Edith Walton became worried about the fact that her uncle had not yet returned from his hedging work. In the winter, he usually knocked off at 4 p.m. It is what happened later that is peculiar. She had seen Edith's fiancé, Edgar Goode, in Stratford 'at about 4 p.m.'. The town is 8 miles away from Lower Quinton and if Charles Walton was dead by 2 p.m., that would have been ample time for Goode to have got to Stratford, either by car or bus. Why did he call at Mildred Nicholls' house at 9 p.m. and why did he believe it was *Mildred* who had bad news about Edie? In any case, the *really* bad news was about her uncle, as Goode corrected himself. Most bizarrely of all, Goode does not appear to have explained what he was talking about and the implication from Mildred's statement is that she only learned of Charlie Walton's death later.

DS Jenkins does not seem to have asked for clarification of any of this. And, in one apparently simple statement, we have an example of a major problem in handling cold cases years after the event. Virtually everybody living in the area in February 1945 is now dead; certainly, the key players are. All we have to go on is the evidence collected at the time and that is where the difficulties begin. A number of senior policemen in the case refer to the 'demeanour' of witnesses. This corresponds with the legendary intuition which detectives are supposed to possess. The problem is that it is not evidence, we do not know exactly what is meant by it, and nothing of the kind would be acceptable in a court of law.

For me, the starting point in any enquiry of this sort is the various books written on the case over the years. I begin with the most recent and work back, noting where ideas and phrases come from. Today, it is relatively easy to detect plagiarism in blogs and articles by checking against other online content. Older books are more difficult to check, of course, unless they have been digitized – rare in the case of books on a relatively unimportant case. Even so, trends often emerge and when something crops up time and again, it is not that difficult to track them to their source – some authors do still give sources, though this is becoming rarer online.

Today's publishing world has gone quietly mad. Anyone with a computer can 'publish' a book and the reading public has no idea of the credentials of the author. Celebrities whose faces are known from television inveigle actual publishers to produce their efforts and they usually sell purely on the well-known face; the actual writing is often woeful. To save money, many publishers these days do not even employ editors, so typos abound and facts remain unchecked. In the world of true crime, where evidence is vital, this leads to all sorts of errors: sources are not always given so original material cannot be found.

The first full book on the murder of Charles Walton was Donald McCormick's *Murder by Witchcraft* (1968). In that, the author discusses two Midlands murders – Walton's in 1945 and that of an unknown woman whose remains were found in Hagley Wood, Worcestershire, in the year before the Lower Quinton killing. The *first* book on any case is usually the most important because it forms a starting block for all those that follow. McCormick's is so bad that I have included a whole chapter on it later in this book. He muddies the waters in both cases, while claiming that they have nothing in common and produces a wealth of improbable speculation based on spurious and unacknowledged sources.

To find out what *really* happened to Charles Walton, we have to go back before McCormick to investigate the sources he might have used. Unfortunately, as we shall see, the media of the 1950s became hopelessly infatuated with the idea of a supernatural element to the murder, aided and abetted by 'academics' who should have known better. Witchcraft and stories of 'things that go bump in the night' sold newspapers and journalists, then as now, are quite prepared to put spin on their stories to boost sales. Even with today's technology, finding contemporary newspaper articles is surprisingly difficult. For years, the British Newspaper Archive was at Colindale in London; that has now moved. Such copies online are a work in progress; they have not all been digitized. The *Police Gazette*, for example, which was a communication tool between various police forces, is only available online up to 1918; to all intents and purposes, 1945 does not exist.

Newspapers, however, can only take us so far. Contemporary copy, the first stories to hit the headlines, were hampered by the reporting restrictions of the time. The war, although coming to an end, still had weeks to run and all journalese was strictly censored. Today, Charles Walton's murder would be front-page headline news, with television crews swarming all over Lower Quinton, hovering as close as they could to the blue and white crime scene tape. In 1945, the best that local papers could manage was a single column on page four. On the day that Walton was killed, an estimated 150,000 died in the RAF/USAAF bombing of Dresden; a single Warwickshire hedger easily disappeared in all that.

And that takes us back to the *original* coverage of the case, by the Warwickshire Constabulary and the Metropolitan team from Scotland Yard called in to join them. Throughout the war, police forces up and down the country were stretched to breaking point. A whole raft of legislation, covering everything from blackout regulations to Fifth Columnists, ended up on the desks of chief constables. And everybody, the detectives in their informal uniforms of trilby and trench-coat, the boys (and the handful of girls) in blue who walked their beats, had to be alert and ready for anything at all times.

'Calling in the Yard' was standard procedure in those days, because the Met, with its vast records and forensic expertise, had the edge over provincial forces more used to handling crimes of trespass and petty theft, with perhaps a little Black Market activity on the side. When a man met his death in mysterious circumstances, everyone in the area at the time became a suspect. Children could be ruled out; no one in the Quintons under 10 seems to have been interviewed. Such was the ferocity of the murder that women were unlikely to be responsible either, but the police could not rule that out entirely so local women were interviewed too.

The bizarre thing about Charles Walton's murder is that it took place in the open in broad daylight shortly after midday. In keeping with the majority of such crimes, no one saw a thing. Or at least, no one came forward to admit that they had. There may have been unprecedented restrictions on peoples' lives during the war: defeatism was a crime; travelling too far was frowned upon; gasmasks and identity papers had to be carried at all times. That said, reading the statements of locals like Mildred Nicholls, we are struck by how freely – and often – people moved. Mildred and her friends went shopping in Stratford on St Valentine's Day 1945. Edgar Goode, who worked for the Water Board in the same town, was wandering about the place at 4 p.m. There were an unknown number of Italian prisoners of war walking around the Quintons that day, too, even though they were technically held in a prison camp and, until very recently, had been the enemy in a world war. Then, there was the parochialism of the village bobby. The performance of PC Michael Lomasney from Long Marston, the first copper at the murder scene, was, as we shall see, lamentable, but men like him had a difficult tightrope to walk. He was on first name terms with local men, any one of whom could have hacked old Charlie Walton to death.

At each stage of their enquiries, it was the job of investigating officers to write up reports and take statements. There were 493 inhabitants of the Quintons in 1945. Allowing for a percentage of children, there ought to be over 400 locals' statements in the file at the National Archive (formerly the Public Record Office); in fact, there are fifty-eight! It does not help that Detective Chief Inspector Robert Fabian, leading Scotland Yard's enquiries, claims in the first of three books on his career – *Fabian of the Yard* in 1950 – that over 4,000 statements were taken and enquiries made as far afield as Salisbury. There is no mention of that town in the police files as they stand today.

Still more disappointingly, crime scene photographs have vanished. Seven of these were taken at the time, by police photographer Arthur Nicholls, three of the body in situ at the corner of Hillground, two of the ground itself minus the body and two of the corpse in the Stratford Hospital Mortuary. Only two of these have survived, one simply a flattened area of grass which has no evidential value whatsoever.

The tools which became weapons in the murder of Charles Walton – the billhook and the pitchfork – were certainly in the possession of Warwickshire Constabulary in the mid-1990s (a senior officer was filmed holding them for a local newspaper article), but there is no mention of these weapons in the reply given to me by the Freedom of Information Unit.

Whoever was responsible for collating the original material on the Meon Hill murder has done a woeful job. And this is by no means unique. I carried out research some months ago at the Worcester Hub while writing a companion volume to this book – *The Hagley Wood Murder* (Pen & Sword 2023) – and found that the police files there were even thinner than on the Walton case. There are multiple photocopies of items that have only tangential relevance and crucial pieces of information, such as the coroner's inquest on the woman's body found stuffed into a hollow wych elm, are not there at all. In that context, the inquest into the death of Charles Walton, for which I had to pay a not insubstantial amount, is actually just a series of photocopied statements from the National Archive. I had expected a verbatim transcript of the proceedings, as in actual murder trials; it is nothing of the sort.

How much help, outside the remit of the police investigation, is other archival evidence? There was a time when the inhabitants of the Quintons would have been born, lived and died in the village and their details would have been written down longhand by the vicar or his curate and kept in ledgers in the church vestry. These have now been routinely removed for 'safe-keeping' and partially digitized online. This actually means that they are almost impossible to find. Various websites, cashing in on the public's fascination with family trees, provide this information but it is scanty and at best unhelpful, at worst just wrong. Census records have been kept since 1801, but the most recent information is not available. The National Archive is currently widely advertising the release of the 1921 census, the most recent available since the law of the land (as always outdated and often ludicrous) decrees that this information cannot be published in the context of anyone still alive. There was no census in 1941 because of the peculiarities of wartime, with people in the armed forces, for example, scattered all over the world. There was a Register taken in 1939, the year war broke out and I have been able to find the relevant information for the Quintons. However, that was last updated in 1991 so of the 440 names listed, seventy-five have been redacted – 'This record is officially closed' – because in 1991 those seventy-five were still alive. Now, however, thirty years on, they probably are not, but their names still remain a closed book, unless a researcher can prove they are dead, in itself a gargantuan task.

One local, commenting on the Meon Hill murder to a local newspaper reporter in 2018, said it was time the case was closed and forgotten. I cannot agree less. Justice was not served in the case of Charles Walton. The police at the time failed to do their job; worse they (or an archivist somewhere in the past) failed to record all the evidence they had uncovered. That leaves a mountain of ignorance for us to climb – me, as writer; you, as reader.

Even so, let me see how far we can get.

Chapter 2

Valentine's Day

There is only one photograph of Charles Walton alive. We do not know when, where or precisely why it was taken, but it shows a man in his forties or fifties with a rough thatch of forward-combed hair, deep set eyes squinting into the sun and a huge walrus moustache. He is wearing a jacket and waistcoat over a collarless shirt, the sort of clothes he wore every day for most of his adult life, and behind him, appropriately enough, considering his job and where he died, there appears to be a hedge.

All his adult life, Charlie Walton had been grappling with hedges and on 14 February 1945 he would be doing it again, splicing the boughs, bending twigs, cleaning debris with a skill now almost lost to the world. It was a way of life he had inherited from his father and grandfather in that world where nothing changed, come what may. Men like Charlie Walton were the salt of the earth; they were the fabric of villages like Lower Quinton and thousands of others all over the country. And St Valentine's Day that year would be just like all the others, too.

Walton had been awake for over an hour before he got up and got dressed. The thatched cottage which he shared with his niece Edith – the middle one of three, standing opposite St Swithin's Church – had no upstairs bathroom and the old man almost certainly washed in an outhouse next to the kitchen. Over his woollen long combinations, he put two shirts, one of them short sleeved, then his tweed trousers and blue overalls and his flannel body belt. Despite the fact that February that year was exceptionally mild, Charlie Walton was 74 – he felt the cold these days and needed the warmth. He pulled his heather-mixture cardigan on and sat down in the kitchen where Edith was busy with his breakfast.

The woman was 33 and had lived with old Charlie for the past thirty years. Though technically his niece, she had been adopted by Walton and his wife Alice when she was 3, so doubled up in her role as daughter and housekeeper. Edith's mother had died and her father – Charles's brother – seemed incapable of bringing up the little girl on his own. At the time of Charles's death, he was still living in Stratford. Edith, Charles and Alice had lived at 15 Lower Quinton, the thatched seventeenth-century house, since the First World War. She worked as a printer's assembler in the eighteenth-century Palladian building called Quinton House (today a care home along the main road through the village), which was then temporary home to the Royal Society of the Arts, moved to the village from London to escape the Blitz. Did she get a Valentine card from her fiancé, Edgar Goode, that morning? We do not know. They would marry two years later.

As part of the morning ritual, Walton ate his two rounds of toast and drank his coffee. Not much of a rules man was Charlie Walton. He never carried any personal papers, even though war regulations insisted he carry an Identity Card at all times. He had long ago abandoned, if he ever carried it at all, that other vital wartime adjunct to every adult's and child's life, his gas mask. How he felt about rationing and coupons we do not know, but nothing must be allowed to come between him and his coffee and toast.

Walton would be gone all day until darkness fell, unless the weather took a turn for the worse and drove him indoors. Edith wrapped a piece of fruit cake in a blue sugar bag and the old man was good to go.

He left home about 8.30 a.m., according to Edith – although, as we shall see, recollections vary about this – using two sticks to help him walk. One of these he had bought. The other shorter one he had fashioned himself from a hedgerow. He was, as usual, carrying no money and had no tools; these – his pitchfork and his billhook – were stashed under the hedge where he had left them the day before.

This was a field called Hillground on the slopes of Meon Hill, an Iron Age fort site that brooded over the adjacent settlements of Upper and Lower Quinton. To get there, he had to cross the road and pass through the churchyard of St Swithin, the village church whose bells had been silent for the past five years. We have no idea whether Walton was a churchgoer. He had not married in this church, though he would be buried in its churchyard. He would have seen the building every day of his life and heard its bells, six of them dating back to the 1620s, ringing throughout the years. The fact that there is no marked grave for Alice, implies no links with the church. Beyond the graves and the church gate, he was out in the open, making for Hillground where a hedge lay half-finished in the weak February sun. One account from an eyewitness says that he was carrying a knapsack, which may have contained a pair of hedging gloves and perhaps his 'file', a whetstone for sharpening the billhook's blade.

A recent writer on the case, Paul Newman,[3] contends that Walton's rheumatism meant that he was bent and crippled, which is Edith's testimony, but no one as infirm as that could spend all day in the fields, where, by necessity, he had to kneel and move with a certain agility.

Two older Lower Quinton residents, Miss Charlotte Byway, 73 and Joseph Walters, 83, saw Walton pass through the churchyard, although, intriguingly, their times differ by half an hour. There is nothing sinister in this; one of them simply got the time wrong – these things happen. Charlotte had been a children's nurse, working for Mrs Smith at the Manor House in Lower Quinton. She told Sergeant 165A Hinksman of the Warwickshire Constabulary days later that Walton 'had a sack over his shoulder but it didn't look to have anything in it'. This one little piece of evidence I believe to be crucial to the events that followed that day.

The nearest house to Hillground was a cottage – number 30, Upper Quinton – owned by 33-year-old Feronia Gough, who had a temporary,

---

3   *Under the Shadow of Meon Hill*, Abraxas & DGR Books 2009.

billeted wartime lodger, 59-year-old Walter Weaver. As we shall see in the next chapter, the pressures of wartime meant that billeting occurred everywhere in the 1940s. Refugees, essential war-workers, even troops, found themselves in somebody's spare room, joining families for meals and doing the washing up. It made the job of any police force, investigating a murder, for example, all the more difficult.

It is difficult to pinpoint individual buildings today. Only the church spire, 127 feet high, would have been clearly visible from the murder scene. Any view from the village of the actual site would have been screened by the hedge itself. Weaver worked as a printer for the RSA in the same establishment as Edith Walton. Feronia cleaned and cooked for a number of local people and on the 14th was at Mrs Nicholls' house, Valender's Cottage in Upper Quinton. She washed clothes there until 12.15 p.m., then went home, collecting pig meat from her aunt, Mrs Roland Simmonds, on the way. She was back at her cottage by 12.30. Weaver went home on his bike for lunch at 1.08 p.m. with his landlady and they both left at 2 p.m., Feronia going back to Mrs Simmonds' house. Neither of them saw Charles Walton all day.

Across the fields from Hillground was a caravan belonging to Flight Lieutenant Thomas Woodward and his wife Maud. The aerial photographs taken in February 1945 under instructions from the police do not identify this clearly. Unless it was a considerable distance away, it, too, would have been concealed by the hedge. The Woodwards lived there with their baby and the flight lieutenant saw Walton while waiting outside the caravan for a lift to Long Marston airfield, 2 miles away, where he was based. According to his statement to the police, Woodward saw Walton pass the caravan at 8.15 a.m., yet Edith says that he had not left home by then. It is a small but telling example of how bad humans are as eyewitnesses; it did little to help the police with their enquiries. The flight lieutenant was sure of the time, he told police, because he was waiting for a lift to his base at Long Marston airfield which was due at 8.30 a.m. Mrs Woodward saw no one at all, presumably having her hands full with the baby.

George Purnell was more observant. Like Walton, a labourer who worked for Alfred Potter at the Firs Farm to the east of the village, he was out on Meon Hill that morning and about eleven o'clock saw a civilian in the company of an army officer, distinguishable by his khaki battledress. As things turned out, the civilian was actually Sergeant George Mills of the Royal Warwickshire Regiment wearing denim overalls. The officer was Lieutenant Alan Edwards of the 22nd Infantry Training Centre and with him were not one, but two other soldiers, although Purnell did not mention them. Sergeant George Mills and Lance Corporal George Hobbis had been removing booby traps set the day before because Meon Hill was a training ground for troops on manoeuvres – 'schemes' as they were called in the 1940s. All the soldiers left the area soon after 11 a.m. and were out of the district completely by 2 p.m., heading back to Budbrooke barracks near Warwick.

Corporal Hobbis saw another man, riding a tractor and ploughing a field on Meon Hill. This was Basil Hall, according to later police enquiries, the son of famer Richard Hall and he was at work all day between ten in the morning and six at night. Young Hall saw no one in that time except a man standing about 350 yards from him by a hedge and looking out over the village and its church. The man was there for about half an hour and this was at three o'clock. Unfortunately, Hall did not clarify which hedge he was referring to and later police reports doubted the lad's accuracy anyway; he may have been thinking of the wrong day.

The eagle-eyed Hobbis saw two more men in the fields. The first was in the late morning and he was probably in his sixties. He was 5ft 4in tall with a flat cap and walking stick, the typical labourer's dress of the time. He was walking along a hedge in the direction of Meon Hill. This turned out to be John Field, 64, employed to tend the cows of farmer Frank Stanley, who had land on Meon Hill.

The only other person known to be in the vicinity that day (working in a barn 300 yards away) was 72-year-old George Higgins, perhaps Charlie Walton's only friend in the world. He lived at Fair View, Lower

Quinton and worked for Allan Valender, farmer and baker. He had started work at half past eight that morning. He had lunch that day in Valender's bakehouse and worked on until four o'clock. During the course of the police enquiries that followed, it transpired that he and Walton had had a falling out at Christmas time and had barely spoken since. Before that, they often worked hedges together and since their schooldays had operated as a two-man hedging team.

By six o'clock, Edith Walton was back home from her day at Quinton House. There was no sign of her uncle who usually knocked off outside work at four. By this time the sun was setting and the typical deep twilight of February was giving way to complete darkness. Although she was aware that Charlie knew those fields like the back of his hand, he had no torch with him and she became concerned. The usual routine was that Edith would leave the old man's tea plated up and he would eat it as soon as he got home, before she arrived. On 14 February, it was untouched.

Wartime Lower Quinton was black as pitch and Edith did not feel comfortable traipsing the fields alone, so she called on her next-door neighbours, Harry Beasley and his wife. Beasley had known Walton for years – they were, in fact, distant relatives – and had lived next door to him for twenty-three of them. He had not seen Charlie since the previous day but the couple were happy to help Edith in her search, no doubt trying to allay her fears. She only knew the vague area where her uncle had been working so the logical thing was to talk to Alfred Potter, Walton's employer. On the way to The Firs, they spoke to Flight Lieutenant Woodward, who had got back to his caravan by 5.30. No, he had not seen the old man since the morning. Again, we have a time discrepancy. Paul Newman, quoting Edith's police statement, says it was 'around 7 p.m.'[4] when the pair reached The Firs; author

---

[4] Paul Newman *Under the Shadow of Meon Hill* p. 14.

Simon Read claims it was 6.15 p.m.[5] Such inconsistencies are probably unimportant, but they cannot both be right and in a case like this, accuracy is everything. The Firs, now gentrified and available for bed and breakfast in 'Shakespeare's Land', so beloved of Japanese and American tourists, stood to the east of the village, about a quarter of a mile from Walton's workplace that day.

Potter told them he had last seen Walton at lunchtime and he brought his torch to join the search. He knew of course the stretch of hedge that the old man had been working on and strode off with Beasley while Edith struggled to keep up. Various commentators years later expressed surprise that Potter knew precisely where Walton had been working, but this is hardly a mystery and certainly not sinister. He was Walton's boss; he had arranged the whole work schedule that day. In perfect conditions, which rarely prevail, a young, fit hedge-layer can manage around 60 feet per day. Hedge-laying is a lost art today. It took time and was designed to last. The hedge on which Walton was working and others circling Hillground, still bear the signs of his work after seventy-five years, albeit with later maintenance work also visible. Nowadays, farmers and councils alike merely mangle an overgrown hedge with machinery, to save time and money. Even if Walton could manage 60 feet – and it is likely he would be achieving about half that – he would be easy to find as he would not have moved far since midday.

As the little search party trailed the hedge on Hillground, moving west in open country, they were joined by labourer Harry Peachey, coming from the opposite direction and on the far side of the hedge; no doubt he was intrigued by their probing flashlights, although Harry Beasley later told police he had no idea why Peachey was there at that time. Intriguingly, the police do not seem to have followed this point up. The work that Walton had already carried out would have left spaces at the base of the hedge where the torch light could be seen.

---

[5] Simon Reed *The Case That Foiled Fabian.*

They found Charles Walton lying close to the hedge he had been working on. He was on his left side, his left arm pinned under his body with hand raised. In the eerie, probing beams of their torches, Potter and Beasley could see that the old man's throat had been cut with his billhook still embedded in the wound and his head was pinned to the ground by his pitchfork, its prongs thrust through his lower jaw. There was blood everywhere and the old man's trousers were undone …

Edith screamed …

Chapter 3

There Was a War On

During Charles Walton's last night on earth, 773 Lancasters of the RAF's Bomber Command obliterated the German city of Dresden. On the day that he died, the 8th US Airforce followed up the attack. Six square miles of the Medieval city centre were left smoking ruins. The number of dead was estimated at anything between 30,000 and 200,000, victims of the terrifying fire storm that engulfed buildings and streets in minutes. Eighteen months later, 21,000 bodies had been recovered from the shattered debris, with many more waiting to be found.

Dresden had a population of about 400,000 but in February 1945 there were an additional 600,000 refugees in the city, running from the Russian Red Army advancing from the east. The Church of Our Lady had gone; the opera house was burned out; the royal palace devastated. After the war, people began to question the morality of this. The city was known for its educational institutes, its art and porcelain. Like all German cities, it had gone over to war production, but not in a major way. It is only recently that Bomber Command, with its 55,000 wartime deaths, were given their own memorial. People who had never fought a war pontificated against 'Bomber' Harris, the Air Marshal in charge, who in turn was abandoned even by the prime minister, Winston Churchill. Everybody, it seemed, blamed Harris for a disproportionate use of force.

But we should see this in context. What the combined air forces of Britain and the United States did to Dresden in 1945 had already been done to Britain by the Luftwaffe, in the skies over London, Hull, Plymouth and, above all, Coventry.

On the night of 14 November 1940, had Charles Walton looked north-east out of his home in Lower Quinton (as he probably did), he would have seen the sky glowing red with the fires of Coventry, 25 miles away. The Heinkels and Dorniers that droned over the city that night were using the new Knickbein system which allowed raiding aircraft to co-ordinate beams of light to hit targets in the dark. At that stage of the war, only London had experienced the Blitz;[6] now it was Coventry's turn. The city of the three spires was an important centre of arms production, especially aircraft and it paid the price. The elegant, graceful fifteenth-century cathedral of St Michael was left a smouldering shell. The Guildhall, with its Medieval glass and fine tapestries was gutted. Four hundred and nineteen German bombers dropped 503 tons of bombs, 881 incendiaries and 64 fire bombs. Five hundred and fifty-four were killed, a further 865 were seriously wounded. Two thousand two hundred and ninety-four buildings were destroyed with a further 45,704 damaged. All railway lines were cut, as were six out of seven telephone lines. With most buses bombed out of existence, the city's transport system had virtually ceased to exist.

Between four and five hundred shops were out of action the next day and rationing, already a central part of everybody's lives, was suspended. Over 100,000 loaves of bread were brought in by whatever transport was available to the stricken city. Drinking water had to be boiled. In the streets, WVS soup kitchens provided food. The three Mass Observation Unit correspondents who reached Coventry on 15 November reported the thick smell of smoke 5 miles out from the city centre and witnessed the extraordinary behaviour of locals who were suffering the same shell-shock as those in Guernica in Spain nearly four years earlier when Germany's Condor Legion had unleashed the first ever blitzkrieg raid on civilians. Women in particular were screaming,

---

[6] From the word '*blitzkrieg*' (lightning war) used by the military theorist Karl von Clausewitz to describe the tactics and astonishing success of Napoleon Bonaparte.

crying, shaking, hitting the people of the emergency services who were trying to help them.

German propaganda invented a new phrase – *coventrieism*, to Coventrate, to destroy a city totally. And everywhere the day after the raid, with glass like crystals in the street, jam and butter running in the gutters and with a night-like fog at midday, the Mass Observation people heard the same thing – 'Coventry is dead. Coventry is finished.'

Of course, it was not. It was simply one of the most appalling nights in the people's war, a war of which Charles Walton never saw the end. But by the time he died, he had lived through nearly five years of it.

The first criminal casualties of the war occurred, ironically, in Coventry and no doubt Charles Walton and many other people in Lower Quinton read about them with horror in the papers. On Friday, 25 August, nine days before war was actually declared, a bomb went off in Broadgate in the city centre. It had been left in the basket of a bicycle parked on the kerb outside Astley and Sons, paint merchants and at 2.32 p.m. precisely, the package blew up, shattering the windows of twenty-five shops nearby and leaving the shopping centre looking like a battlefield. There were five dead and seventy injured; for Coventry, a grim foretaste of the future. But this had nothing to do, at least directly, with the Nazis; this was the work of the IRA, bent on causing murder and mayhem to add to Britain's fears.

When the German chancellor, Adolf Hitler, refused to withdraw his troops from Poland which they entered illegally on 1 September, the British prime minister, Neville Chamberlain, declared war and broadcast it to a worried nation – 'I have to tell you now that no such undertaking [troop withdrawal] has been received and that consequently this country is at war with Germany.'

Evacuation of children from the major cities was instant, thousands of bewildered youngsters armed with suitcases and sandwiches, packed on to buses and trains and shipped out to safety in the country. The bombing of Guernica had convinced everybody that 'the bomber will always get through' and that total urban destruction was on the cards. Hundreds of thousands of cardboard coffins were rushed into production. And then … nothing.

The 'phoney war', known in France as the *drôle de guerre* (funny war) and in Germany as *Sitzkrieg* (the armchair war) was a surreal lull before the storm. That was because the Germans were busy in the east where the Wehrmacht, to create Hitler's *lebensraum* (living space) had teamed up with Stalin's Red Army to obliterate Poland. When the Third Reich's war effort swung west in the spring of 1940, the results were devastating. No one was prepared for the speed and accuracy of blitzkrieg, as Heinz Guderian's panzer divisions crashed their way past the 'invincible' Maginot line of French defences. One by one, and in a matter of weeks, the Western nations fell to Hitler – the Netherlands, Belgium, Luxembourg, France. Only Britain held on, because Britain had 21 miles of sea defended by the Royal Navy – the most formidable in the world – and that had proved an impossible obstacle for many an invader.

The difference now was aircraft and the Battle of Britain, in the summer of 1940, was fought in the skies over the south of the country, Churchill's 'few' exhausting themselves and their materiel in keeping the Wehrmacht out. Winston Churchill had replaced Chamberlain in May 1940 as the British Expeditionary force limped back from Dunkirk. Such was the desperation of the time – and the ebullient mood of the nation – that Churchill's bulldog rhetoric turned what was actually a shambolic defeat into something like a victory.

When the Luftwaffe lost more planes than the RAF, the Reich changed tactics and what everybody assumed would happen from the first day of the war now became a nightmarish reality. In September 1940, the Luftwaffe turned its attention from the airfields of Fighter Command to the towns and cities. The front was now the high street, the battle-zone the market square and very few people got off scot-free.

There was, for four years, an atmosphere of barely suppressed hysteria. Everyone was convinced that there was a 'Fifth Column' operating inside the country. Several of Hitler's Fascist ideas struck a chord with Britons of all classes and backgrounds. The East End was not overfond of the Jewish community living in its midst, even though it had been there for at least sixty years. Money men and the aristocracy had a terror of the Bolshevik threat posed by the USSR; Hitler was seen as a bulwark against that.[7] There were nationalist elements in Scotland and Wales and much more strongly in Ireland that might be harnessed by the Reich to rebel, or at least sow discord, against the British war effort, as the Broadgate bombing in Coventry proved.

So began an unprecedented propaganda campaign, posters warning about casual conversations that could be overheard by spies and reported back to Wilhelmstrasse in Berlin. Mr Knowall, Miss Leaky Mouth, Mr Pride in Prophecy, Miss Teacup Whisperer and Mr Glumpot were all stereotypes dreamed up by Alfred Duff Cooper's Ministry of Information. Such stereotypes were all too real, the deadly cancer in the British body politic. As A.P. Herbert, that incomparable, if maverick, commentator of life in the 1940s, wrote: 'Bold is the citizen who makes a public utterance in the present war. If we say "It is a fine day," we are "complacent"; if we say "it is raining", we are "defeatist"; and if we say "it looks like rain" we are "Fifth Columnists".' Churchill's government was missing the point (even though the prime minister wanted Herbert in his cabinet) – in making gossip and a bad mood crimes, it was actually turning Britain into Nazi Germany. It was the beginning of an attack on the freedom of speech which has never quite gone away.

And with the propaganda came a raft of legislation to make sure that the economy could survive and that people, by and large, behaved themselves. Nobody was much concerned by the curtailing of freedom under Regulation 18B by which potential traitors, Fascists and far Right supporters were rounded up. There was not much of an outcry either

---

[7] The alliance between Germany and Russia in the secret Ribbentrop-Molotov Pact was only ever a temporary arrangement to give Hitler time to launch his attack on Russia, Operation Barbarossa, in June 1941.

when foreigners, particularly Germans, Austrians and later, when they joined the Reich, Italians, were rounded up. Ice cream parlours vanished overnight, but that went largely unnoticed because most seaside towns were no-go areas anyway, with barbed wire, gun emplacements and searchlight batteries all over the place.

What really hit hard was rationing. Country folk like Charles Walton did not feel the full impact of this, with regular access to milk, eggs and poultry. In the towns and cities, however, coupons could only buy so much. From December 1939 butter and bacon were rationed; from April 1940, meat. Powdered egg, snoek (tinned fish) and sickly whale meat were not really substitutes and most people hated them. Radio chefs, a new breed of broadcaster, advocated spaghetti, gnocchi and noodles. Everybody had a wireless set and relied on it for news, but few people had ever heard of food like this and it was not readily available. Most people pulled in their belts, made do and mended and went hungry, especially mothers.

In June 1940, clothing coupons were introduced. Out went the huge 'Oxford bags' popular with men-about-town in the 1930s and everything was 'utility' – frills disappeared from knickers, turn-ups from trousers, pleats from skirts. Bright young things went bare-legged because there were no nylons and they got their friends to draw up the backs of their legs with eyeliner to create faux seams and an air of normality. Queues were everywhere, from people waiting for fresh water after an air raid to desperate housewives asking harassed shopkeepers – 'AUC?' (Anything Under the Counter?).

Everybody, even babies, had to have a gas mask and to carry it in public at all times. It was an appalling waste of money and time; no gas was used in the Second World War. Armies of petty officials, from cabinet ministers to air-raid wardens, strutted about in tin hats (which actually gave very little protection from anything), barking orders and blowing whistles – 'Put that light out!' Small wonder they became known as 'Little Hitlers'.

The BBC, in the days before it became a political behemoth, provided entertainment and vital news. In fact, it was spewing out propaganda but rather more subtly than Josef Goebbels' Ministry of Information in Berlin. On the worst night of the Blitz, 10 May 1941, when London was left in tatters, the BBC claimed that twenty-eight enemy planes had been shot down; the actual figure was seven. Everybody made allowances for this – morale was an important factor in winning a war, especially when the front line was made up of civilians without the training or usual stoicism of the armed forces. The Home Service's Alvar Liddell and other newsreaders were as famous as Winston Churchill, perhaps more so, because they spoke to the nation every day. Children could enjoy Uncle Mac – 'Hello, children, everywhere' – and the adults laughed uproariously at Tommy Handley's *ITMA* (*It's That Man Again*) with its catchphrases that became legend – 'Can I do you now, sir?' 'It is my duty', said Handley at the Ministry of Aggravation and Mysteries in December 1939, 'on the umpteenth day of the war … to explain to you that I have 700 further restrictions to impose upon you … some of the most irritating regulations you have ever heard.' Henry Hall's big band sound soothed the adult population as did the oily singing voice of Hutch. Vera Lynn towered over all other radio performers as the forces' sweetheart, looking forward to a time when bluebirds flew over the white cliffs of Dover rather than the Spitfires and Hurricanes that were actually there – ironically, the lyrics were written by an American and the Americans were not part of the war – yet.

In January 1940, 2 million brown envelopes hit doormats all over the country and men between the ages of 19 and 41 were called up. At 69, Charles Walton was far too old for that and anyway, farming, like mining, was a reserved occupation, so there was no chance of the old man being directly involved in any action.

The average British family was living on less than £5 a week. Rent was 10s 6d, clothes 9s 6d, fuel and light 6s 5d, food £1 14s 1d. Charles Walton got £3 a week from farmer Potter as well as his 5s pension, but his income must have been enhanced by whatever Edith earned at the Royal Society of Arts down the road.

In the middle of all this – *because* of all this – war-weariness became a problem. Molly Lefebure, the 22-year-old secretary to Home Office pathologist Keith Simpson wrote of it:

> It was a real illness ... and as the war went on, almost everybody fell victim to it. Some it made drink a lot. Others took to bed – with others – a lot. Some became hideously gay [happy] brave and hearty. Others became sardonic and bored. Some seriously depressed ... A few took to prayer.[8]

And then, the Americans arrived. The satirical magazine *Punch* summed it up:

> Dear old England's not the same,
> The dread invasion, well, it came.
> But no, it's not the beastly Hun,
> The god-damn Yankee army's come.

Churchill had done his best to draw America into the war earlier, but President Franklin D. Roosevelt was assailed by a powerful pro-German lobby and an even larger one of American moms who did not want to see their boys slaughtered in a war that had nothing to do with them. That all changed on 7 December 1941 – 'a day that will live in infamy' as Roosevelt said, when Japan attacked the American naval base at Pearl Harbor in Honolulu, Hawaii. Since Japan threw in its lot with Germany, that meant that the huge resources of the United States were now not only at Britain's disposal, but on their way to Britain like an army of occupation.

---

[8]   Molly Lefebure *War on the Home Front* p. 103.

The bottom line of American involvement was that it was vital for the war effort, but there were teething troubles along the way. The average GI earned three times the pay of his 'Tommy' counterpart; his uniform was smarter, his style at once more attractive and direct. Thousands of impressionable young girls brought up on heart-throbs like Clark Gable learned the jitterbug, for which dance floors had to be reinforced, inveigled candy, gum and nylons out of the 'overpaid, oversexed and over here' Allies and generally caused a lot of trouble wherever the Americans were based. Inevitably, London was the biggest magnet for servicemen and camp followers alike and the Americans policed themselves with their white-helmeted 'snowdrops', the Military Police. Over 1,100 cities, towns and even villages became temporary homes to this invasion force, occupying 100,000 buildings including schools, country houses, aircraft hangars and Nissen huts.

There were racial issues too. The 'coloured' community in Britain was very small and isolated before the war, but the American forces had black units still officered by white men, and the memories of the Civil War were still relatively fresh. 'What do you call a Negro with a Purple Heart?' one joke ran. 'A fiction.' Britain was outside all this, but trouble spilled out into city centres from time to time as in the 'Battle' of Bamber Bridge in Lancashire. The whole American army was banned from Manchester for two weeks in 1945.

As D-Day dawned on 6 June 1944, at least the end of the beginning was in sight. A number of books written recently have given the impression that by the time Charles Walton died, the war was virtually over and everybody was planning street parties to celebrate its end and to stage the brave new world that would follow. That is seriously jumping the gun, if only because a second Blitz had replaced the first.

A week after D-Day, with the Allies having a tentative foothold in 'fortress Europe', the first V1 rockets fell on London. They were called 'pilotless planes' and 'flying bombs' and were potentially more deadly than anything seen before if only because no German airmen were involved to be shot down. The rockets could be shot down, either from the ground or by aircraft, but that could cause as much damage as if they had hit the ground unexploded. Their noise was sinister – a 'grating growl' which became a 'most menacing roar', then silence just before they dropped. The people called them doodlebugs or buzz bombs and they rained down during the day when the population was trying to work. 'It was as impersonal as the plague,' wrote Evelyn Waugh in his book *Unconditional Surrender*; 142 V1s fell on Croydon, with over 1,000 homes destroyed and 5,700 more damaged. By the middle of July 1944, anti-aircraft guns massed on the coast were bringing down over half of them over the sea, but no one knew how many more Hitler had in his arsenal.

How was Charles Walton's Warwickshire affected by all this? We have seen already the appalling casualty rate and psychological damage done to Coventry, and Birmingham, although not hit as badly, was the country's second largest city and, like Coventry, a major industrial contributor to the war effort. Lower Quinton, like every other village in the country, would have had more than its share of government leaflets – 'What to do if the Invader Comes'. Road signs disappeared, so that should what many saw as inevitable actually did occur, the Wehrmacht's progress would at least be slowed down. St Swithin's bells were silent, only to be used in the event of an invasion. Huge silver barrage balloons floated over cities and towns. Sandbags lined key buildings, like Leamington Spa police station under the railway arches in the town. Leamington became one of a handful of centres that housed the Civil Defence Camouflage Establishments, based in the Regent Hotel and the Roller-Skating Rink in Dormer Place. Camouflaged tanks were on display in the art gallery and the girls' school next door – so much for wartime secrecy! Everybody stuck tape over their windows to reduce the impact of flying glass in the event of an air raid. The area police, men like Constable Michael Lomasney from Long Marston, were on constant alert, to the extent that the man drove a car on duty; most bobbies patrolled by bike or on foot. Royal mail pillar boxes, bright scarlet in peacetime, were now painted green with anti-gas paint designed to combat mustard gas, used widely in the First World War. Villages like Lower Quinton had their Home Guard units, men from the area formed as Local Defence Volunteers, generally older men or those unfit for active duty. Sixty-five was a guideline but there was no upper age limit, so even Charles Walton *could* have volunteered. The Register of 1939 lists eight ARP (Air-Raid Precaution) wardens for the village.

Boy Scouts in the area were marshalled to act as aircraft spotters, ready to do their bit in whatever capacity their troop leaders saw fit. Concrete pill boxes and gun emplacements appeared in corners of farmers' fields. Farmers braced themselves for their tractors and horses being commandeered for war service.

Some people dug their own air-raid shelters at the bottom of their gardens and watched the night skies anxiously between 1939 and 1942 to check the enemy aircraft roaring overhead. The larger Victorian houses had cellars that would serve the same purpose, but cottages like Walton's did not possess them and survival against the Blitz was largely down to luck.

Petrol was rationed so travelling by car was limited. Very few people owned cars in the 1940s (certainly, Charles Walton did not) and the 'little Hitlers' swarming everywhere would continually ask drivers 'Is your journey really necessary?' Trains had blacked-out windows for night journeys and could only manage 15mph in places because of bomb damage. Unbeknownst to most people, there was another war going on at the time – between the railway services and the government.

Women in Warwickshire formed knitting circles, making socks, cardigans, jumpers and balaclavas for men serving who knew where around the world. By 1945, there were over 12,000 members of the Women's Voluntary Service across the country, with a clothing centre for refugees which opened in April 1941. In December 1942, Stratford ladies were darning or knitting 250 pairs of socks a week. By 1944, most recipients of this work were European refugees whose lives were now being managed by the American Red Cross.

Locals remembered the sense of tension in Stratford during the war years. There was little direct bomb damage, despite hits on some housing in a Stratford suburb but Coventry was *very* nearby and outbreaks of diphtheria, typhoid and scarlet fever did little to calm anxious mothers and their children, many of whom were having to cope without their menfolk.

Intriguingly, the Midlands in what was 'fortress Britain' by 1940 became home to large numbers of outsiders. Apart from evacuees from blitzed Coventry and Birmingham, Canadian troops were stationed in Stratford. As a working and loyal part of the empire, the Canadian government under Governor-General Mackenzie King put the armed forces on a war footing. The first of them arrived in December 1939 and were dispersed all over the country. Disaster befell over 5,000 of them on 19 August 1941 when the 'reconnaissance in force' raid on Dieppe went badly wrong. It was a lesson on how *not* to invade Europe. In Stratford, their usual watering hole was the Red Horse and many of them, along with the Americans when they arrived, got their quota of culture at the Shakespeare Memorial Theatre.

The building was brand new at the start of the war; the older theatre was gutted in a fire in 1926. Everybody expected it to close for the duration, but, like the famous Windmill vaudeville theatre in London, it never actually closed but continued performances. In the month after Charles Walton died, the Memorial Theatre was busy as ever. It put on: *Henry VIII*; *Much Ado About Nothing*; *Hamlet;* and *Twelfth Night*. The Shakespeare Company had always doubled up its actors to save money, but conscription in wartime meant that men on stage were in short supply. Andrew Faulds, who would go on to become MP for Stratford long after the war, played four roles in *Henry VIII* and Howard Worrell-Thompson as stage manager, had walk on parts as well. In papers released long after the war, it was revealed that Stratford was classified in secret papers and the theatre, in the autumn of 1940, was to become the new home of the Houses of Parliament, the bombing risk to the original being so high. Both Houses could be accommodated as well as offices for various officials like the Speaker. Local hotels would become the permanent/temporary homes for MPs and peers. In the event, cool nerve prevailed and the government stayed put in the capital, albeit sandbagged and gun-emplaced.

One institution that *did* make a move, however, was the Royal Society for the Encouragement of Arts, Manufacturers and Commerce (RSA) founded in 1754 and receiving its royal status in 1908. It was originally housed in John Adam Street and was a sitting duck for Luftwaffe bomb-aimers just west of the Thames as it curved at Westminster. In 1945, the RSA's president was E.F. Armstrong. The only building large enough in the Lower Quinton area was Quinton House and two people involved in the story of Charles Walton's death worked there; one was his niece, Edith.

Only a few fields away from Lower Quinton was Long Marston, home of No. 1 Royal Engineers Supply Depot with its handy railway line and its own airfield. Towards the end of the war, this huge site housed both Italian and German prisoners of war.

Look again at the people out and about in Lower Quinton that day in February 1945 when somebody killed Charles Walton. Apart from the villagers, there was at least one airman, a scattering of soldiers and a surprising number of Italian prisoners of war. There was also, although he was never identified, one killer. The quiet, almost Medieval village which had barely changed with the centuries was transformed by the bizarre conditions of war. In every way, it was an unlikely setting for a murder.

Chapter 4

'The Work of a Maniac'

O n 14 February 1945, as the beams of torches flashed on Hillground below Meon Hill, the first task was to get the hysterical Edith Walton away from what was clearly a crime scene. In one of those bizarre conversations that often take place in moments of shock, Beasley told Edith 'My God, he's gone.' Edith asked 'What's he done?' Beasley told her, in a classic piece of understatement and false information, 'He's cut himself.' The next task was to call the police.

We have become used to instant communication. Today, Alfred Potter or Harry Beasley would have ferreted out their mobile phones and the response would have been immediate. As it was, in the early spring of the last year of the war, life was rather slower. Potter, as a local landowner and Walton's employer, naturally took charge and told Harry Peachey to run to Valender's farm, the nearest to the murder site and to call the police. Even the famous emergency call sign of 999 was only nine years old and nobody, not the operator nor the desk sergeant, expected news of a killing in Upper Quinton.

As Harry Beasley led a sobbing Edith back towards the churchyard, they met two women coming towards them. One was Lilian Potter, Alfred's wife, coming from The Firs, and the other a Miss Savory who was either lodging with the Potters or a neighbour. Aware that the search party had gone out minutes earlier, they had decided to join in.

Allan Valender was as shocked as everyone would be by the news. In his statement to the police, made five days later, the baker/farmer explained that Peachey had been concerned about 'something wrong with a girl. I think it's Edie Walton'. Valender had been sitting in his living room at about 6.45 p.m. when Peachey knocked on his window. '"Phone the police immediately. Mr Potter asked me to come down to you." I realized that Mr Potter would not have sent Mr Peachey … unless it was something urgent.' Earlier that day, during her lunch break from the Society of Arts, Edith had gone to see him to buy a radio he had for sale. They had agreed a price of £7. Valender rang the police and reached the local bobby, PC173 Michael Lomasney at nearby Long Marston. The call was logged at 6.50 p.m.

Lomasney's statement, not taken until 1 March, filled in the details. 'This is Ray Valender, Jim,' the farmer had said. 'I have been told by Harry Peachey that there is a girl at the foot of Meon Hill and that there is something seriously wrong with her. I've been asked by Alf Potter to send for the police.'

'All right, Ray, I'll come at once.'

'You'd better come to me at my place and I'll come along with you.'

Either Lomasney had astonishing powers of recall or he essentially made up this conversation. There was no mechanism in a local police station in 1945 to record such messages and the conversation had taken place two weeks earlier. That said, the call illustrates the point that local bobbies were at once a blessing and a curse. The first name terms imply that these men knew each other – 'Ray' when the full name was Allan Raymond; and that Lomasney would know who Harry Peachey was. This was a useful situation in that local knowledge could go a long way. It was a problem, however, when the bobby might have to arrest a friend, someone he was possibly at school with. It was a matter of walking a tightrope – and Michael James Lomasney was not very good at it.

Valender's message was garbled. He had not seen Walton's body and extraordinarily, Peachey does not seem to have mentioned it; perhaps he had not seen it either. Lomasney got to Valender's farm at 7.05 p.m. and, with Peachey leading the way, went back to the hedge, the fourth and fifth set of footprints (other than Walton's and his killer's) to contaminate the crime scene. They found Potter, having climbed over a boundary fence (no longer there). The farmer was standing about 25 feet from the corner of the field, near an RAF cable pole. Still believing that the point of his visit was the screaming female, Lomasney asked, 'Where is she, Alf?' Potter said, 'Look over there in the corner.'

Even allowing for the fact that it was dark and everybody was shocked and working by torchlight, Lomasney's lack of professionalism was astonishing. He assumed that the dead man was an airman, probably because of the blue overalls, even though the rest of his clothes were clearly those of a civilian.

'It's an airman,' the constable said, obviously struggling with the lack of light. He flashed his torch and realized that he was looking at a dead civilian. He asked Potter who it was.

'It's old Charlie Walton. He had been working for me at trimming the hedge.'

Valender saw 'the body of Mr Walton lying alongside the hedge in the corner of the field. I saw a hay fork sticking in his face and a slashing hook stuck in the throat. The head was covered in blood.'

Lomasney's second impression, having got the man's profession wrong, was to assume that he was looking at a suicide. 'I looked in the man's pockets to see if there was a note. I did not find one.' In doing so, of course, Lomasney must have moved the body from its original position. In all, Walton had at least five pockets in his clothing. If Lomasney searched them all, he would have had to have turned the body on to its back, even if he then tried to put it back as he found it. At no point in his statement did he say he was wearing gloves. Because this statement was made so late in the enquiry, elements crept in which could have had no significance at the time. Lomasney found the watch chain in the bottom right-hand waistcoat pocket, but no watch. By 1 March, this watch had assumed an importance out of all proportion to its value and even existence. He found a blue sugar bag containing a few crumbs in the left-hand jacket pocket. 'In my search it is quite likely that I put my hand in the back pocket of the man's trousers.

I am positive that I had no blood on my hands.' He was careful to add that the photographs subsequently taken were of the body 'exactly as I found it' but this cannot have been the case.

Lomasney then checked the weapons still embedded in the body – '... the blade of a hedging hook and the tine of a two-tine fork were inserted into the man's neck and throat. I felt the handle of the fork near its extreme end and found that it was firmly fixed in the hedge.' Rifling pockets was one thing; handling a murder weapon was in an altogether different league. 'It was then obvious to me that there had been foul play [!]' He told Valender to call police headquarters at Stratford and to send someone in authority. Valender called the superintendent at Stratford and waited at home for the cavalry to arrive.

That left Lomasney and Potter alone with the body. The policeman asked the farmer when he had last seen Walton alive.

'About ten minutes or a quarter past twelve when I came to feed the cattle and sheep down there.' He was pointing towards his farmhouse. Lomasney flashed his torch over the murder scene. About 3½ yards from the body, he saw Walton's walking stick.

'I picked it up and found blood and hairs adhering to the handle end.' He showed it to Potter. 'Look at this blood and hair.'

Potter's comment was, 'It is, as well.'

Not content to handle one murder weapon, Lomasney now handled another. Harry Peachey was still present, but hovering in the background. Potter was shivering and complaining of being cold.

Looking back [by 1 March, Alfred Potter was a person of interest] I think Potter appeared more worried than one would have expected of him. I have known him for over five years and he is not a demonstrative sort of fellow. He is used to seeing animals slaughtered and is accustomed to the sight of blood. He said, 'It's a devil, this happening on my land. What will the public say? You know what they are round Quinton.'

We will analyse Alfred Potter's reaction in Chapter 7. With hindsight, dark rumblings of the Devil and the attitudes of the locals took on an altogether more sinister aspect which I very much doubt Potter intended.

Stratford-upon-Avon is 8 miles south-west of Quinton, already famous as the birthplace of Shakespeare and in peacetime the focus of considerable tourism. Relatively safe from direct bombing (although some Luftwaffe crews jettisoned their bombs there on their way back from raids on Coventry), the town was crowded with refugees from Birmingham and Coventry itself, adding considerably to the 12,000 inhabitants. Most families had lodgers, either the homeless or forces staff drafted in from all over. RAF officers had taken over the Falcon and the Red Horse, two of the town's largest hotels.

Peter Sumerton was a child in Stratford during the war. He remembered skating on the Avon in the unusually cold winters of the 1940s and the American Military Policemen who were billeted with his family. His father, a veteran of the First World War, was a sergeant in the Home Guard and the Sumertons' air-raid shelter was their cellar. The Americans liked the town's Black Swan pub so much that they renamed it affectionately the Dirty Duck and did not complain over much about the warm beer! By February 1945, of course, most of them had gone with their units via the Normandy beaches like 'bloody Omaha'.

The police officers who arrived at Valender's Farm, Lower Quinton that St Valentine's night were Inspector Chester and Sergeant Bailey, probably driving a black Railton, the ubiquitous vehicle of the wartime CID. By the time they got to the murder scene, to which Valender had taken them, Harry Beasley had come back along with his brother Frederick and another villager, Mr Nicholls. His Christian name does not appear in the police files, but the 1939 Register lists two men by that name – Joseph and George – living in Friday Street behind Charles Walton's cottage. Looking at the men's ages, I believe that this was George, clearly Joseph's son, who was in his thirties. Lomasney contended that Beasley and Nicholls had turned up at 7.45 p.m. along with a local farmer, Joseph Stanley.

> Potter said, 'I'm famished. I'll be getting home.' He then left. It struck me at the time as being odd that Potter should leave without waiting for the Stratford police to arrive. His complaint of feeling cold ['famished' in the area means cold as well as hungry] I considered a strange excuse from one who was used to attending to animals at all hours and in all kinds of weather, especially as the murdered man was his own employee and had been murdered on his own land.

In the very next paragraph, Lomasney gives the lie to his previous testimony in that Chester and Bailey had already arrived before Potter left, as had the forensic team involved. Stanley and Nicholls left with Potter, no doubt believing that the experts were all there and that they, at least at the moment, were superfluous.

Nicholls and Bailey had brought a hurdle to take the body away, perhaps a five-barred gate dragooned into use. Tot up the crowd at this point – Potter, Harry and Frederick Beasley, Peachey, Lomasney, Chester, Bailey and Nicholls; sixteen feet trampling evidence to oblivion in the chill of a Warwickshire night, all of it contrary to police procedure at a crime scene.

The first medical man on the scene, other than the ambulance men who arrived later, was Dr A.R. McWhinney, driven there by PC Benton. The doctor had a practice in Stratford at 7 Rother Street. He was effectively the police surgeon, the go-to doctor in all cases of violence which needed a medical input. His preliminary report was important because it was made with the body in situ. We do not know whether he realized that Lomasney had already disturbed the corpse but it meant that the photographs taken later were not reliable or accurate in what they showed.

Charles Walton lay on his left side a yard from the hedge he had been working on. His knees were bent and his left arm was under the body. His cap had fallen off, almost certainly because of the blows to his head and it lay close to the body. There was a deep gash to the right side of the neck and the cut ends of the 'main vessel' and trachea could be clearly seen among the blood by the probing beams of McWhinney's torch. The curved blade of Walton's billhook was still embedded in the wound, the tip at least 4 inches into the tissue. It was this that led the media and various later commentators to imply that there had been an attempt to decapitate him. Walton's head was turned to his left, towards the hedge and the handle of the billhook lay across his face, parallel to 'the long axis of the body'. The subsequent photograph does not show this; the billhook's shaft is approximately 30 degrees to the body axis.

The dead man had been impaled with the pitchfork, one prong on each side of his face. On the right, the point of the tine's entrance was just below the angle of the jaw; it was lower on the left. The fork's handle had been deliberately pressed back, tangled in the hedge, making it difficult later to remove it.

More police arrived. The Warwickshire Police Archive has a flurry of activity going on in the form of telephone calls. Someone called Stratford Police HQ, effectively giving a precis of what was then known. A civilian had called (this was Ray Valender) and the body had not officially been identified. He may have been dead seven or eight hours (McWhinney's initial observation) 'cutting tool stuck in his neck, also the prong of a fork in his body. Not known how the instruments [*sic* – this should read wounds] were made. PC [redacted] guarding the scene [this was Lomasney]'. Detective Superintendent Alec Spooner, the force's most high-profile detective, based in Stratford, was informed and told to report to the murder scene with PC Arthur Nicholls, who photographed the body. 'This,' said a message sent to the chief constable at 8.15 p.m., 'is a most brutal murder.'

Alec William Spooner was not a local man. Born in Amington, near Tamworth, he was the son of a hospital labourer and had been a miner before joining the police in Solihull prior to transfer to Sutton Coldfield. He became head of Warwickshire CID in May 1939 and various books have him based in Leamington Spa, Warwick and Stratford. This most dogged of detectives would continue to visit Lower Quinton long after any new information came to light on the murder.

Crime scene photographs are vital because they freeze the moment in time that cannot be reconstructed later. Famously, of the five murders attributed to the Whitechapel murderer in 1888, only one, that of Mary Kelly, was photographed on the bed on which she died in her grubby little room at 13 Miller's Court, Dorset Street. In all other cases, the Ripper's victims were photographed in the mortuary, at least two of them with their bodies covered in blankets to preserve their modesty. With all due respect to the sensitivity of the Victorians, preserving modesty does not catch killers. Nicholls took three photographs of the body in situ, which he showed to the coroner's jury days later. Those that have survived show the body viewed from behind. The other two were taken in daylight the next day once the body had been removed.

In one of the three photographs available to the public (the others are of the hedge without the body), Charles Walton's hair still appears dark, although whether this is blood is difficult to tell. His jacket and waistcoat were unbuttoned and his braces were undone at the front and torn at the back. His belt lay across his thighs and his trousers were undone and his flies open. It is clear from Nicholls' photograph that the weapons were still in place at the time. The long handle of the pitchfork was clearly home-made, almost certainly by Walton himself and can be seen to the left of the picture, alongside the billhook.

At 11.30 on what was proving a long and difficult night, Professor James Webster, the Home Office pathologist, arrived from his base at the West Midlands science laboratory of Birmingham University. A car from Solihull had collected him and taken him to Stratford police station where Inspector Chester met him. The first half of the century, and the war years in particular, produced a crop of extraordinary pathologists, many of whom became household names. The doyen of these was

Bernard Spilsbury, a native of nearby Leamington Spa, who had made his name in the Crippen case of 1910. The 'mild-mannered dentist' (actually a pharmacist) was hanged for the murder of his wife, Belle Elmore, almost entirely on Spilsbury's say so. In the 1930s, pathologists Glaiser and Brash made headlines by identifying the butchered remains of Mrs Ruxton and her maid, who had been killed by the Parsee doctor, Buck Ruxton. Traipsing over murder scenes from squalid bedsits to leafy glades, Keith Simpson and his indefatigable secretary, Molly Lefebure, cracked difficult cases that led to the hanging of the Canadian soldier August Sangret and the creepy fire-watcher Harry Dobkin, both of whom killed the women they claimed to adore.

James Webster was the equal of these colleagues, but he was far more modest. Whereas Simpson – as well as his colleagues Francis Camps and Donald Teare – went into print with exciting accounts of their cases, Webster did not. He dominated the murder scene in the Midlands in the 1940s and on that Warwickshire night was still wrestling with the identity of a murdered woman found stuffed into a wych elm in Hagley Wood in Worcestershire two years earlier. She would never be identified.[9] The first thing that Webster saw, apart from the body, was a considerable amount of blood on the ground. There was no possibility that Walton had been killed elsewhere and his corpse dragged to this spot. Webster removed both the pitchfork and the billhook with considerable difficulty and noted that the fork's tines had been rammed into Walton's face for three-quarters of their length. That would have taken considerable strength and an astonishing ferocity. Because the fingers and small joints were showing signs of the advent of rigor mortis, the pathologist estimated that Walton had been dead no more than ten hours. He took the body's temperature 'per rectum' and recorded it as 88 degrees. In fact, when he first arrived, he thought he could detect some warmth to the skin.

---

[9] But see my *Hagley Wood Murder* published by Pen and Sword 2023 and Chapter 10 in this book.

It was technically the next day, the early hours of Thursday, 15 February, when the pathologist ordered the makeshift ambulancemen to take the body to the mortuary at the General Hospital in Alcester Road, Stratford. According to Lomasney, the body was placed on a stretcher and lifted over the fence at 1.30 a.m. It was then placed on a handcart (presumably Nicholls') and transferred to the ambulance permanently stationed at The Firs as a wartime precaution. The guard at the murder site stayed put, with Lomasney, who had been there since mid-evening, until 3 a.m. He was relieved by War Reserve Constable 245 Harris and two hours later, PC 12 John West took over. The War Reserve had been set up in May 1938 as a precautionary measure as tension built in Europe. It took men over 30, at first in the Metropolitan districts and then in the provinces. By 1945, this back-up force was virtually interchangeable with the police proper.

West's statement was not made until 13 April, nearly two months after the murder. All was quiet in Hillground until about 7.40 a.m. and it had been daylight for twenty minutes. A man came walking along the hedge and West told him not to come any closer. There was no routine use of 'crime scene' tape in the 1940s, hence the need to maintain a police presence. The pair exchanged pleasantries about the recent sharp frost and the man introduced himself as Alfred Potter, who had found the body.

'It was a mess,' Potter told West, 'and I didn't touch him, but I did just put my fingers on the stale [shaft] of the pitchfork.' Potter had shouted to someone in the next field [Harry Peachey] to fetch the police and Lomasney duly turned up. The farmer told West that he had seen Walton working at the hedge earlier in the day and while he was talking, Potter was continually looking at the murder site. ''Cause these blasted Italians are poaching all over the place and it might be one of them. By the way, his stick and file they were looking for are up the hedge there. I saw them when I came along just now.'

This piece of evidence is extraordinary. Potter's condemnation of the Italians is hardly surprising, given their proximity to Quinton in their camp, but the police later took this to be an attempt to distance himself from the crime. The stick, however, was potentially a vital piece of evidence, if it was the one used to attack Walton; it was last seen in Constable Lomasney's hands. If it was the *other* stick, however, the one made by the dead man himself, why was it overlooked, even in darkness? The file that Potter referred to was almost certainly the whetstone that Walton used to sharpen his blade.

Potter gave West a Players cigarette and asked him if he had been on duty all night. After a few more generalities about the weather (traditionally, of course, the passing Englishman's *only* topic of conversation) Potter went back the way he had come. Later, when Alfred Potter became the *only* person of interest (see Chapter 8), this returning to the crime scene took on a sinister aspect. The farmer's reason for it was that he had come to check on his sheep and calves, as he did routinely.

Lomasney and Constable Barrett arrived shortly afterwards and West told them about the conversation with Potter. He also showed them a snare he had found. When other officers arrived (including Nicholls and Denton to take two more photographs of the site) that and Walton's stick were taken as evidence by Inspector Jones. Nicholls' daytime photographs, while it was right and proper to take them, provide no useful evidence. It is ironic that what we are looking at, in the flattened grass in front of the hedge, are the murderer's footprints but these have been obliterated by everyone else's.

Professor Webster began work on the post-mortem of Charles Walton at noon, accompanied by Dr McWhinney, who naturally had an interest in the case. If either man got any sleep before that it must have been very little. Thanks to television cop shows we all have what we think is a very clear, familiar view of crime laboratories. In fact, they are usually small, cramped and rather grubby, the smell – of formaldehyde and other chemicals – impossible to remove. And some of them are not what they seem. The laboratory used in the *Silent Witness* series, for example, is a permanent film set and despite the rows of refrigerated cubicles for the storage of bodies, only one of them works; the others have false doors and are merely cosmetic!

Authorization for the work was granted by George Lodder, coroner for South Warwickshire. Webster began by describing what he had seen at the crime scene, including the presence of Walton's left hedging glove near his left elbow. The right glove lay near his groin. 'The front of his clothes were undone and the top part of his fly was also open.' Webster had had some difficulty in removing the end of the pitchfork from the hedge – the body had to be depressed to enable this to happen.

The pathologist did his best to straighten out the body on the mortuary slab. Clearly, rigor mortis had not quite worn off. He washed it, removing the dried blood and found that the deceased was 'a little, rather bent old man, with a certain amount of lateral and antero-posterior curvature of the spine'.

Webster was working, not in the white or green coat and specialist clothing that television shows us, but in a leather apron more reminiscent of a Victorian butcher than a scientist at the forefront of his profession. Walton had been 5ft 6in tall, with calluses on the soles of his feet. Webster described the injuries he saw. There were four bruises, sustained during a struggle before death, on the back of the dead man's right hand and forearm. There was a small cut on the right elbow and a flap laceration on the back of the left index finger. All these would have been sustained during Walton's attempt to defend himself.

The slight abrasions to the left shoulder would have been caused by the tine of the pitchfork. There were seven lacerated wounds to the back and top of the head, none down to the bone. Below these were deep-seated bruises to the scalp. The left clavicle had been severed from the sternum and several ribs were broken on the left side. The wounds to the neck consisted of one that ran from about an inch below the point of the chin to the suprasternal notch. This had been made by several slashes to the throat and had left a hole 4¼ inches by 3½ inches. 'The tissues on the front of the neck were grossly cut about.' To the left and right side of this hole were the puncture marks of the pitchfork.

Clearly, these wounds and the story they told were of most interest to the police, but in autopsies, pathologists routinely cover all aspects of a body's condition, in case any of them are relevant to the cause of death. The heart and major blood vessels were healthy for a man of Walton's years, but his trachea had been badly damaged by the billhook and pitchfork. Most of the torn tissue lay to the dead man's left, including the broken ribs, but the lungs were healthy. The old man's stomach contained a 'farinaceous meal' including currants, clearly Edith's cake. The spleen, liver and intestines were all healthy, as was the bladder and kidneys. Walton showed symptoms of osteoarthritis, which presumably explained the sticks that he carried and his 'bent' appearance.

Webster wrote in his report:

This had been a remarkably healthy old man for his age. The cause of death is quite clear He died from shock and haemorrhage due to grave injuries to the neck and chest. Those injuries had been caused by two types of weapon, namely, a cutting weapon and a stabbing weapon such as the two weapons I found in situ in the field. Further, the cutting weapon had been wielded at least three times and with great violence. The old man defended himself, as shown by the cut upon the left hand and the bruises on the back of the right hand and forearm. Death had occurred in my opinion somewhere between 1 p.m. and 2 p.m. on the 14th February.

Perhaps oddly, there seems to have been no consideration of whether the murderer was right- or left-handed. The intensity of the attack to Walton's left would indicate a right-hander and in the 1940s, for reasons of tradition and superstition, there were fewer left-handers than today. Crucially, Webster concluded elsewhere that the order of attack was as follows. First came the blows to the head from the old man's own walking stick. Then, when he was on the ground, the pitchfork to the throat. Finally, the hacking mutilations to the neck. Those who, years later, tried to read something sacrificial about this murder, have ignored this sequence entirely.

While Webster was conducting his post-mortem, his West Midlands laboratory in Birmingham was carrying out work on Walton's clothes, walking stick and fingernails. In fights to the death, people often scratch their opponents and residue under their fingernails might have yielded clues as to the killer. The definitive corroborative evidence of DNA still lay forty years in the future.

It is always extraordinary how much detritus ends up at crime scenes. In an open area like a country field there would be less of this than, say, in an urban street. Even so, some items did not make sense. Walton had been wearing a cardigan and he carried a red handkerchief in its left pocket. In the right pocket were three pieces of string and the foot of a sock. The jacket had a whetstone (clearly a back-up to the file that Potter had found) for sharpening the billhook and a piece of rope with a hook attached (this was for pulling down high branches). There were three more pieces of string here too. In the left bottom pocket of the waistcoat was another sock foot and a pocket knife. In the top pocket was a length of watch chain, but no watch and a tin containing four gun licences with relevant identification numbers. Countrymen like Walton often owned shotguns and used them, for instance, to shoot crows, magpies and other pests. Police discovered later that Walton was a crack shot but he did not own a gun. In the blue overall trousers' right pocket was a piece of rag and in the left a receipt marked No. 20 for 8 shillings.

On 16 February, DI B. Toombs of the Warwickshire Constabulary handed over a number of items belonging to the dead man to the West Midlands Forensic Science team. Most of these were garments that Walton was wearing when he died, but they included the overcoat of an Italian prisoner of war with the name G. Bianco inside and a sample of hair found at the scene. There were seven other garments belonging to Italians, proof positive that, as early as two days after the murder, the police were highly suspicious of the prisoners from Long Marston, echoing Alfred Potter's words to Constable West.

Two days later, Alan Gemmell, staff biologist at the West Midlands laboratory, sent a report on all items to Professor Webster. They were a little disappointing. The hairs clinging to the walking stick were indeed Walton's, as was fairly obvious. The dead man's fingernails were inevitably covered with soil (that went with the job – he would only have worn gloves in *very* rough conditions) but there were also woollen fibres of a reddish-brown colour, light blue, crimson, green and yellow. Gemmell's limp explanation is that these fibres may have come from other garments of Walton's that he was not wearing on the day he died or may have been present in the soil!

This is actually far from satisfactory. Depending on how personally clean Walton was, some of the fibres were almost certainly from the killer. The only clothes we *know* he handled were the ones in which he was found and the fibres did not come from there. Unless the old man had not washed his hands since the previous day, why should the fibres from his *own clothes* be under his nails? And how could such fibres end up in a hedge and ditch where only he worked? Pioneering work on evidence like this had been carried out by Dr Edmond Locard, who had set up his own forensic laboratory in 1910. The Locard Exchange Principle that 'every contact leaves a trace' would have been well known to Webster. 'It is impossible,' Locard had written, 'for a criminal to act, especially considering the intensity of a crime, without leaving traces of his presence.'

Not only would there have been traces of the killer on Walton's body, traces of Walton would have been all over the killer's clothes. The crime scene photographs showed that Walton's trousers were undone, his braces loosened and broken and his belt lying across his thighs. What with the missing watch added to the mix, it looked as though someone had rifled the dead man's clothes, perhaps looking for money.

As to the Italian greatcoat belonging to G. Bianco, it is not clear from police files where this was found. Several high-profile killers during wartime, including the 'Blackout Killer' Gordon Cummings, were caught because they left named items at the scenes of their crimes. The hairs on Bianco's coat were either pig bristles (presumably from a clothes brush) or human hairs that did not come from the head of Charles Walton. None of the fibres from the dead man's fingernails had any connection with the other Italian garments examined.

It goes without saying, of course, that PC Lomasney had routinely checked Walton's pockets. Today, his DNA would have been found all over the body. No one, least of all the pathologist himself, seems to have checked how much interference with the corpse had been carried out by Lomasney. At the very least, and on his own admission, he had handled the shaft of the pitchfork and gone through the dead man's pockets.

The local press were on to the story by the next day, but who informed them is unknown. Police forces routinely worked with journalists and by and large the media was more inclined to toe the establishment line than today, especially because of the dangers of misreporting during the war. News itself was curtailed, partly because of the need for secrecy and partly because newsprint itself was expensive.

The *Coventry Evening Telegraph*, more used than most to covering the horrors of war, came out with the banner headline – Hedge-cutter Dead in Ditch – on 15 February. The article is basically correct, but it would be fascinating to know who told the reporter that Walton was 'a friendly old man without an enemy' as that certainly did not square with the later police enquiries. The *Birmingham Mail* opined the same day that 'the police regard the crime as the work of a lunatic or someone maddened by drink'. The *Evening Despatch*, having repeated the gory journalese that Walton was almost decapitated, rather coyly added 'foul play is suspected'.

The next day, Friday, 16 February, the *Birmingham Post* added nothing to the bare facts of the case, but the *Coventry Evening Telegraph* reported that the police could not establish a motive for the murder. The *Birmingham Gazette* that day gave out the information that the police were carrying out enquiries at a camp. This was Long Marston, but there are no details in the paper.

At 10.55 a.m. on Thursday, 15 February, E.R. Kemble RN, the chief constable of Warwickshire, sent a telegram to Scotland Yard – 'The deceased is a man named Charles Walton, age 75 [*sic*] and he was killed with an instrument known as a slash hook. The murder was ... committed by a madman ...'

Chapter 5

Calling in the Yard

For the duration of the war, all police forces throughout the country were stretched to breaking point. Today we have a misty, nostalgic view of that generation of coppers. From the red-cheeked, huge-waisted caricatures of Lawson Wood's cartoons in the 1930s to the avuncular 'Mind how you go' Sergeant Dixon of Dock Green (as played on television by Jack Warner) twenty years later, they were a rock in a sea of troubles. Armed only with a 14-inch wooden truncheon and patrolling at a regular 2½mph, they walked their beats, told people the time, checked on safety and knew everyone.

If Wood and Warner represented fictional stereotypes, the reality threw up heroes (and some heroines) aplenty. In 1923, PC George Scorey, riding a grey horse, kept order at a rowdy pitch invasion at Wembley and prevented a catastrophe. Four years later when thugs Browne and Kennedy shot and killed PC Gutteridge of the Essex force, the whole country was outraged. Symbolically, the ex-cons had shot out both Gutteridge's eyes. Even other villains regarded them with contempt.

There were 60,000 police persons in Britain at the outbreak of war (of whom 282 were women). Nine thousand of that force were war reservists, which meant that, young and able-bodied, they were likely to be called up because conscription into the armed forced kicked in immediately on the outbreak of war. Recruits for the police came from four sources. The Police Reserve was made up of retired coppers, 10,000 of them, and they were immediately recalled to the nearest station. Special constables made up another 130,000, doing, as we have seen, all the work that the regulars did. The Police War Reserves brought in thousands more and, after much campaigning, the Women's Auxiliary Police Corps. It was a sign of the times that until the thin blue line was stretched to breaking point, most of these women typed the reports, answered the phone and made the tea. By 1941, there were more police in uniform than at any time in the country's history – 92,000 regulars.

Peacetime officers carried a copy of Cecil Moriarty's *Police Law*, a manual by which they operated. Cynics reminded everybody that Moriarty was the 'Napoleon of Crime', Sherlock Holmes's nemesis as written by Arthur Conan Doyle. *This* one, however, was chief constable of Brighton in 1939. To a bewildering series of crime categories, including assault, murder, rape, abduction, prostitution, breaking and entering, larceny, malicious damage, coinage, forgery and poaching were now added specifics relating to wartime. Twenty pages dealt with regulations relating to alcohol. Cameras had to be checked, the blackout enforced, docks and factories guarded and aliens investigated.

On the other hand, in some respects the pressure on police forces lessened. An unknown number of criminals were taken off the streets and wrapped in khaki, airforce blue or navy blue en route to various theatres of war. Traffic problems lessened because petrol was rationed and there were fewer cars on the roads. Against that, no force could ignore the threat of a shadowy Fifth Column operating in their area and the cities in particular became aware of a growing rate in juvenile delinquency, now that Dad's belt or slipper was not around.

The police were always at the forefront of air raids, often the first on the scene, with the heartbreaking job of finding bodies and counselling the wounded and bereaved. Such men had to be able to put out fires before the Fire Brigade arrived, patch up the injured before the ambulance got there. Every city and many large towns – certainly Birmingham and Coventry – had such 'incident officers' and the toll on them was tough.

The greatest strain was inevitably felt by the Metropolitan Police. Formed by the Home Secretary Robert Peel in 1829, it was designed, by the sheer physical presence of uniformed constables, to deter wrongdoing.

It struggled to be accepted at first, but by the mid-nineteenth century had become the model to which county constabularies, most of which were set up in 1856, aspired. In the first year of the war, ten Met officers won the Police Medal for bravery, often facing down and arresting armed thieves and killers with nothing but their truncheons or even just fists. In 1940, the George Medal was established for police bravery – eighty-two were awarded in the next five years, along with 276 commendations. 'It is no exaggeration,' wrote Herbert Morrison, the Home Secretary, 'to say that the reputation of the British police for service to the community stands higher than ever before.'

The 'Mobile Patrol Experiment' of 1920 had morphed into the Flying Squad by 1935. The 'Heavy Mob' could now rival the best-equipped city gangs with modern vehicles fit for purpose. Their Railtons could reach speeds of over 100mph. The emergency call sign '999' was established in 1936, five years after the Highway Code laid down the rules of the road. When the system opened on 1 July 1937, 1,336 calls were logged. A number of these callers dined out on the fact that they were the first to use the number!

At the pinnacle of the Met was Scotland Yard, a constantly shifting headquarters in the capital which originally housed visitors to Elizabethan England from James VI's Scottish court. During the war, the headquarters building was across the road from the Houses of Parliament and backing on to Whitehall and the Thames Embankment. It had originally been planned as an opera house in the 1890s but other than the Met's Glee Club, not a single note was ever heard in the place. Its famous telephone number – Whitehall 1212 – was soon known countrywide.

It is no disrespect to the Warwickshire Constabulary that it decided to call in Scotland Yard. Perhaps it was the ferocity of Charles Walton's murder, perhaps because his force was physically and mentally exhausted, that the chief constable decided immediately to send for the specialists. The Home Office was duly informed, as a matter of routine and Warwickshire CID arranged cars to collect the Yard men when they arrived. We do not know how local CID officers like DI Toombs and Superintendent Spooner felt about this and the Yard knew perfectly well that kid gloves would be necessary. If an arrest was to be made, it would be made by the local officer, not the Met. The London force's expertise in forensics like fingerprinting and handwriting analysis gave them the edge. The Detective Branch itself was set up in 1842 and although there was considered something 'sneaky' about a plainclothesman, in terms of crime detection, it was the obvious way forward. Most of the requests from county forces were in connection with murder cases and the original four-man team sent out into the sticks came to be known as the Murder Squad; it was never an official title. Under Superintendent Frank Froest were DCIs Fox, Arrow, Kane and Dew, the last made famous for catching Dr H.H. Crippen in 1910.

In February 1945, the two officers assigned from the Yard to assist Spooner were Robert Fabian and his number two, Albert Webb, two highly efficient and experienced detectives. The Walton case, everyone felt confident, would be cracked in days.

We know more about Fabian than arguably any other Scotland Yard detective because he not only wrote three books on his career, but went on to become the first of the television detectives, in a series of half-hour episodes in the 1950s in which an actor played him and he himself spoke to camera at the end of each programme. Just as pathologists were household names, appearing regularly in the media, so too were detectives. Their 'uniform' was instantly recognizable – a trilby hat, trench–coat and probably a pipe.

In his first book, *Fabian of the Yard*, published five years after Charles Walton died, the detective paints a domestic picture of himself. His wife, Winnie 'a most important part of a policeman's equipment'[10] suggested he write an introduction. He pointed out that everyone who gets his name in the papers says that their favourite hobby is gardening, they are pretty good at snooker, hope to back a

---

[10] All quotations in this chapter are from Fabian's books unless otherwise stated.

Derby winner and detest the skin on boiled milk! *Fabian of the Yard* is not an autobiography but a description of some high-profile cases, including the murder of Charles Walton, with a chapter title 'Under the Shadow of Meon Hill'.

Fabian was born in Ladywell, London, on 31 January 1901 as the century opened. He had originally planned, like his father, to become an engineer. He enrolled at Borough Polytechnic at the age of 12 with that in mind and began a dull job as a draughtsman, sitting at a high stool like something out of Charles Dickens. A chance discussion with a family friend in 1921 gave him a change of direction. Inspector Frederick Rolfe talked Fabian into joining the police. He duly turned up at Lewisham Police Station and went through his physical. He was tall enough at 5ft 10in but a little light at 10 stone 4lb. Form A1/R8 elicited from Fabian that he was of British birth and descent, could read and write and showed 'a reasonable proficiency in ... simple arithmetic'. The examining doctor was satisfied that the new recruit had never been ruptured, nor suffered from flat feet, tumours or facial deformity.

Fabian reported for duty at 2 p.m. on 17 May 1921. Years later he could still remember the 'indefinable smell' of a police station – 'a mixture of scrubbing soap, disinfectant and typewriter ribbons'. His first posting was Vine Street station behind the Piccadilly Hotel in the heart of C Division. It had been a parish watch house before the first commissioners took it over and had been rebuilt in 1868. The Man in the Moon pub next door must have been Fabian's local when he was off duty (there were strict rules against drinking in blues) but in 1931 this became a typing office for the Met. In 1940, because of the peculiarities of wartime, it became the Aliens Registration Office.

Fabian became used to beat patrol, especially at night – 'Each doorway, shadow at a window, hurried footstep or meaningful glance may have a tale to tell.' Before long, Fabian found himself attached to Vice. Journalists and the public loved the phrase 'Vice Squad' because it appealed to the prurient and sold newspapers. In fact, it was never a formal title. What Fabian actually joined was C Division's Clubs Office, because Soho and the West End were littered with them, centres of illegal gambling, drinking and prostitution. The Section House for young, single constables like Fabian was at Beak Street, in the centre of all this. The pay was £3 a week.

Two years later, the now experienced constable applied to join the CID. The Criminal Investigation Department was born out of scandal. The Detective Branch created in 1842 was small and by 1877 had become increasingly corrupt. When a number of detectives were found guilty of fraud, an untried civil servant with a military and journalistic background offered an alternative. He was Howard Vincent and the CID was his brainchild. In time, every force in the country would have a similar organization. Fabian made a point of getting inside the minds of criminals. He knew that they were not stupid and learned quickly by experience. But he also knew that London's underworld was a 'dismal, sordid, petty place. Few high-powered glamour-boy crooks live outside of Hollywood.' One of his first arrests in plainclothes was when he was off duty, in fact on his way to the pictures with Winnie, not yet his wife. He arrested two car thieves and held on to them while Winnie went in search of a uniformed copper!

Fabian's training as a detective took place at Hendon college. Since this was not opened until 1933, we know that the courses he followed there were ongoing refreshers, as police procedure, like much else in those years, was changing all the time. As we shall see, Fabian was to use the latest Hendon technology in plotting people's movements on the day that Charles Walton was killed.

In 1929, when the Met was a century old, Fabian was transferred to New Scotland Yard (Norman Shaw's never-opened opera house) working in Criminal Records. Before the advent of computers, the details contained in shoeboxes and filing cabinets, including fingerprints, formed an invaluable database of all known criminals in the country. It was here that the detective realized how crimes are solved – 'by the mobilisation of an intricate machine which makes use of ... the skill of the chemist, the photographer and pathologist, in addition to a well-tested system of analysis of evidence'.

Fabian worked his first murder case in 1926, as a 'ghost', still unknown to Soho criminals. The killer, who shot a fellow snooker player dead, was Emile Berthier, known, appropriately enough, as Mad Emile. He was caught on a ship from Newhaven trying to flee the country. Exhilarated, Fabian rang Winnie, now his wife – 'Winnie! I've just solved my first murder case!'

'That's wonderful – you'd better come and tell your son all about it.'

In June 1939, three months before war was declared, bombs exploded in London. By this time, Fabian was a Detective Inspector and he was typing up a report on his battered old Remington when an explosion from Piccadilly Circus shivered his windows and ruffled his papers. The government, in preparation for what everyone feared was coming, had already issued gasmasks; Fabian grabbed his and fought his way through an incredulous and ghoulish crowd who would soon be inured to such scenes. Shattered glass, cigarettes and cigars, along with silk lingerie were scattered all over the pavements. Piccadilly Circus, usually bright with neon lights, was in virtual darkness. As his eyes became accustomed, Fabian saw a brown-paper wrapped parcel. Urging his two sergeants to keep the crowd back, he cut the parcel tape with his pocket knife and knelt there, looking at a lump of Polar Amnon Gelignite. There were six more like it in the paper. Using the knife, he flicked the fuse out of each one, not knowing that the blade's contact with any of these could have blown him sky high. With the sergeants' help, he got the gelignite to Vine Street and dumped it into fire buckets. There were six more explosions in London that night – the work of the IRA – and most of the suspects, straight off the boat from Dublin, were caught and imprisoned. On 6 February 1940, Robert Honey Fabian was presented with the King's Police Medal for Gallantry for his fast (and some would say, reckless) action that night. It obviously meant a lot to him, but perhaps not as much as the packet given to him by a gang-lord whose name he does not divulge. Some of his boys had been at the 'Dilly on that night and thought that Fabian might have saved a few lives. In the packet was a bronze medal, inscribed 'To Detective Inspector Bob Fabian, For Bravery, 24-6-39. From the Boys'.

Fabian got home late on the night of 15 February 1945. He had recently been put in charge of the Flying Squad, the Sweeney that put the fear of God into London's underworld. He was also feeling a little smug because of the cracking of a case against a violent London gang which had netted £4,000-worth (£170,000 today) of stolen goods. It was Buller, his overweight bulldog who greeted him because his family were in bed. A note on the telephone table read 'Telephone the CID Commissioner'. There had been a request for help from the Warwickshire Constabulary. He phoned the night duty inspector at the Yard on the famous number Whitehall 1212 and checked that the murder bag he would be taking with him had a torch. This equipment had been ready for immediate use for the first time in 1925. Each of the nine still available twenty years later contained rubber gloves, magnifying glasses, tape measures and other measuring devices, containers for bodily fluids and hair samples, first aid equipment, stationery and equipment for fingerprint taking and footprint cast-making, along with handcuffs in the event of an arrest. Fabian asked that a screwdriver, awl, nails, hammer, wrench and non-spillable ink bottle be included. He had never worked with Warwickshire CID before and had no idea what to expect. With him, as he travelled north, was Detective Sergeant Albert Webb.

Like Fabian, Webb was a Londoner, born in Bethnal Green in 1904. His family were of immigrant Huguenot stock who had settled in the area in the 1680s. Webb's father made brushes and, as was customary in the 1920s, it was natural for young Albert to follow in the man's footsteps. His education was undistinguished, although he had a love of literature that stayed with him all his life. The mid-1920s was a hard time economically; there were nearly a million men unemployed and Webb had no real qualifications to speak of. Cheap Japanese imports were already taking the place of British-made goods and there was a deep irony in that many people bought cheaper German-made brushes than those made by the Webbs. After defeat in the First World War, Germany was already bouncing back under the new democratic Weimar government.

Webb never intended to become a policeman. The only book on him – Gerard Fairlie's – is called *The Reluctant Cop* for good reason. But the job offered £1 a week more than most working men could get and it carried with it free accommodation. Based in Peckham, Albert Webb, brushmaker, became PC Albert Webb, 807P.

The free accommodation turned out to be a little less than advertised. Each recruit had a narrow, hard bed and a small locker for personal items. There was no heating and no decoration. But at least he was better off than the miserable marchers on London's streets at the time, men who could not find work, a situation which would explode into the General Strike of 1926.

Webb's first move from Peckham happened because of one of those periodic scandals which continue to haunt the Met to this day. The Macmillan Committee, prompted by press reports of police overzealousness, had enquired into professional standards in 1927–8. Despite the whitewash result of no wrongdoing, it was clear that there were plenty of rotten apples in the force; none more so than Sergeant George Goddard of Vine Street. Anonymous letters implied that Goddard was on the take, turning a blind eye to shady Club activities, especially those of Kate Merrick, who ran the Cecil Club in Gerard Street. Gambling, obscene stage shows, after-hours drinking and prostitution were all going on, the letters said, under Goddard's lack of watch. The Flying Squad (not yet under that name) led by Inspector Fred 'Nutty' Sharpe, investigated and Mrs Merrick was sent down for six months. Goddard, it emerged, owned a house worth £2,000, drove a car and had two bank accounts containing a total of £2,700. This was, of course, way beyond his salary, made all the more unlikely when he was found to also have £12,000 in cash in a safety-deposit box at Selfridge's Hotel, in the false name of Joseph Eagles.

Goddard was found guilty under the Corrupt Practices Act and served eighteen months, his police career clearly over. Apart from the fact that the press was now routinely suspicious of all London coppers, there was need for a reshuffle in Goddard's C Division and Webb volunteered. He was now based at Great Marlborough Street and was soon involved in Winter Patrols, where constables operated in plainclothes to mingle with crowds, especially at Christmas time, to arrest pickpockets and thieves. With this experience, he volunteered to join the CID, working for two years as an aid to detectives, which was the norm. In 1932, newly appointed DC Webb was posted to K Division, based first in Limehouse, then West Ham. Five years later, he was Detective Sergeant 2nd Class and early in 1941 was transferred to the Criminal Records Office at Scotland Yard.

The war, as we have seen, hit the police forces in the country like the bombs raining over the cities. The particular aspect of policing that Webb was involved in was the huge rise of dodgy charities that sprang up overnight. 'There is no one so virulently uncharitable,' wrote Webb's biographer, 'as one Charity Organizer about another Charity Organizer'[11] and it took up all of the DS's time.

Travelling with Fabian to Meon Hill was not the first time that Webb had been involved in provincial cases when the Yard had been called in. In November 1941, the Met had been asked in by the Buckinghamshire Constabulary. Two little girls, Doreen Hearne, 8, and 6-year-old Kathleen Trendle were found dead in Rough Wood near the village of Penn. They had both been stabbed several times in their throats. The case was handled by Chief Inspector George Hatherill who wrote his autobiography many years later, in 1971. The only obtuse mention that Webb gets is that he was 'a junior officer who was to assist me'. This lack of generosity compares sharply with Fabian who makes Webb a very human character. It points up another flaw in police autobiographies – a probable tangle of untold politics

---

[11] Gerard Fairlie, *The Reluctant Cop* p. 34.

and bitchiness which never sees the light of day and which may well have hampered police enquiries.

In fact, the 'junior officer' had brought the car to Hatherill's house and with him was Sir Bernard Spilsbury, the leading Home Office pathologist of the day who gave Webb some advice he would never forget. The DS had suggested that the girls' killer must be mad. 'Not *mad*, Webb,' the great man had said. '*Bad*. Just *bad*.'

Unlike the Charles Walton case, the murder site had been left largely intact, as per Hatherill's instructions. Although the girls' clothing was disturbed, there was no sign of sexual interference, one of the most common motives in child killings. There were, however, clues, especially a handkerchief with a laundry mark, RA1019, which immediately pointed in the direction of the Royal Artillery, based at a camp nearby. It was wartime and all street lights had been removed. So had road signs and even the Flying Squad driver, ferrying Hatherill and Webb around unfamiliar countryside, got lost. At one point, they drove through a live minefield that had already claimed one victim in the form of a brigadier. All that was found of the man was his cap and that was buried with full military honours!

In his account of the case, Hatherill makes great play of clever forensics and astute police work, but as Webb makes clear, there was only one suspect. He was 26-year-old Harold Hill, a gunner often seen in the girls' company; the handkerchief was his. His counsel attempted a plea of schizophrenia, but the jury did not buy it and Hill was hanged at Oxford on 1 May 1942.

Days after this, Webb was back in action on another call-in case, of the murder of a 6-year-old girl at Riddlesworth, near Thetford, Norfolk. His guv'nor this time was DCI Barrett and Webb used his considerable powers of chatty persuasion to break down a soldier, Private Wyeth, who was stationed near the murder scene. While Webb clinched the charge, by retracing Wyeth's steps on the day in question and proving that the murder could have been done in a twenty minute 'window', Wyeth was found guilty but insane and sent to Broadmoor. Many years later, now a superintendent and nearing retirement, Webb visited the man and they chatted in the asylum grounds like two old friends.

In May 1943, Webb was instrumental, under DCI Peter Beveridge, in bringing to justice Trevor Elvin, who bludgeoned his girlfriend, Violet Wakefield, to death near a fairground in Barnsley, Yorkshire. Thomas Pierrepoint hanged him at Leeds on 10 September. One of the most unpleasant cases that Beveridge and Webb worked on was the murder of little Dawn Digby, just 3 weeks old. The girl's father, Ernest, was a bigamist who, by the time the police investigated, was serving in the army at Witney, Oxfordshire. He made three statements to the detectives, each more unbelievable than the last. First, he claimed to have abandoned his first child (by his first marriage) and had no idea what happened to the second one! Finally, he told police that he had been carrying Dawn when he stumbled and dropped her. He left her in some woods and went back the next day to check on her and, unsurprisingly, found her dead. He carried her body in a suitcase and buried her in a 'rabbit hole'. Digby was executed at Bristol, but, oddly, his second wife, Olga, in terms of the law as guilty as he was, was reprieved.

George Fairlie's coverage of the Charles Walton murder is fleeting – the man's name does not appear in the index; neither does Meon Hill nor Lower Quinton. 'There was a short delay before calling for the assistance of Scotland Yard,' Fairlie writes, although to be fair, most of the damage to the crime scene had been done by the finders of the body which would have happened whether the Yard were called in or not. It may be that this delay was caused by the sheer volume of work that the Warwickshire Force was obliged to undertake. The police files contain two pages of frantic telephone calls on 15 February showing that officers detailed to give evidence in court that day had to be substituted. There are two minor discrepancies in Fairlie's account which, bearing in mind the thirteen-year gap between the murder and the book, is unsurprising. Edith Walton was not technically Charles's daughter, but his niece and he was not killed in the 'middle' of a field, neither was it 'well away from the hedges he was trimming'; PC Nicholls' photograph shows it within a couple of feet. The fact that the search party on 14 February found the body so quickly is that Alfred Potter, Walton's employer, knew exactly where he had been working.

Fairlie's conclusion to this case, accurately but infuriatingly, says 'Why that old man was so savagely killed, and by whom, remains a mystery.' Three months later, DS Webb was promoted to Detective Inspector.

Superintendent Alec Spooner met the Yard men at Leamington Spa on 17 February, allegedly today one of the most haunted railway stations in the country, and they drove via the Stratford HQ to Lower Quinton, parking, as my wife and I did on our visit, near the churchyard. It was not yet dawn. In the small windows of a dozen thatched cottages, oil lamps were being lit. 'They're waking up,' Fabian remembered Spooner saying. 'And eating breakfast,' Webb added, having had nothing at all that morning.

'In the field under Meon Hill, a young constable stood guard over thick clogged bloodstains upon the grass,' Fabian wrote ten years later. This may have been Constable West, the third guard at the crime scene; everybody else had gone. The detectives talked about motive; who would want a 74-year-old man dead?

According to Fabian, it was now that Spooner gave him not one, but two books. The first was *Folk Lore, Old Customs and Superstitions in Shakespeare Land* by J. Harvey Bloom, MA. The second was Clive Holland's *Warwickshire*. Both allegedly referred to a much earlier murder that took place near Lower Quinton, that of Ann Turner in 1875. Webb 'laid a mock sympathetic hand upon Superintendent Spooner's shoulder. "The mad, hectic life of the country is proving too much for you, sir." Alec Spooner, a highly scientific policeman, smiled patiently. "You wait and see, my lad!" he said.'

Little of this rings true. According to Fabian, Webb was 'one of the most astute and cheerful investigators in the Murder Squad'. Even so, was it likely that he would have been quite so flippant as to adopt a patronising tone to a senior officer who outranked him and whom he had only just met? And, even more outstandingly, would that senior officer thrust two books on folklore into the hands of the Met men standing in a Warwickshire field on a winter's morning? All this is, I suspect, an ex-copper's licence, spinning a good yarn for the amusement of his readers. I have no doubt that both those books came Fabian's way eventually and they probably came via Spooner, who, as the local man, would possess such arcane – and, as it turned out, irrelevant – knowledge.

And this, of course, is the problem with former policemen's accounts of cases. They are uniformly written years later, without access to case files and they are based on memory. There had been a time when retired coppers were banned from writing their memoirs – the powers that be took a dim view of them. Inevitably, however, a trickle of such books began to leak into the public domain. In the 1890s, Inspectors John Littlechild and Maurice Moser both wrote accounts of their careers in the Met. Walter Dew waited twenty-five years before he published *I Caught Crippen* (1935) which is riddled with inaccuracies.

Fabian was at least guilty of concertinaing time. According to the Met's logbook (a copy of which is in the National Archive), the Yard men left Paddington at 9.10 a.m. that Friday and reached Leamington Spa two hours later. There was no dawn over Meon Hill, no waking up of Lower Quinton. Allowing for the 8-mile drive to the village and a brief visit to Stratford, it would have been after lunchtime before the Yard men got there. We followed Spooner and Fabian's route as faithfully as we could in 2022, but the volume of traffic was far greater than in wartime and road layouts have changed. And there were not just three of them at the murder site, but five – Kemble, the chief constable, and Superintendent Simmonds were also there.

All in all, as faithful descriptions of a murder case go, Fabian's account is not a good start.

That day (17 February) the *Coventry Evening Telegraph* carried the headline 'Scotland Yard To Join In Hunt'. It is a reminder of the nature of wartime news reporting that the story is confined to page 8; today it would be front-page headlines. Four days (the paper wrongly told its readers) of enquiries had led nowhere, but Italian prisoners of war had been interviewed. Fabian's overall report on the case explains that all prisoners away from the camp on 14 February (see Chapter 7) had been searched, interviewed (with an interpreter) and nothing had come of it. Tellingly, the article concludes, 'The police are of the opinion that the crime was committed by someone who knows the neighbourhood.'

The *Birmingham Mail* of the 17th was prepared to speculate on the details of the case, even though the inquest had yet to be held. Because both the pitchfork and the billhook had long handles, the murderer would probably not have bloodstains or tears in his clothing, the *Mail* averred. This is amateur speculation, but it pales into insignificance alongside another theory reported by the paper that the crime may have been committed by someone who was 'bi-minded'. This is almost certainly 1940s-speak for schizophrenic and it was no doubt an attempt to explain a sudden, ferocious attack that came out of the blue in an otherwise idyllic country setting.

How accurate the description was remained to be seen.

Chapter 6

'Murder by Person or Persons Unknown'

Before the Yard arrived, Warwickshire CID had begun their own enquiries. It is important in a case of murder to strike quickly. It is also nonsense that – as quoted in many a crime novel and television detective series – if a murder is not solved within forty-eight hours, it never will be.

On 15 February, the day after the murder, Warwickshire CID were back at Hillground using a range of equipment – metal detectors, cameras, shovels, even magnifying glasses. Constable Arthur Nicholls was with them, taking two photographs of the now empty field, with the body gone. These have survived the passage of time and are in the Warwickshire Police Archive. One is available on the internet. As Peter Arnold, a Crime Scene Investigator for Yorkshire and Humberside put it in 2015, 'The crime scene is the silent witness. The victim can't tell us what happened, the suspect probably isn't going to tell us what happened, so we need to give a hypothesis that explains what has taken place.'[12]

The detectives working under the leadership of Superintendent Spooner were perfectly familiar with the work of Edmund Locard, referred to earlier. His famous dictum – 'every contact leaves a trace' – meant that Charles Walton's killer had left crucial evidence over the weapons, the grass and the hedge that made up the crime scene. He may also have touched the dead man's clothing or skin.

Today, the CSI pattern is rigid and almost universal. The body is found, uniformed police arrive, a detective of the rank of DI or above determines whether it is likely to be a case of murder, suicide or accident

---

[12] Quoted in Val McDermid, *Forensics, the Anatomy of a Crime.* p. 4.

and the crime scene is cordoned off with the famous blue and white tape. Everyone attending the scene after this is meticulously logged. How much of this went on in February 1945 is anybody's guess. There is no mention of this sort of detail in the files of the Metropolitan Police in the National Archive. Nor in the Warwickshire Archive. In all probability Constable Nicholls left a camera bulb behind (it was found later) but there is no record of it by the police.

I have in front of me the police training manual of the West Riding of Yorkshire Constabulary, published in 1938. It covers everything from initial cadet training to specialist work within departments and something very similar would have been implemented by all police forces in the country. There were refresher courses for uniformed men at regular intervals up to the first two years in the job.

Of particular relevance to the Meon Hill case was the six-week training course for detective inspectors and sergeants. How much of this went on in the emergency conditions of wartime is difficult to say. No doubt, personnel were in short supply and corners were cut, but the manual listed lectures stressing the importance of 'a careful and exhaustive' search of a crime scene, marks of footprints, weapons involved and signs of violence. Dust, dirt and debris were all relevant, leaf fragments, insect debris, fragments of skin, hair and clothing. Even before a pathologist arrived, a detective was supposed to note pressure and impact marks on bodies, nail and teeth marks. He had to be aware of the type of wounds inflicted – bruises, scratches, lacerations, punctures, a cut throat. And he had to be aware of the changes to the human body after death – cooling, rigor mortis, hypostasis. Although it was the pathologist who determined time of death, the senior man on the scene would already have an idea of this at least. The phone calls flying between stations in Warwickshire on the 14/15 February 1945 indicate that this had been done.

We have seen how many shoes and boots trampled the grass and how many fingers may have touched the hedge. At least four people (other than the murderer and Walton himself) handled the murder weapons.

Presumably, the purpose of leaving uniformed constables on duty at Hillground was to monitor and/or deter visitors, but, as we shall see, that was less than helpful. It is unlikely that Constables Lomasney, West et al. stood stock still on a February night; their footprints were everywhere.

The problem with an outdoor murder scene, especially in winter, is that the weather can destroy evidence quickly. One badly informed website on the Meon Hill case today has an atmospheric photograph of a pitchfork plunged into ground covered in thick snow. There was no snow in that specific area in February 1945. In fact, after a typically cold January, February was exceptionally mild, with temperatures normally associated with late spring or even early summer. Charles Walton was wearing a jacket, cardigan, two shirts and overalls because it was his custom and he was elderly, not because it was cold.

Today, we have the full fig of protective clothing at crime scenes. The Crime Scene Manager and his team wear a hood or hairnet, two pairs of protective gloves, overshoes and a surgical mask. Some of this is to prevent contamination of DNA but of course in 1945 this was entirely unknown. There was no attempt to preserve the scene because, despite Locard, ideas like this were not in tablets of stone and were not universal. Even more, new scientific ideas, especially when they came from abroad, were treated with scepticism by hard-bitten coppers looking for murderers. The whole notion of detection came from a French thief, Eugène-François Vidocq, fifty years before the plainclothes idea was accepted in Britain. Locard was a Frenchman too, so his ideas were suspect. Cesare Lombroso, who tried to work out criminal 'types' by their physical appearance, was Italian; ignore him. Even in what may be called our own times, the tried and tested criminal profiling techniques of the FBI were resisted by umpteen British police forces for years, in part because they were American.

Photography was important. Ideally, Walton's body should have been photographed from every angle, yet today there is only one available – taken from behind as he lies on the ground with his back to us. We know this is the position that PC Lomasney left him in; but did he find him in exactly the same position? Several contemporary newspaper accounts refer to his body 'under a hedge' as if there had been some attempt to hide it. There is no discernible ditch in this photograph (although there is one today) and it would not have been possible to push the body 'under the hedge' in any meaningful sense. Constable Nicholls took three photographs of the body 'in this position' and another two in the Stratford hospital mortuary later that day, by which time Professor Webster had carried out his post-mortem.

Spooner's team would have carried out a fingertip search, already routine by the 1940s, which involved uniformed officers on their hands and knees on the damp grass, feeling for anything that felt out of place. In a field, this was an easier job than in a house or flat, where all sorts of random bits and pieces might be found that had nothing to do with a crime at all. In particular, Spooner's men were looking for Walton's watch, the only item we *know* he had with him which was missing. The watch itself was not old or valuable, but it might carry fingerprints if found or even point to a motive for the killer to take it with him. Metal detectors were readily available in the area; the Royal Engineers, camped only 2 miles away at Long Marston, provided their mine-sweepers which gave off a clicking sound in the presence of any kind of metal.

While all this was going on, the Warwickshire force were going house to house, knocking on doors and taking statements. It was slow and painstaking but it was vital work. There were 493 people living in Lower Quinton; surely, *somebody* knew *something*. According to one account, everybody over the age of 10 was questioned.

Detective Inspector Toombs interviewed the farmer Alfred Potter at 11 p.m. on the night of the murder, visiting him at his farm, The Firs, and taking notes in shorthand. The Warwickshire Police Archive has a redacted, typewritten version of these notes. It is worth quoting, with redacted names replaced, as they are in fact in the public domain, because this is the first interview in the murder enquiry and because Alfred Potter was clearly a person of interest.

> Been at the farm about 5 years and had known Walton all that time.
>
> Employed Walton casually for about 9 months. Walton worked when he could, that is, when it was fine weather.
>
> Had been engaged during the last few months hedging and had done all the hedging and was on the last field known as Hillground.
>
> Was in the College Arms with Mr Joseph Stanley of Upper Quinton, left at twelve o'clock – specially noticed the time. Went straight across to a small field adjoining Hillground. Could see Walton about 500 to 600 yards away.
>
> Noticed that Walton had about 6 to 10 yards of hedge to cut and when Potter found the body later, about 4 yards of hedge had been cut round the corner, which would be about half an hour's work.
>
> Knowing Walton's habits, Potter knew he would stop about eleven o'clock for lunch [tea break] as he did not stop for dinner [lunch] and then finished about four o'clock.
>
> Inoffensive type of man but one who would speak his mind if necessary.
>
> About quarter-past-six, Mr Beasley and Miss Walton came to Potter and said Walton had not come home. All three went and found him in the corner of Hillground.
>
> Potter stayed at the scene while Mr Beasley and Miss Walton went to fetch assistance.

Potter's age was anything from 37 to 42 years old, depending on which document you believe. He was married to Lilian (40) and ran the farm on behalf of his father, L.L. Potter, who had set up a family concern years earlier. Much of The Firs was still owned by Magdalen College, Oxford, and technically, Potter paid rent to them.

Potter did not give Toombs his detailed itinerary for the day of the murder but it emerged in later interviews. He had been working on the farm after breakfast and at 11 a.m. went home to collect tools to castrate some cattle ('punch' was the Warwickshire word), which he did regularly. At 11.45, he went to the local pub, the College Arms, with another farmer, Joseph Stanley. The pub was originally a sixteenth-century farmhouse. By 1897, it had become licensed premises but was still owned, like much of the village, by Magdalen College. This seems to have been Potter's local, although the village's other pub, the Gay Dog (now gone) was nearer to The Firs, behind Charles Walton's house, along Friday Street. Potter must have downed his two pints of Guinness quickly because he had left by twelve o'clock. In a second statement given to DS Webb on the 17th, he said that ten minutes later he walked across his fields to Cacks (or Cocks) Leys to check his sheep and tend some calves. Crossing a field next to Hillground at about 12.20 p.m., he saw Charles Walton working on the hedge 500–600 yards away. He estimated that he had about 10 more yards to go before he finished the job. It was the first time Potter had seen Walton working in his shirt sleeves and was quite surprised by that, thinking to himself, 'He's getting on with it today.'

'I would have gone over to him,' the farmer told Webb, 'but I had a heifer in a ditch nearby which I had to attend to. I went straight back home and got there at about twenty to one. I then went to see about the heifer.'

From the south, that is, Meon Hill, the fields are very open and murder in such an exposed area must have been highly risky. It all depends on exactly where various witnesses were on 14 February. If Basil Hall had been driving his tractor on the northern slopes, he should have seen Walton clearly. If, on the other hand, he was preoccupied with his work or on the far side, he would have seen nothing at all. The fact that he told police that he saw someone standing by a hedge and looking towards the village, indicates that he *did* have a view of the murder site, at least at about three o'clock. As we have seen, Hall was not exactly sure of the date when he saw this man or indeed the time at which he saw him.

The statement made by Harry Hall, Basil's brother, still in the National Archive, is not helpful. DS Jenkins of the Warwickshire Constabulary took it on 28 February. Harry was helping Basil on the top of Meon Hill between eleven and twelve, at which point he went back to his father's farm. The only person he saw was a soldier (Corporal Hobbis) collecting booby traps, at about eleven o'clock.

When Potter got home again, lunch (which he called dinner) was not ready, so he went off with a labourer, Charles 'Happy' Batchelor, to pulp mangolds, presumably in the farmyard. Batchelor gave his statement to DS David Saunders of Special Branch, whom Fabian had brought in to interview the Italian prisoners of war, and DI Toombs of the Warwickshire force, on 23 February. Batchelor was 38, born in Pebworth, Worcestershire, just over the county line from Warwickshire and had lived in Lower Quinton for three years. He had been Potter's cowman for three months. He had known Charles Walton for about a year and 'have always found him to be a happy, jovial type of man. He seemed quite contented and always minded his own business.' He had never seen the old man working in his shirtsleeves.

On the day in question, Batchelor saw Alfred Potter at The Firs about ten in the morning, then again at 12.40 when he came into the 'mixing house' where he (Batchelor) was 'pulping the mangels'.

> I remember the time exactly because I asked Mr Potter the time and he replied 'I'm not sure but it must be getting on' ... We then both walked into the yard and looked at the church clock. It was 1 p.m. Mr Potter then went towards his house, as far as I know to have his dinner.

Batchelor had known about the heifer in the ditch since the previous day. This animal, which had accidentally drowned in the ominously named Doomsday ditch, loomed large in the police enquiries, both in terms of Potter's alibi and in the supernatural claptrap which emerged years later. Batchelor could not tell Potter about the death on the 13th because the farmer was busy in Stratford at the time. The dead animal was finally removed, according to Batchelor, by Potter and Mr Mace, driving a tractor belonging to Tom Russell, another farmer. Half an hour later, Mr Perkins, 'the knackerman', took the animal away. Batchelor had talked to Potter at 2.15 p.m., to discuss the heifer's removal. The farmer drove to Russell's farm to borrow Mace and a tractor because Potter's own tractor had metal wheel-casings that would destroy the road to the ditch. Potter had come back to The Firs about four o'clock, went into the house for a few minutes and worked with Batchelor in the milking shed until at least 6 p.m., when Batchelor knocked off for the day. It was not until 6.30 that Harry Beasley and Edith Walton came, hammering on his door in search of Charles.

As the police should have realized, assuming that Professor Webster's time of death, between 1 p.m. and 2 p.m. is correct, then farmer Potter could not have killed Charles Walton. Leaving aside the problem of motive, in terms of practicality, the farmer had an alibi at 1 p.m. – 'Happy' Batchelor, the church clock and mangolds – and from then until 3.30 p.m. in the form of his wife Lilian, who claimed that he was at home. The problem, of course, is that times of death, even when decided by experienced pathologists, are *not* precise. And wives, when it comes to protecting their husbands, do not make the most reliable witnesses.

'By afternoon [on 17 February],' boasted Fabian, 'we had brought the twentieth century to Lower Quinton like a cold shower-bath.' The implication was that the local plod had little idea of what to do (always the problem when outside 'specialists' are brought in) and that the 'big boys' had arrived. An Avro Anson was brought in from the RAF air strip at the edge of Leamington Spa and flew over the murder scene, taking photographs that were of such clarity that the bloodstains showed clearly. The airfield was at Whitnash, 17 miles from Lower Quinton and

Avro Ansons were multi-purpose bombers first flown ten years before Charles Walton's murder. It seems likely that the Yard men used pre-existing aerial photographs too, taken before the war, which gave an unusual and comprehensive view of the crime scene. The bizarre thing about the killing is that it took place in the open and in broad daylight; and yet nobody under Meon Hill had seen or heard a thing.

The only one of these photographs to have survived (there is none in the Archives) is that in Fabian's 1968 book *The Anatomy of Crime*. Only an expert could tell at what height it was taken but it shows the whole Upper and Lower Quinton settlement and is far too high for any signs of the bloodstains that Fabian claims could be seen, presumably at those taken at lower altitudes. The spot where the body was found was marked with a white cross but no buildings have been identified on the photograph which is, to say the least, unhelpful.

'We persevered,' Fabian wrote, 'took 4,000 statements, traced tinkers and gypsies ... I had tramps retained in Somerset, boot-repairers questioned in Salisbury ...'

This is one of the most disappointing aspects of the Charles Walton murder case. I had expected the police file in the National Archive to run to several boxes. In fact, it is only a plumpish folder containing seventy-nine documents as well as sixty-eight Italian statements. Several of these are very brief, less than a page long and with minor exceptions, are very much confined to Lower Quinton and the day of the murder. Allowing for the fact that children of 'tender years' (Fabian's phrase) were not interviewed, we might expect about 400 statements from villagers alone, not to mention troops and strangers in the area. In fact, we have only 126 and that includes sixty-eight Italians! Either the 4,000 statements were a figment of Fabian's imagination or the National Archives file is a woeful example of somebody's poor record keeping.

Our experience at Kew was excellent. Bearing in mind today's irritating technology and a natural need for security and common sense post-COVID, we sailed through the process effortlessly. It was a *little* annoying at first when the wrong file was brought up for us, a very thin folder on the murder of wartime prostitute Olive Balchin, but the officials apologized and produced the right one in minutes. Clearly, not *every* piece of paper from an eighty-year-old crime can be stored (although is that not what computerisation is for in this instance?) but who knows what vital piece of information may have been thrown away?

There is no reference whatever to tinkers or gypsies in the archive, even though both groups were regarded as undesirables at the time and for centuries earlier. There *were* bands of travellers in the Midlands in the 1940s, but in a country paranoid about spies and a possible Fifth Column of Nazi collaborators, the existence of such people in the Quinton area would surely have been commented on and police action taken. The only tramp in the archive is Frederick 'Ginger' Sandford, aged 55, who carried out labouring work for farmers. According to Fabian, he was interviewed and his statement taken, but it is no longer in the file. There is nothing to link Sandford to Somerset and the only mention of boots refers exclusively (and exhaustively) to those worn by Italian prisoners of war in Warwickshire, not Salisbury.

The Warwickshire Archive contains three documents (22/3 February) relating to 'Ginger', although his name and nickname have been redacted. In the context of the Walton murder:

It is desired to trace a man of the tramping class [?] 50/60 years, hair ginger, moustache ginger, wearing old coat and cap and carrying a sack. Is of filthy appearance. This man slept in a hovel for two nights near the scene of the crime and left in the morning of the 14th instant for Cheltenham.

If the timing is accurate, 'Ginger' could not have murdered Charles Walton because he was already on his way south-west by then.

Clearly, 'Ginger' Sandford got about. A 'man answering his description' was seen in Cheltenham at 5 p.m. on 16 February heading for Chepstow. He left the Don lodging house at Godregaig on 6 January on his way to Brecon. He is now described as '5ft 7–8, fresh, full face, wearing old dirty overcoat and cap, black boots in worn condition'. His ginger hair was turning grey and he was stone deaf. He told the Gloucestershire police that he regularly travelled the roads from Brecon to Mold and on 23 February there was a warrant out for his arrest. The previous day, a man had been interviewed at Pontypridd police station, South Wales, but was younger and clean shaven. He admitted to knowing Ginger but had not seen him for some months.

It was right and proper for the police to check on Sandford. If Walton was the hapless victim of a wandering, opportunistic thief, then Ginger no doubt fitted the bill. On the other hand, he was a classic example of 'stranger danger' with which the police were – and still are – obsessed. No one from the Quintons could have killed old Charlie Walton. It had to be an outsider. And one with a disability as well! What could be more likely?

In fact, there are only three examples of documents in The National Archive file that stray out of the county. One comes from Lincolnshire three years after the murder and will be discussed in the final chapter. Another concerns Alfred Potter's finances and involves the London branch of his business. And the third is a telegram from Scotland Yard, dated 27 February 1945, asking for pawnbrokers and jewellers to keep a eye out for Charles Walton's missing watch which itself had received a mention in the nationally available *Police Gazette*.

The police enquiry into the case was thorough and exhaustive; there really was no need for Fabian to big it up as much as he did.

The Yard men had been given an office at the headquarters of the Warwickshire Constabulary in Stratford. At the end of each day, they liaised with Spooner and Toombs, comparing notes, swapping ideas. In no sense was this the Met pushing their experiential weight about; it was co-operation all the way. Fabian used the Hendon method of elementary mapping, the latest thinking in murder investigation from the detective training school. All over one wall of the incident room were maps and photographs, both aerial and from the ground. Using pins and coloured thread, the team was able to establish a pattern of everybody known to be in the area on the day that Walton died, noting how near the threads passed by the x-marked murder site. This was an early form of geoprofiling or murder mapping, actually more useful in hunting serial killers with multiple murder sites than a 'one-off' like Charles Walton.

Fabian's report, very detailed at twenty-five pages and covering every aspect of the case, is dated 5 April 1945 and contains reference to the very map we are talking about. Because this has not survived, because the area has changed almost beyond recognition today, it is not possible to recreate 1945 Quinton with any accuracy.

The Waltons' home opposite the church was marked Number 1, approximately three-quarters of a mile from the murder scene. The nearest cottage, Feronia Gough's, was Number 2, 300 yards away. Number 3 was the Woodwards' caravan containing the flight lieutenant, his wife Maud and their baby. The churchyard of St Swithin's was marked as Number 4. The barn where George Higgins was working on 14 February was labelled Number 5 and Valender's farm and bakehouse was Number 6. Valender's bean field (Number 7) was next to Hillground where the body was found. The Firs, Potter's farm, was Number 8, along the main road from Number 9, the College Arms. Cacks Leys, the field to which Potter was going when he last saw Charles Walton alive, was Number 10.

To superimpose the actual positions of locals out and about on 14 February was obviously more difficult, but I suspect that Fabian, Webb and Spooner gave it their best shot.

In the meantime, speculation was growing in the media. In Birmingham's *Evening Dispatch* of Monday, 19 February, an article on page 4 was headed 'Man with "Staring Eyes"'. He was wanted by the police in connection with the murder of 55-year-old Red Cross worker Mary Hoyles in a cul-de-sac in Southampton. She had been strangled and was last seen in the company of an American soldier with the eyes that made the headlines. There are no links whatever between this unsolved murder, that took place on 12 February, and that of Charles Walton, but for some reason the *Dispatch* wrote in the same article, 'Scotland Yard and Warwickshire police are also making camp investigations in their search for the murderer of the lame hedger …' From such bad journalism emerge non-existent links which future writers craft into 'hard evidence'.

What nagged away at the detectives was motive. One of the most common reasons for one man to kill another was money and it was obviously with that in mind that Fabian interviewed Edith Isobel Walton again on 23 February, nine days after the murder. No doubt still in shock from recent events, she told the police that the Waltons had lived at 15, Lower Quinton, since the First World War – in other words, all her life. Her uncle never worked at weekends. He was also something of a fair-weather worker. If it was wet, he did not work; if it was windy or foggy, likewise. Neither did he venture out in snow or ice. In winter, in particular, he worked little, rarely a full week at a time. In the recent past, he had been off work ill for a fortnight and his doctor, Dr Van der Meyn of Mickleton, a village nearby, came to treat him. Bearing in mind Professor Webster's post-mortem findings on the man's health, Walton's problem was likely to be a bad chest.

Walton, Edith said, was usually paid on a Saturday and he would go to Potter's farm to collect his wages. She had no idea how much he got, but never remembered him whingeing about it or being short of money. As far as Edith knew, her uncle had never lent money to anybody; neither did he have any IOUs.

Charles Walton's finances came under Fabian's scrutiny early on in the enquiry. He received 5s a week in Old Age Pension as well as the pay he received from Alfred Potter. Details of his bank account, at the Midland Bank in Chapel Street, Stratford, are included in the police archive. When his wife Alice died in 1927, she left him £297, a not inconsiderable amount. In June 1929, he still had £227 10s of that left and the total dwindled as time went on. By 1938 he was down to

£11 11s 9d, ad by June 1940, £2 13s 9d. This remained fairly constant throughout the war, with the final balance at the end of 1944 at £2 15s 6d. The accounts do not include the £44 he received in 1936 from a benevolent club to which he belonged. Neither do they include the regular payments he received from Alfred Potter.

The detectives checked the accounts of L.L. Potter and Sons, which the manager, Norman Hitchman, was happy to provide. Walton's pay was erratic because of his working habits, but having interviewed Alfred Potter, Fabian believed the farmer was claiming more than he actually passed on to the old man. Technically fraud, this was standard practice for many employers and usually no questions were asked. If Walton was aware of it, he certainly never complained to Edith or in her presence.

For seven years up to the autumn of 1944, Walton worked for another farmer, Frederick Frost of Magdalen Farm in Lower Quinton. His take home pay for the whole of that time was £3 a week. 'Charles Walton,' Fabian wrote, 'was a man of most frugal habits. His rent was but 3 shillings a week and his total outgoings at the most cannot be estimated at more than £2 a week.' He paid Edith £1 a week for housekeeping and he bought the weekly coal and meat.

Holding a bank account was not common practice for an agricultural labourer in the mid-twentieth century. Every transaction involved a cash economy; only the wealthy used cheques. This led Fabian to believe that Walton had money lying about the house or hoarded somewhere else. In the cottage itself, Fabian found 30 shillings in a dresser and the same amount in a purse in the old man's bedroom. Such small amounts of cash were kept by everybody to pay local tradesmen, but there was no sign of larger sums and there had been no large deposits or withdrawals at the bank for a considerable time.

It is difficult to know what Walton spent his money on. He did not own or drive a car and, unusually for a man of his class and time, did not smoke. The question of his drinking remained up in the air. On the one hand he was very rarely seen in the College Arms or the Gay Dog.

On the other, Lilian Potter had given the old man a glass of cider in the days running up to his death as if this was a common occurrence. One local told writer Donald McCormick years later that Walton used to drink at home and once dragged 96 pints of cider back to his cottage in a wheelbarrow! As we shall see, not all of McCormick's recollections were very accurate.

Various people were surprised that Walton had not left any money in his will. Robert Hemmings, of 4 Lower Quinton, had known the area for years and told police that, at some time in 1943, he had been working with Walton when Horace Yates, another employee, had lost a pound note. 'You shouldn't carry a lot of money about with you,' Walton had said. 'I never do. I'm not short of two or three hundred pounds.' But in fact, he was; at least according to his bank account. In 1943, his balance was £2 14s 9d. Emily Neal, of Park Farm, Henley-in-Arden, was the old man's niece. He stayed with her as a holiday every year and worked on her husband's farm. Although he kept his private life to himself, she was under the impression that, according to Fabian, he 'had a few hundred pounds saved up'. John White, a scavenger (rag and bone man) of Birmingham Road, Stratford, was related to Walton by marriage and agreed with Mrs Neal. Edith and her fiancée, Edgar Goode were surprised (and possibly rather miffed?) that he had nothing to leave them. Edith told police that Walton's money belt was for carrying personal items, not cash. The dead man's old friend, George Higgins, believed that he only carried 'an odd shilling', never notes; he would have nothing to spend money on working in the fields.

Harry Beasley's wife, who had lived next door to the Waltons for twenty years told Fabian, 'I did Charles's bit of shopping for him and I am convinced he had no more than a few shillings in his belt.' The police were doubtless intrigued by the fact that Walton's clothes were disturbed as though someone had been rifling his belt and pockets in search of money. Given this belief, it is difficult to see why Fabian lighted on a chief suspect in this context (see Chapter 8).

Meon Hill, Warwickshire. The hill fort above the village of Lower Quinton. Taken from the murder site of Charles Walton. *Author*

Charles Walton's rented cottage in the 1920s, where he lived with his wife Alice and niece Edith.

The Tudor coat of arms in St Swithin's church, Lower Quinton, which writer Donald McCormick found 'demonic'. *Author*

A brass rubbing of the tomb of Joanna Clopton, 1430, St Swithin's Church, Lower Quinton. According to author Donald McCormick, she became a witch after the death of her husband. In fact, she became a nun. *Author*

Is this the grave of Charles Walton? The headstone was allegedly removed by his family to deter ghouls. *Author*

: God loue our nobie Queen. Elizabeth Amen

The hedge at Hillground where Charles Walton was murdered in 1945 as it is today. Signs of his work are still there. *Author*

The only known photograph of Charles Walton.

A two-tine pitchfork which was a common tool of agricultural labourers. Charles Walton was pinned to the ground with his. Was this the last thing he ever saw? *(Author's collection)*

This wall of implements from an agricultural museum shows the type of billhook used in the murder (the two long handled, curved implements) as well as short-handled versions (with tang) which many people think was the type used.

(Bluebells Museum, Isle of Wight)

One of five police photographs of the dead man taken by PC Arthur Nicholls, 14 February 1945. The handles of the pitchfork and billhook can be seen to left of the picture.

Farmer Alfred Potter, the prime suspect in the murder of Charles Walton (Unknown newspaper source).

Detective Chief Inspector Robert Fabian, the most high-profile 'copper' of his generation.

Detective Sergeant Albert Webb worked with Fabian on the Walton murder. This photograph was taken years later after his retirement.

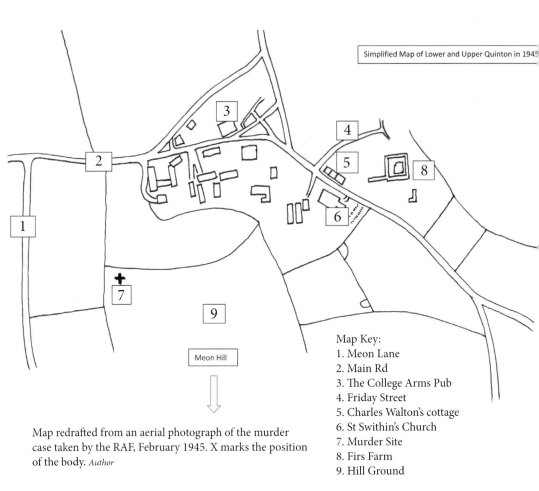

Meon Hill

Map Key:
1. Meon Lane
2. Main Rd
3. The College Arms Pub
4. Friday Street
5. Charles Walton's cottage
6. St Swithin's Church
7. Murder Site
8. Firs Farm
9. Hill Ground

Map redrafted from an aerial photograph of the murder case taken by the RAF, February 1945. X marks the position of the body. *Author*

The College Arms, Lower Quinton today. Prime suspect Alfred Potter drank here on the day of the murder. *Author*

Gerald Gardner, 'king of the witches', thought the witchcraft link with Charles Walton was nonsense.

Donald McCormick, the 'fantasy historian' who wrote the first book on the Meon Hill murder.

Dr Margaret Murray, Egyptologist and anthropologist, believed that the Walton murder was linked with witchcraft.

Italian prisoners of war often worked in farmers' fields in the mid-1940s. Several were seen near the murder site.

A view of a 'laid' hedge near the murder site. When properly done, the foundations of such work can last for decades. *Author*

The view of St Swithin's church across Valender's bean field, which still shows the ridge and furrow of the Medieval three field system. *Author*

Sketch of Charles Walton as he would have appeared on the day of his murder. *Author*

But there was a sub-text to Charles Walton's finances which was never explained at the time and which I believe has a bearing on his killer's motivation. As Fabian said in his final report:

> The closest enquiry had been made into the activities of Charles Walton with a view to discovering how he could have spent the money which appears to be missing, but no explanation has been forthcoming ... Neither is there any evidence that he ever had any financial dealings with anybody. Walton was a *secretive type of man* [my italics] and the mystery surrounding his money is almost as great as the mystery surrounding his death.

There were rumours in the local village shops that the old man was cashing cheques for more than he appeared to need. This was happening regularly in the months leading up to his death and the possibility exists that he was paying someone. If the money he cashed was not in his home, nor in his money belt, where was it? No IOUs were found on Walton's premises, but if my theory is correct (see Chapter 13) that is hardly surprising.

The coroner's inquest opened at Stratford Town Hall on 20 February with George Lodder in the chair. The County of Warwick's Southern District inquest opened with the basic information relating to Charles Walton's death. The deceased was found dead in a field on Potter's farm in the parish of Quinton at 7.15 p.m. on Wednesday, 14 February. The medical staff who had examined the body were Doctor McWhinney and Professor Webster. Walton had no life insurance and was in the General Hospital mortuary in Stratford, awaiting burial. 'Negligence or blame' was alleged against someone, listed as 'Not known'. Friends wished to bury the old man as soon as possible. At that stage, the senior police officer handling the case was Superintendent Herbert Simmonds of Stratford. There were seven jurymen (the numbers in coroner's court juries vary), all male, with corporation toll collector Joseph Hobday as foreman. As was to be expected, they were all Stratford residents, with a variety of occupations.

The first witness was PC 148 Arthur Nicholls who took six photographs of the body. Numbers 3, 4 and 5 were taken in situ by the hedge, clearly using a flash because it was by now midnight. The next day (15 February) Nicholls took two more photographs (6 and 7) and finally 1 and 2 taken in the mortuary. These photographs were shown to the court and jury, but only one (3, 4 or 5) seems to have survived. There are no more in the police files at the National Archive.

PC Michael James Lomasney told the court that he took a phone call at 6.50 at his Long Marston station. He joined Valender as requested and went with him to the murder scene – 'I saw the apparently lifeless body of Charles Walton. I made a cursory examination … and was satisfied that life was extinct.' For reasons that are unclear, Lomasney added 'when I arrived at the scene, Mr Potter was standing about 25 feet from the body … In consequence of what I saw I arranged for a doctor and senior police officers to attend the scene.'

The rest of the inquest file now in the hands of Warwickshire County Council is extremely disappointing. Paul Newman, writing on the case in 2009, quotes what appears to be a verbatim account of the proceeding in *Under the Shadow of Meon Hill* but this question and answer between the coroner and Alfred Potter, appears nowhere in the records, either of the inquest or in the National Archives' files. The Warwickshire Archive contains a three-page (redacted) account of the inquest, but it, too, is clearly incomplete. The coroner asked Potter if he had been told that Walton had no shirtsleeves. Fabian refers to this in his report.

On 17 February, the farmer had told DS Webb that he could not be positive, but 'I am almost certain it was Walton whom I saw working at the hedge … Whoever it was appeared to be trimming the hedge.' Three days later, Potter told coroner Lodder that he had seen someone in shirtsleeves in the field and 'the person he saw did not move'. The time had changed from ten past twelve (Webb) to 12.30 (coroner). But

Potter had actually told Webb that it was 'about' 12.10 p.m. and in all his movements that day, it was clear that the farmer was not wearing a watch, so his timings could only be approximate.

By the time of the inquest, the farmer had been shown the dead man's clothing and could presumably see what the coroner was getting at. He definitely saw someone in shirtsleeves and whoever it was did not appear to be using tools. He did not move. Potter told Lodder that he had not touched the body but had 'got hold of the trouncing-hook'. 'You cannot help further, can you?' the coroner asked. 'I am afraid not, sir,' Potter said. 'I wish I could.' The farmer claimed that he never had a row with the dead man and that he trusted him to get on with his work.

Fabian pointed out that Potter's account did not tally with various statements he had made to the police. The farmer acknowledged this, admitting confusion and swore that his current testimony was the correct one. Fabian's interjection was odd. Had the inquest not been adjourned, the Yard man would have had his chance to testify.

'One has to give you credit,' Lodder told Potter, 'for being detached.' This is interesting because it is a reasonable and humane observation, totally at odds with the police view. Everybody, from Fabian to Lomasney, expected Potter to be hard as nails about the whole episode. 'I don't know what I felt,' the farmer said, 'I was so cut up.' And, tellingly, 'It was the first time I had seen a dead body.'

The rest of the inquest file as it exists now consists of copies (typed and handwritten) of statements made to the police by various people involved with the case. Professor Webster wrote to Lodder expressing his willingness to appear at the inquest at twelve noon and enclosed a copy of his post-mortem report (see Chapter 4). All these statements are analysed elsewhere in this book. One intriguing handwritten note, with no signature or identifying marks, but which may come from the coroner himself, carried the line, 'Lomasney – any interference?' It is gratifying to note that I am not alone in finding the local bobby's behaviour unacceptable.

The *Birmingham Evening Dispatch* was there to cover the inquest. Harry Beasley, as one of the finders of the body, gave evidence, as did Professor Webster. Matters were suspended, as was routine, to give police time to investigate further. Robert Fabian estimated that a month should be sufficient for this. As it turned out, of course, eighty years would not be enough!

The *Birmingham Mail* was accurate in its reporting of Webster's findings that the pitchfork was thrust into Walton's throat to hold him down while the attack with the billhook took place. Later writers, with their own increasingly deranged agendas, have made the assumption that the pitchfork thrust was delivered last (see Chapter 10).

On Tuesday, 20 March, various local papers reported the closure of the inquest. With no new leads and inconclusive interviews, the inevitable result was 'Murder against some person or persons unknown'.

Chapter 7

The Enemy Within

How often have you read, in today's newspaper accounts of murders, the line 'This sort of thing doesn't happen around here'? Murder is always somebody else's problem. It happens elsewhere. Not in my backyard.

The truth, of course, is very different. And it is a falsehood to claim, as some recent writers have, that Charles Walton's murder shattered the peaceful idyll of a rural community. The war had shattered that idyll five years earlier and signs of it were everywhere. The searchlights that probed the night sky, the roar of the bombers bound for Coventry, the whine and sudden silence of the doodlebugs, the tramp of marching men. There had been a time, certainly in Charles Walton's memory, when the only soldiers people saw were the Warwickshire Regiment or the Yeomanry on manoeuvres, the Territorial Army at the Drill Halls in Stratford and Leamington Spa, the smug ceremonial of a country that had not been successfully invaded for 900 years.

By 1945, all that had gone. There were no less than eight exiled governments based in London, each with its military hangers-on. The Free French, the Czechs, Poles and many more did what they could to remain fighting fit and several of them joined the D-Day landings in June 1944. On top of that, there were colonial troops – Canadians, Indians, South Africans – and, from early 1942, the Americans, overpaid, oversexed and over here.

So, if the people of Lower Quinton could not, in all conscience, claim that murder did not happen in their neck of the woods, at least they could point the finger at strangers, outsiders who had no right to be there in the first place.

Soldiers had always had a bad reputation. 'The brutal and licentious soldiery' were feared and hated by communities with long folk memories they did not even know they possessed. When the Manchester and Salford Yeomanry had corralled a 40,000-strong crowd in St Peter's Fields, Manchester in 1819, the crowd booed them. After they charged, killing eleven and injuring 400 more, they – and by association all other Yeomanry regiments – were called 'Piccadilly Butchers' after the area of Manchester where the incident happened. Because the day ended with a show of force from the 15th Hussars, who had fought at Waterloo four years earlier, the Manchester debacle came to be known as Peterloo.

The only man in the British army to rise from private to field marshal was William Robertson, who joined the 16th Lancers in 1877. His mother was distraught when he joined – 'to go for a soldier' was a shameful thing. The attitudes of the 1940s had softened this, if only because in the Second World War conscription meant that the size of the armed forces was vast and these were ordinary boys in uniform.

But the pressure on these boys was often too much. Even for those who had never heard a shot fired in anger, the stresses of war service were real and could be profound. The phrase and concept of post-traumatic stress disorder did not exist in the 1940s, but there were other terms for it. Professor Keith Simpson, the Home Office pathologist who handled many high-profile murder cases in London and the south, wrote:

> Emergency regulations, uniforms, drafting, service orders and a life of discipline cramp the freedom of many young men and during the long periods of wartime training and waiting, not a few of them got bored – 'browned off' was the common term. Some missed their wives or girlfriends and got into trouble with local girls and camp followers ... urged on by long periods of sex starvation ... there was a steady flow of rapes (some with strangling and other violence), of assaults (some fatal), of abortions and infanticides, of breaking into 'deserted' houses

(sometimes with violence), all arising from the changes in life that were thrust by service conditions on ordinary people.

The statistics of murder in wartime make interesting reading. If we take a six-year period (the length of the Second World War) and apply it to the 1930s, 1933–38 saw fifty-nine people hanged for murder, three of them women. The total victim count is sixty-eight. The youngest killer was 20; the oldest, 62. In terms of motive, the most common by far is domestic – husbands and boyfriends killing their partners in a row. Then comes theft and then sex crimes. Three victims died in fights, four appear to have no motive at all, and there is only one for gain. Battering to death is the most common cause of death. Ten were strangled, with ligature or manually. There were nine fatal stabbings and seven shootings. The geographic pattern is random – there is no 'murder capital' in the 1930s; London accounted for only nine of the killings.

The six-year period immediately after the war (1946–51) saw ninety-seven people hanged, including two women; and this was a time when Clement Attlee's government was halting the death penalty wherever possible. The victim number was 109, but six of them were down to one man, the 'acid bath murderer' John Haigh (caught, incidentally, by DI Albert Webb – see Chapter 13). The average age of the murderer was 33, the youngest 19 and the oldest 59. Domestic violence again leads the field in terms of motive, with theft, sex and fights following in descending order. Twenty-seven were battered to death, twenty-six strangled, twenty shot and twelve stabbed. With the slight increase in gun crime (almost certainly a legacy of the war) there is little difference in the pattern of murderous behaviour between pre- and post-war societies.

What about the war itself? Between 1939 and 1945, 112 men were hanged and no women. The average age was 31, the youngest 19 and the oldest 62. Domestic violence ranks highest, at 28 per cent, sex crimes at 20 and armed robbery 16 per cent. The pattern is inevitably slewed to an extent because 22 per cent of those hanged were spies.

What is interesting about wartime murder is that it did not increase exponentially. The enormous loss of life in various theatres of war did not lead to an increase in murder at home, on the grounds that life had become cheap. In essence, it was business as usual.

Even so, of the eighty-nine hanged for reasons other than espionage, forty-eight wore uniform. Stanley Boon and Arthur Smith were regulars in India before the war began. They were hanged at Wandsworth by Thomas Pierrepoint in October 1939 for the murder of 44-year-old Mabel Bundy, whom they had raped and battered near Hindhead in July. Clifford Holmes, of the Royal Engineers, shot and stabbed his wife at their home in Longsight, Manchester that same month. He had been knocking her about for four years – 'You won't get a penny out of me. I'll do you in first.' Samuel Morgan, of the 1st Battalion the Irish Guards, strangled 15-year-old Mary Hagan in a concrete blockhouse in Waterloo, Liverpool on Saturday, 2 November 1940 (a day, incidentally, that the Italians call the day of the dead).

The list goes on, depressing as it is repetitive, but in no single instance is the victim a 74-year-old man living in a country village. The arrival of the Americans changed the dynamic in terms of crime. In American cities, gangsterism and violence was a way of life; all over America, there were racial tensions and inevitably this situation came over with the 'Allied invasion' of 1942. Most US servicemen, at least until late 1944, were tried by their own court-martial system and punished accordingly. Of the eighteen hanged for rape between 1942 and 1945 (all at Shepton Mallet prison, Somerset), ten were black and three Hispanic. Rape has never been a hanging offence in modern Britain, but the American penal code is different. Even allowing for a more draconian regime, the figures make grim reading. Over a three-year period, American troops committed twenty-six murders, thirty-one manslaughters, twenty-two attempted murders, 126 rapes and over 400 sexual offences.

Of the eighteen executed, only one, Private David Cobb of the 827th Engineer Battalion, had his exhumed body sent home from Shepton Mallet. All the others were reinterred in the American cemetery at

Oise-Aisne in France. They lie in a special section, the 'dishonoured dead', with their backs to their comrades who died honourable deaths in combat. No Stars and Stripes flies over this section of the cemetery.

What relevance has any of this to the murder of Charles Walton? The 407 Company, Royal Engineers was drafted in to minesweep the area of the crime. They were camped nearby at Long Marston, within easy reach (2 miles) of the murder scene. These men were not locals; who knew what motives and drives lurked under the ubiquitous khaki? It would not be the first or last time that a killer has voluntarily helped in the search for his own victims or looked for clues that he himself has left lying around.

Troops were all over Warwickshire in the winter and spring of 1945. Apart from Long Marston, there were Americans based near Stratford – Fabian and Webb were sharing a hotel with some of them – and not everybody had a very high regard for them. Then again, there was Flight Lieutenant Thomas Woodward, in his caravan with a clear view of the murder scene. You could not make such analogies, of course – although people did – but six airmen were hanged for murder during the war, the most notorious of them, Aircraftsmen Gordon Cummings, the 'blackout killer' responsible for the deaths of up to six women in the summer of 1942. Less spectacularly, David Williams killed his girlfriend Elizabeth Smith in the same year because she had broken off their relationship; and Charles Koopman hammered to death his mistress Gladys Brewer and her 2-year-old daughter, Shirley. In Lower Quinton, there was never any suggestion of any involvement of the Woodwards, but look again at Chapter 2, at the list of people out and about in the area on the day that Charles Walton died. Lance Corporal Hobbis of the Royal Warwickshire Regiment based at Budbrooke Barracks in Warwick, was removing booby traps on the slopes of Meon Hill in the mid-morning. Sergeant George Mills was there too, as was Lieutenant Alan Edwards of the 22nd ITC. All three men were interviewed by Fabian and Webb and did not arouse the Yard men's suspicions.

Second Lieutenant Edwards, of F Company, stationed in Budbrooke was in charge of a 72-hour 'scheme' that began on 12 February. The next day he sent Hobbis up to the pylon on Meon Hill to plant booby traps for the operation due to commence that night. Fighting in the dark was always a tricky operation and the more practice the troops had, the better they were likely to perform in the real thing. On the day of the murder, Edwards's platoon took part in an exercise in Wimpstone near Preston-on-Stour, leaving Hobbis behind to recover the booby traps he had laid the day before. He was wearing denim overalls and a soft cap, so it is entirely likely that eyewitnesses would have taken him for a civilian. No one involved had seen anything suspicious. Hobbis backed this up entirely.

Sergeant 5121389 George Mills of the Royal Warwickshire Regiment had left Budbrooke at 8.45 on the morning of 14 February. His commanding officer, Lieutenant Paddock, does not seem to have been interviewed. Most of Mills's scheme happened some miles away and he did not reach Lower Quinton until 3.30 p.m. He saw two Italian soldiers walking towards the main road. He described them as both dressed in khaki greatcoats and caps. One was slight and swarthy, only 5ft tall; the other stockier, 5ft 6in, and with a round face. Mills also saw children in the school playground, one of whom was almost certainly Margaret Peachey (see below). The only other people he saw were two men pushing bikes and driving a herd of cattle. None of Mills's men left the unit at any time and they all were very distinctive, in full combat 'greens' with helmets and blackened faces.

The Long Marston camp itself, 2 miles from Lower Quinton, was a 455-acre site next to the railway line that ran through that village and was designated Number One Royal Engineers Supply Depot. To that end, it had an airfield, built in 1940 and large blocks of warehouses, sheds and Nissen huts. Towards the end of the war, the airfield was taken over by the American air force, although no one from this unit seems to have been interviewed, if indeed they were there at the time. This was Camp 6 Ordnance Depot according to the OS maps of the time, although this, in wartime, was top secret. Next to it was a German working Prisoner of War camp by 1945, designated Camp 685.

The telegram that the Yard had received from Chief Constable Kimber had been very specific – 'The murder was either committed by a madman or one of the Italian prisoners who are in a camp nearby.' There were Slavs and Ukrainians at Camp 685 too, although it is interesting that Kimber singles out the Italians, perhaps because they were in the majority. When Inspector Toombs interviewed Alfred Potter on the day of the murder, the farmer suggested the killer might be one of those 'blasted Italians'. In the first full book written on the murder, Donald McCormick wrote, 'There was an undercurrent of resentment against the prisoner-of-war camp – oddly enough supported by the local vicar who was firmly convinced that an Italian was the killer and that this method of killing was peculiarly Italian.' This is not quite what we may expect from an Anglican clergyman steeped in God's love, but the war affected people in different ways. It may be that the vicar was thinking of the legendary use of stilettos by the Italian Mafia in its ongoing blood feuds, but it did not fit the pattern and there were plenty of murders during the war years that were just as grisly. Apart from the sadism exhibited by Gordon Cummins, Edward Anderson smashed his blind uncle to death with an axe in June 1941; and John Smith stabbed his girlfriend Christina Dicksee thirty-four times.

The resentment hinted at by Potter and McCormick is not generally borne out by contemporaries. Italy had been on the Allied side in the First World War, but their lack of territorial gains under the terms of the Treaty of Versailles helped to give rise to the Fascist dictatorship of the journalist Benito Mussolini. Il Duce waited until June 1940, when Nazi Germany had overrun the whole of Europe other than neutral Spain and Sweden, before joining the 'Pact of Steel'. The Italian war effort was feeble, giving rise to all sorts of jokes – How many gears does an Italian tank have? Four: one forward and three reverse. It was only in the Mediterranean where the Italian navy was remotely formidable and the fact that Italians had overthrown Mussolini and pulled out of the war by 1943 makes their commitment to it doubtful in the first place.

The first large influx of Italian prisoners arrived in July 1942 with several thousand captured troops in the Middle East where Mussolini had been trying to recreate the Roman Empire. When the country surrendered, a further 100,000 volunteered as 'co-operators' with the Allies and this was the general attitude of prisoners of war in the 1940s. In his report, Chief Inspector Fabian calls them 'collaborators', which had a rather different connotation. There were other camps in Warwickshire – a German one on the current site of Warwick School, past which Fabian and Spencer would have driven on their way to the murder scene; another on Warwick racecourse. There was a large German contingent kept under guard at Merevale, near Atherstone, at a camp from which the Italians had been moved on. One ex-inmate of the Merevale camp, a German, remembered excellent relations with the locals. The prisoners played football matches with local lads, built a theatre and put on shows for the villagers, complete with a 'big band'. The locals gave them fresh eggs and the prisoners made toys for their children at Christmas 1944.

The love-hate relationship that all this engendered was difficult. A month after Walton's death there was an attempted break-out at Merevale, quickly coped with and the German camp at Bridgend, South Wales, housing the eminent Nazi general Gerd von Rundstedt, was the scene of serious trouble. A year after Walton was killed, with camps and prisoners still in Britain even though the war was well and truly over, Shaftesbury town council in Dorset lodged an official complaint about an extra 150 prisoners being brought in. It was claimed that local women had been molested. And at Stoneleigh, in Warwickshire, rumour had it that babies were conceived through the metal fencing around the camp there!

While Fabian and Webb focused their attention on the locals, Spooner and his team tackled the Italians. Fabian himself, however, had foreseen the problem and sent for DS David Saunders from Special Branch, who was a fluent Italian and German speaker and could make himself understood in Ukrainian too. The Branch was originally the Special Irish Branch, set up in 1883 to gather intelligence on the terrorist group, the Fenians, who brought a bombing campaign to mainland Britain during that decade. By the late nineteenth century, it continued its counter-intelligence work, shifting operations against whoever the dissidents were (largely Anarchists by then) and also supplying what was effectively a bodyguard service for royalty and visiting dignitaries.

Special Branch had been monitoring Fascist movements in Europe long before the outbreak of war, but in the war itself, each of the armed forces had its own intelligence units, as well as MI5, MI6 and Churchill's own brainchild, the Special Operations Executive. Saunders was a highly competent officer working under the command of DCI Leonard Burt.

There were 1,043 prisoners at Long Marston and presumably Saunders had to interview them all. Their names are duly catalogued in the Archive files. There were thirty-nine more at a hostel in Shipston-on-Stour and another twenty at the Long Marston airfield. Of the airfield contingent, Sergeant 1003845 Thomas Atkinson, who supervised them, told DS Thomas Medley of the Warwickshire Constabulary on 22 February that all twenty 'Co-operators' at his station were accounted for. Their only time 'off' during the day was on a Sunday. Wednesday, the day of the murder, was a 'Domestic day' which involved the inmates working late. None of them left Long Marston on 14 February and this was co-signed by Atkinson's superior, Adjutant Sheppard.

Local labourer George Hopkins of 10, Council Houses, Mickleton, a nurseryman who was a year older than Walton and probably knew the dead man as well as anyone, saw an Italian on 14 February walking quickly across a field in the direction of the camp. He greeted Hopkins with a cheery 'Afternoon'; one of the basic English greeting words that most prisoners picked up. The statement, given to Inspector Jones of the Warwickshire Constabulary, is marked with an X. This is the only one in the record pointing to illiteracy. Spooner's team, led by Sergeant

165 Hinksman, took plaster casts of footprints around the murder site and elsewhere, but an army boot is an army boot and it was not even clear whether the prints were Italian or British. Neither could it be determined exactly when they were made.

Margaret Peachey, the 11-year-old daughter of the labourer who had been present when Walton's body was found, saw two Italians at 12.10 p.m. walking across Upper Quinton village green before turning into a field entrance. She saw them again at 4.20. These times seem remarkably accurate. Even assuming that a schoolgirl had a watch (not that likely in 1945) why would she check the times of her sightings? They sound like the result of some fairly intrusive police questioning, although they may be guesswork based on the timings of the local school. Ten past twelve would be shortly after the end of a morning's session; twenty past four would be soon after the end of the school day.

Margaret was clearly interviewed at the school on 19 February, while the Italians were very much uppermost in the minds of the police. Her statement makes it clear that the headteacher, Arthur Dobson, had 'asked all the school children whether they had seen any strange people about in the village. I know why the schoolmaster asked us because my mother had told me before I left home that Mr Walton had been found dead across the fields.' It would be fascinating to know if this urging came from Dobson or the suggestion of the police. Once again, even allowing for a rather naïve interpretation from an 11-year-old, we are in the realms of the mindset mentioned at the beginning of this chapter; murders are carried out not by the man or the woman next door, but by the wandering maniac who is a stranger to the area.

Mrs Annie Norton, of Upper Quinton, had seen the same pair of Italians between 12 and 1 walking towards the Green. Margaret told Superintendent Spooner that she had been cycling home for lunch when she saw the pair walking near Mr Valender's shop from the direction of the hill. This was clearly too early for the murder itself, according to Professor Webster's expert opinion, but it had to be followed up. They both wore uniforms and top coats 'the same colour as English soldiers'. This is not *quite* correct – Italian troops' tunics and jackets were greener than the British khaki. One had a willow stick, which looked as if it had come from a hedge, which must have rung all sorts of alarm bells in Spooner's mind.

Since the Italians were, by definition, in custody, however lax, it was not difficult to arrange identity parades. One was arranged by Spooner at the Italian Working Company Headquarters at Long Marston on 16 March. It was now over a month since the death of Charles Walton and it is of great credit to Margaret Peachey who picked out 27-year-old T.38323 Rodrigo Brunelli, who told police that 14 February was his rest day and that he left Camp 685 at 2 p.m., walking to both Quinton villages where he met fellow prisoner T.251721 Mario Chicolli. The pair had bought cigarettes at Lower Quinton Post Office and this was corroborated by Phyllis Collett, who ran the place. The discrepancy of the timing was probably not important, but the CID were well aware of Professor Webster's 'murder window' of 1–2 p.m. as the likely time of death. The Italians effectively alibied each other, but the smart money was that it may have taken *two* men to batter and slash Charles Walton and it would not be the first or last time that a soldier refused to give evidence against a comrade.

Ernest Cranke was the next witness to examine the parade. He lived at the Bungalow, Meon Hill and had seen Italians nearby on the day in question. He could not identify anyone.

At his headquarters in Stratford, Fabian had marked all these sightings on his 'murder map'. Brunelli and Chicolli were taken separately by police car to retrace their route on 14 February; they coincided exactly, but Chicolli's contention that he did not leave Long Marston until three o'clock that day ruled him out as being the man seen by either Margaret Peachey or Annie Norton, who could not identify anyone either.

Two other Italians came under suspicion. As Fabian puts it in *Fabian of the Yard*,[13] John Messer, a baker's delivery man, saw the pair sitting on the verge along Meon Lane at about 1.30 p.m. One of them was wiping his hands while the other one seemed to have just broken through the hedge. Messer's description of the men was extraordinarily accurate – 'even down to his teeth' – and one of them looked 'as if he did not want to be seen'. Fabian dismissed Messer as 'a most unsatisfactory type of witness and I consider that little reliance can be placed upon what he says'. Perhaps Messer was rabidly anti-Italian or even that he had some sort of grudge against the man in question. I shall return to John Messer later because I believe that Bob Fabian had an altogether different reason to doubt him. The man seen washing blood off his hands was Annunzio Duchetta. He was seen again cleaning his clothes in camp, but the blood turned out, when tested, to be rabbit blood. The engineers even found his snares with their metal detectors. Technically, poaching was illegal, and the Italian had no idea what the punishment might be had he been caught. Statements were taken, mostly by DS Saunders, of fifty-five other Italians who were off duty on 14 February. Such was the laxity of the camp and such the ambivalence of attitudes towards them that they came and went relatively freely, both on foot and on bicycles.

There was another Italian at large on 14 February. Calogero Bonano cycled into Lower Quinton at least twice during the afternoon to visit the village shop even though it was not a rest day. He had bought needles and pins from Phyllis Collett at the post office and was clearly a regular, serving as batman to Major Whitworth at Long Marston. The postmistress knew him as 'Miss', although whether this was because of his politeness or his penchant for sewing, we shall probably never know! Saunders was happy with the answers Bonano gave, as he was with all the others he investigated. Probably exhausted by two weeks' intensive interviewing, Saunders made a laconic judgement call at the end of

---

[13] Fabian p. 127.

each one. The demeanour was either 'quiet' or 'frank', depending on how forthcoming the prisoners were. Fabian's conclusion was clear:

> From enquiries I made in this matter I have been unable to establish that any of these Italians have ever resorted to violence during their stay at Long Marston and cannot find an authentic case of them even being discourteous to the local villagers. The result of these intensive enquiries into the movements of Italians on the 14th of February, 1945, does not reveal any evidence which could connect them with murder.

As it happened, a sizeable contingent from the Italian camp were in Stratford on the day that Charles Walton died. Some of them went to the Memorial Theatre to see Moliere's *The School for Husbands*. A seventeenth-century French comedy translated into English does not seem the most relevant or exciting fare for Italians, but the prisoners were all too prepared for the relaxation and the chance of a day off. Others 'went to the pictures' as the phrase went, to see Felix Aylmer (already something of a national treasure) in Teddington Studio's *Mr Emmanuel*. This was a pure propaganda piece, about a Jew who goes home to Germany in the pre-war period to find to his horror what is already happening to his people. Several of the Italians interviewed referred to it, but none to the Moliere! A bit player in the film's cast was Louis de Wohl, an astrologer turned spy who worked for the British Secret Service's black propaganda department. He played Hermann Goering!

A separate yet connected line of enquiry concerned the plethora of boot prints at the scene of the crime and a great deal of police attention was focused on them. The only diagram left in the police archive is the sole of such a boot, complete with circular studs. Several footprints had been found at the murder site (many of them, of course, made by the policemen investigating the case) and, to rule the Italians out at least, DS Eric Jenkins of the Warwickshire Constabulary made a plaster cast of a boot impression secured on Hillground by Inspector Jones. Jenkins compared this with impressions in Valender's bean field, behind Walton's hedge, found by Sergeant Hinksman and others found by officers Medley and Croker.

The thinking behind this seems a little off. On 26 March, Spooner and Webb revisited the murder scene and found footprints they believed were freshly made. It was common knowledge that the Italians wandered the fields and some of them were poachers, even having the gall to sell the rabbits they caught to the locals. How these could be distinguished from any made on 14 February escapes me. The clearest impression was a 10½-inch sole belonging to a size 5 army boot, but to all intents and purposes, British and Italian boot soles were identical. At Long Marston, Spooner's men identified ten prisoners with boots of that size, none of whom was in the list potentially identified by eyewitnesses. All this took place over four weeks after a swarm of coppers had examined 2,000 pairs of boots at Long Marston, while their owners were asleep. The result of this was precisely nothing.

In case the police were accused of focusing too narrowly on the enemy within, they widened the net in their investigation. Fox snares along the Quinton hedgerows were found to have been laid by four local boys, 17-year-old Thomas Russell, his 11-year-old brother Frank and Geoffrey Sheppard and Francis Smith, both 17. Sergeant 165 A.J. Hinksman, who had been involved in the footprint waste of time, interviewed these lads on 23 February. A typical statement is that of Francis Smith, an electrician of 21 Friday Street, behind Walton's cottage. 'About five weeks ago' (which would make it the third week in January) he, Sheppard and the Russell boys got some cable from a local workshop belonging to Alec Simmonds and, with Alfred Potter's permission, set three fox snares along the hedge where Walton's body would later be found. They checked on them from time to time but had not been back for at least three weeks.

Hinksman's own statement confirms that the snares he found were amateur. On 16 March, he affirmed:

These snares were very large and of a crude type and appeared to be intended to catch foxes. They were made of brake cable. One set was in a run under some rails in the fence of the field in which the crime took place. Another was set in a run in the hedge a few yards further away… This was secured with a rope to a branch in the hedge. The third snare was set in the hedge in the field just on the Meon Hill side of the scene of the crime and was fastened to a piece of barbed wire

It was the youngest boy, Frank Russell, who took the sergeant to the field and pointed the snares out.

Alec John Simmonds, an agricultural engineer of Friday Street, Lower Quinton, confirmed the boys' story. The 1939 Register lists this man as Alfred J. Simmonds 'master wheelwright' at the same address and his statement is not in the police file. What is unsatisfactory about all this is that the three statements taken from the 17-year-olds and 11-year-old were all identical. Either Hinksman interviewed them all together and produced typewritten copies for them to sign or he allowed far too much collusion in the compilation of the evidence.

Then there was Camp 6's rat-catcher, Private Thomas Davies of the Royal Engineers, father of six. Chief Inspector Fabian, in the police files claimed that Davies was 'an unscrupulous type' (on what evidence is unknown) and he was sometimes seen in the Meon Hill area. His comrades vouched for his presence in camp on 14 February, however, and another line of enquiry petered out. Private 1144046 Davies was 38. He lived at 13 Vine Cottages, Albert Rd, Oswestry on the Welsh border and had been with the Pioneers for two and a half years. He had been at Long Marston for most of that time and seems to have been given a degree of latitude, not parading 'in the usual manner' but carrying out his rat catching 'where I please'. He knew Walton by sight but had never spoken to him. Somehow, Davies had acquired rabbit-catching rights from three local farmers – Potter, Slatter and Huggins – often working with Mr Kimpson from nearby Clopton.

On the day of the murder, the rat-catcher/rabbit-hunter left camp between eleven and twelve. He took his black and white dog with him and a knapsack containing ferrets, nets and rat poison. He borrowed a bike from Mrs Kimpson (for which he paid 6d) and borrowed her dog too. Then he cycled to Pebworth, reaching the Leg of Mutton pub at about half past twelve. He spoke to various people there and left at quarter past two. He worked at Mr Hodges' farm in Pebworth until dusk, returned the bike and dog to Mrs Kimpson and went back to camp. He was nowhere near Hillground or any of Potter's fields that day. His statements concerning his whereabouts at lunchtime were corroborated by Thomas Jardine, a roadman at Pebworth and Jack Jeffrey, son of the licensee of the Leg of Mutton (actually Shoulder of Mutton in Broad Marston) 3 miles from the murder site.

Davies had been stopped the following day by the police who were clearly checking on individuals roaming the area; although this enquiry is an admirable example of no stone being unturned, it is difficult to see in what way Davies was an 'unscrupulous type'. The man's whole existence, however, sheds an unfavourable light on wartime Britain. The Pioneer Corps was an unorthodox outfit but Davies seems to have been allowed to be more unorthodox than most, wandering at will away from camp, making money on the side and no doubt having lengthy breaks from his day job at various public houses.

In his final report, Fabian wrote, 'A careful check was made on all mental defectives living in the locality and missing from nearby institutions on the day in question but as far as can be ascertained none of them has any connection with the murder.' There is a gap in the police files and apparently missing pages which suggests that information on individuals has been removed.

The nearest institution to the Quintons was Hatton County Lunatic Asylum which had opened in 1852. After 1930 it was called the Warwick County Mental Hospital and had a regime of 'moral treatment' which encouraged patients to work and carry out social activities. The hospital had its own farm, laundry and even fire service, containing as it did over

1,000 patients. The site had a chapel and nurses' home and the patients themselves played in an orchestra which sometimes performed for the local community. The pharmacy dispensed drugs daily for severely disturbed patients and the rules for nurses were as draconian in the 1930s as anything known by their Victorian predecessors. Nurses had to be single and lights out was at 10.30 p.m. sharp. There was to be no swearing and 'no patient shall be restrained or secluded except on an order by a Medical Officer'. If a patient escaped (which was the fear in the Walton case) the pay of the nurses on duty was severely hit.

One contributor to a website explained that her mother and father worked at the hospital in the 1940s and discovered to her horror that many patients were incarcerated there for minor problems or petty crimes. On one occasion, an inmate escaped, chased by the website contributor's father for a mile before the escapee stripped and swam the canal. Intriguingly, on her first day at Hatton, the contributor's mother had to push her bike past inmates wielding billhooks to lay a hedge – 'she was a bit worried but soon learnt they were just unlucky'.

This is difficult ground today, when society has become ultra-sensitive about psychiatric illness. New syndromes and conditions have been diagnosed and identified but random attacks and murders still take place, despite an apparent improvement in treatment. The 1940s was not so caring a time; it was still possible for runaway girls, especially pregnant ones, to be incarcerated in an institution merely for being runaways and pregnant. We have not come very far by this time from the wandering maniac everybody expected the Whitechapel murderer to be in 1888, when Isaac Isenschmid, the 'mad pork butcher' of Holloway, could be arrested for odd behaviour and access to sharp objects. If a killing was particularly brutal, as Charles Walton's was, it had to be, in the words of the police at the time, 'the work of a maniac'. There is only one reference to this line of enquiry in the police archive. In 1950, when, as we shall see, interest in the case rekindled, the police received an anonymous letter, postmarked Birmingham, referring to recent attacks by an escaped inmate from what were still called asylums. The writer's geography was not good, he admitted, but was not Birmingham quite close to Warwickshire and could this fact not be connected with the Walton murder? We can only imagine the reaction of detectives of the Warwickshire Constabulary.

There is one reference to Fabian's request for information in the Warwickshire Archive. A report was sent from the Staffordshire police as early as 16 February, two days after the murder. Because it has been heavily redacted, it is of limited value, but the essence seems to be that an inmate had been on parole somewhere in Smethwick, Birmingham wearing his own, as opposed to institution, clothes, and had not returned. He had planned to go to London and was carrying £20 in notes. He had not been seen in his family home since 13 February. The description of him read:

> 5ft 11, medium build, erect but stooped when walking, long, scowling face, fair complexion, clean shaven, brown hair, cut very short, high forehead, thick brown eyebrows, brown eyes, straight nose, large mouth, medium lips, good teeth (have recently been scraped by a dentist) square chin, large ears close to head, no marks.

One cannot help thinking that an institution photograph might have been more helpful to police looking for this man. He had some sort of peculiarity regarding smoking cigarettes but the dreaded black ink of redaction has prevented us from knowing what. Ominously, he was of a violent disposition and 'may resort to force if upset'. His clothes were described in great detail – a navy blue serge suit, grey cap, fawn or dark brown overcoat (he had two), white shirt, black boots and dark tie with white stripe. He had been in and out of his institution nine times in the last twenty years and was always violent when taken back. He was known to have done paid gardening work in the Birmingham area in the run up to the murder, but he had no known links to the Stratford district.

The answer to the mystery, almost certainly, lay among the 493 individuals of Lower and Upper Quinton in that winter of 1945. The nature of the crime was so horrific and vicious that it is most unlikely to have been committed by either a child or a woman. Children kill children if they kill at all; or they murder a family member against whom they have a grudge. When women kill, they usually use a weapon that enables them to distance themselves from their victims – poison or at best, a gun. There is the infamous case of Elizabeth Borden of Falls River, Massachusetts, accused of hatcheting her parents to death in 1892; however, Lizzie Borden was acquitted. Fabian, Webb, Spooner, Toombs and all the others were looking among the adult male population of those villages for the one man who wanted to see Charles Walton dead.

Chapter 8

The Prime Suspect

There is only one photograph of farmer Alfred John Potter, as there is of Charles Walton and he does himself no favours in it. It was taken on a sunny day, probably in high summer and Potter is scowling sullenly at the camera under the brim of a shady hat. He is a thick-set man, running to fat, and looks older than his forty years (although we have no idea exactly when the photograph was taken). Even if we knew nothing about him, Potter looks shifty; his eyes are full of mistrust. Are they also full of guilt?

Potter was, of course, one of the first people to find Walton's body on 14 February. 'First finders' have held a special place in legal circles since the Middle Ages. In terms of modern criminal profiling, it is not unusual for a killer to inject himself into a police murder enquiry, volunteering to join search parties and so on. There is nothing sinister, however – as some writers have alleged – that Potter knew exactly where Walton would be when Edith and Harry Beasley came looking for him; he had employed him to work that particular section of hedge and had seen him there earlier in the day. The police analysed the farmer's movements on 14 February with a fine-tooth comb, from PC James Lomasney's initial chat at the murder scene to interviews with DI Toombs, then Fabian and Webb.

When Lomasney arrived at the site shortly after 7 p.m., Potter seemed to him 'very upset'. He was shivering and complained of feeling cold. Lomasney seems to be that most irritating of policemen – a wannabe detective who was quickly out of his depth. We have already noted his unprofessionalism at the crime scene and the fact that he may have hopelessly compromised it. Now, he was reading something sinister into a perfectly ordinary reaction. It was evening – effectively night – in the middle of February and was undoubtedly cold, for all the weather was atypical during the day. Potter had been standing in open country on Hillground for perhaps an hour by this time. He may have been ill, with a cold or flu or something more underlying. He was almost certainly in shock, as were Edith and no doubt the Harrys Beasley and Peachey who had seen the body and its ghastly wounds. Clearly, Lomasney asked questions on that lonely hillside and Potter told him he had last seen Walton working at the hedge at 12.10 or 12.15 that day. The farmer was concerned what his neighbours would say – 'You know what they are round Quinton.' Alfred Potter had lived all his life in Lower Quinton; he could be expected to understand the foibles of local politics. But Lomasney did not know what he meant by this and did not ask. The phrase hangs in the air like the elephant in the room; we will return to it, but various writers on the case have, I believe, interpreted it the wrong way.

At some point, while the police were called and detectives and doctors turned up, Potter said he was famished (which as we have established could mean he was cold) and had to go home. Lomasney, who, incidentally, claims to have been a friend of Potter's, found this sinister. How could a man used to castrating calves and other animals, be squeamish about blood? The answer is all too obvious; Charles Walton was a human being, with all that that entailed. 'Punching' a calf did not compare with what somebody had done to the old man.

Detective Inspector Toombs visited the farmer at his home at 11 p.m. on the day of the murder. The first official interview was brief, Toombs taking it down in shorthand and it recorded little of interest. From it and subsequent interviews, a chronology for Potter's movements could be worked out and no doubt filled space on Fabian's incident room wall. Potter told Toombs that he left the College Arms at twelve noon (the church clock of St Swithin's is only yards from the pub and nobody could have missed the striking of twelve). He then crossed the field next to Hillground and saw Walton working on the hedge about

500 or 600 yards away. He estimated he had another 6 to 10 yards to cut. At about 6.15 p.m., Edith and Beasley turned up and Potter joined the search party. The original statement is not in the police archive. All Potter's statements refer to 'further' evidence. Consequently, we only have an *assumption* of what the farmer told Toombs initially.

Three days later, a more formal interview was carried out by Fabian and DS Webb at The Firs, filling in missing details. Potter had crossed the field at 12.10 on his way to Cacks Leys to feed some sheep and calves. Ten minutes later, he saw Walton working in his shirtsleeves and was surprised by this; he had never seen the old man do that before. He would have crossed the field to talk to him, but he already knew about the dead heifer in the ditch and time was passing. He got home at about twenty to one. When Webb read the statement to Potter (the routine procedure at the time) the farmer added, 'Although I cannot be positive, I am almost certain it was Walton who I saw working at the hedge at twenty past twelve … Whoever it was appeared to be trimming the hedge.'

In this context, Potter made a second statement, this time to Fabian, at Stratford police station on 23 February – 'I find there are one or two mistakes and I want to put these right.' He told police that, having returned from Cacks Leys, he went home and read the paper for a few minutes before helping 'Happy' Batchelor with the mangolds. The cowman asked him the time and Potter said, 'If we go and fetch some flour we can see the [church] clock.' It was one o'clock and Batchelor went home for his lunch.

Potter took about an hour and ten minutes eating his lunch, which should have ruled him out of Charles Walton's murder if Professor Webster's estimate of the time of death was correct. He then met up with Batchelor again in the yard of The Firs and a complex discussion followed regarding the best way to remove the heifer from the ditch. All this involved the borrowing of Tom Russell's rubber-tyred tractor which was to be driven by Sonny Smith. The whole operation was over by three o'clock and Potter got on with the milking in the cow shed, finishing by ten to six before catching the news on the wireless.

Potter then added details about the finding of the body. Harry Beasley, about to take Edith home, said to him, '"You had better have a look to make sure he is gone." I then walked up to the body and caught hold of the trouncing-hook by the handle at about the middle. I found that it was firmly fixed and then left it alone.' Potter remembered dialogue when PC Lomasney arrived – 'Where is this girl screaming?' and his first (ludicrous) prognostication – 'Oh, Christ, an airman.'

It was clear that Potter was a person of interest throughout. The dead man worked for him and his body was found on his land. Perhaps uniquely, he knew *exactly* where Walton would be and when. If he had a motive for killing him, the times of his day on 14 February could be challenged. In a third interview, on 18 April, Fabian and Webb grilled him again, this time about his returning to the scene of the crime. In all hackneyed police dramas, especially in the golden age of such novels, the criminal inevitably returns to the crime scene and is often caught by police as a result. In reality, some killers find it impossible to stay away in case they have left some incriminating evidence behind. Potter told the detectives that he had gone to the spot at about half past eight on the morning of 15 February and had spoken to a policeman on duty (PC West) and told him that he was on the way to check on his cattle and sheep, 'I remember seeing a broken electric light bulb on the ground and the policeman told me they had been taking photographs.'

This fact raises all sorts of questions. PC Nicholls had yet to return to Hillground on the 15th when Potter saw it, so it must have been dropped by the police photographer the previous night, when he took photos of Walton's body in situ. Presumably, Spooner's team had not yet turned up to begin their fingertip search, yet Potter referred to Walton's second stick, the one made from hedgewood, as something 'the police had been looking for'. The implication is that a search had already taken place and that the light bulb and the stick had been missed by the search party. What else did they overlook?

The police asked around about Alfred Potter and views on him by various locals varied enormously. Three land girls who worked at The

Firs, Margaret Brooks, Lily Chance and Betty Jeynes all liked him. The work of these girls was checked by the police. They were most unlikely murderers, but Land Army girls were physically strong and knew how to handle the tools which had been used to kill Charles Walton. The Archive describes their earlier experience at The Firs in the autumn of 1943. Meanwhile, they had been sent elsewhere – they had not left because of any problems they had encountered at The Firs; Land Girls were relocated as need arose.

It may be one of these girls who gave an extraordinary statement to the police at Henley-on-Thames in 1953. Since her name and many details have been redacted, it is difficult to be accurate but the gist is that she was at The Firs on 14 February 1945 when 'a middle-aged woman [Edith Walton] came to the farm and spoke to [Potter]:

> I understood from the conversation that took place she was a niece of the old man who worked on the farm. She stated that he had not been home to tea that day and she was worried. I cannot remember her name or the old man's. I can't remember that I had ever seen him, but apparently he had been hedging and ditching on the farm.
>
> [Potter] and some of the farmhands then went out to search where this man had been hedging. I did not go.
>
> A short while later [actually, nearly two hours] [Potter] came back saying they had found the old man where he had been hedging. He had been killed with his badging hook.
>
> I was questioned by Scotland Yard officers at [redacted, but presumably Stratford] about the murder, but I could not help much as I had been in the [farmhouse?] until 5 p.m. in the day in question.
>
> I do remember one thing which I forgot to tell the police, that was to my knowledge [redacted] never used the bathroom or had a bath. Only [redacted] and I used the bathroom at [The Firs?].

Between 5 p.m. and 6 p.m. on 14 February 1945 when I went home [to The Firs] I heard someone whistling and splashing in the bathroom. I know it was not [redacted] because she was out or [redacted] because she was downstairs. At first I thought [Lilian?] had visitors, but she said, 'No' so I assumed it must have been [redacted] in the bathroom because there was no one else in the house. From the noise, it sounded as if he was having a bath and this was most strange under the circumstances.

About a year after the murder, I had a letter from [redacted] and in it was reference to the murder, that [redacted] had heard that [redacted] had been carrying on with [redacted] of the murdered man both before and after his murder.

At the time, everyone assumed [Potter?] had committed this murder as it was rumoured he had a blackout occasionally, but all the time I was at the farm I never once heard his voice in anger and he was always very gentle, kind and polite.

What are we to make of this? Fabian makes a reference to Potter as being scruffy in the way that many farmers are, and if it was him in the bathroom that afternoon, he had just helped lift a dead heifer after a waterlogged ditch and he would have smelled to high heaven. The rumour of Potter having blackouts comes out of left field. *No one* mentions this at all, including Fabian who clearly had it in for the man. The 'carrying on' rumour is probably a colossal red herring. It has to refer to Edith, who was engaged to Edgar Goode at the time, but what significance it has to the murder is anybody's guess.

George Purnell clearly hated Potter's guts. On 21 February, he told Webb, '[Potter] was not a good man to work for and frequently threatened to give me the sack and turn me out of my cottage which was on his land.' If this happened, the threat was an empty one – The Firs belonged to Magdalen College; the company merely rented it. 'He would never lend a hand no matter how busy we were but would only grumble if not enough was being done … He was a bad-tempered man and a heavy drinker. He would grumble and order me about especially when he was in drink.' There was clearly a lot of 'form' between the two men. On his own admission, Purnell did not pay rent (6 shillings a week) but worked at weekends for nothing in lieu. He believed that the farmer was short-changing him, paying him for four days holiday instead of seven and not paying him at the standard overtime rate. Purnell's formal letter to Potter had achieved nothing, so the labourer had gone to the War Agriculture Committee to demand justice. This group had been set up in the First World War to oversee all things agricultural.

DI Toombs checked on Potter's reputation with the Warwickshire War Agricultural Committee on 26 February. Inevitably, the people he spoke to and any complainants against the farmer have been redacted, even though the officials themselves can have had no links with the murder whatsoever. Both officials told Toombs that there were no complaints regarding wages or short-changing against Potter, who was one of the best farming employers in the county. Gossip said that he betted 'rather heavily' although we can imagine, as no doubt Toombs did, what short work Potter's brief would make of this irrelevant smear had the case come to trial.

With the typical paper shuffling of wartime red tape, the War Agricultural Committee passed Toombs to the Wages Committee, based in Rugby and the DI discovered that Charles Walton had been dismissed by two farmers over the years but could not explain why. The implication was that theft was involved.

On the day in question, Purnell was working with John Field until ten past one. He then cycled home through Lower Quinton, had his lunch and got back to his ditching at about 2.20 p.m. At four o'clock he went to the farm to help with the milking and knocked off at half past five. He never saw anyone in the fields in shirtsleeves, nor indeed any strangers. In fact, the only person he saw was a local who walked the same way every day from his farm to collect the post. This was at ten in the morning and half past three in the afternoon. Neither Purnell nor this man were anywhere near Walton and they could not see any of Potter's fields from where they were.

John Field, perhaps oddly, did not mention Purnell at all. He had started work on 14 February at Meon Lane, carting straw to Meon Hill, beginning the journey at 11.30 a.m. He passed Hillground but did not notice Walton; neither did he 'see anything out of the ordinary'. At twelve noon, he saw Alfred Potter at The Firs chatting to Joseph Stanley; they were examining a tractor. Field's comment 'I would have had a full view of the field where the body was found' is intriguing. If this was so, why did he not see Walton working there? He was undoubtedly the old man wearing a cap, dark clothes and carrying a walking stick seen by Corporal Hobbis, but he saw no one at all.

William Dyde did not like Potter either. St Swithin's churchyard is littered with the graves of this family, another two of which are listed on the First World War memorial – unlike the Potter family, relatively new to the village, the Dydes had been there for generations. At the time of his police interview, Dyde was working for Frederick Frost at Magdalene Farm and mentioned (why is unclear) that Potter was friendly with Sergeant Edwards from the Long Marston camp.

But being, to some, an unpopular boss, did not make Alfred Potter a murderer. The police needed more. Convinced, as he became, that money was at the bottom of the case, Fabian went over Potter's finances with a fine-tooth comb. They were likely to be complicated, because the firm of L.L. Potter (owned by Alfred's father) owned property all over Warwickshire. On 2 March, Fabian received a telegram to the effect that neither father nor son had any outstanding debts against them. There had been a judgement against Potter senior, but that was back in 1936 and had since been resolved.

Rumours persisted, however, that Potter junior was a bad payer and that, heavily in debt, he not only failed to pay Walton from time to time, but that the old man had lent him money. This would explain why there was so little in the dead man's bank account and also it would provide a motive for murder; Walton called in Potter's debt in the early afternoon of 14 February and paid for his effrontery with his life.

In the statement that Potter made to the police on 23 February, he told Fabian that the £2 15s that he paid the old man on Saturday, 10 February was for a week's work rather than the fortnight he had mentioned in his previous statements:

> Some weeks I had drawn wages for Mr Walton when he has not been at work. My books will show that he had wages every week whereas, in fact, he did not always have wages as he didn't work in very bad weather. There has [sic] been occasions when Mr Walton has asked me for wages due to him and I haven't had the money to pay him as I had spent it. I would then pay him later in the week. The last occasion of this sort I remember was just before Christmas of 1944.

Potter's financial records were in the hands of his firm's secretary, Norman Hitchman of Blockley, Gloucestershire. Perhaps it did not help that Hitchman was Potter's brother-in-law, but the police clearly had to be satisfied that the records appeared to be 'straight'. It may be that Potter was deliberately falsifying accounts and paying Walton less than he should have, but it is worth remembering that Edith had no recollection of her uncle whinging about payment – or lack of it – at any time. Neither did Walton's few friends, especially George Higgins, have any comment on this.

If Potter's financial situation did not shed any light, what about forensics? On 24 February, E.S. Burgess of the West Midlands Forensic Science laboratory took possession from DI Toombs of a white handkerchief, a duster, a woollen pullover, a pair of corduroy breeches and a jacket belonging to the farmer. Unlike detective fiction, the wheels of actual forensic science grind slowly and it was not until 16 March that the results came back from the laboratory. Webster wrote, 'I could find nothing of evidential value upon the garments. There were two areas upon the breeches which gave presumptive tests for blood, but they had been so well cleaned that it was impossible to say whether or not this blood had been human or not.' Given that Potter routinely 'punched' calves, this left the police no further forward. As to the vexed question of the farmer handling the murder weapon at the crime scene, Webster's team found no fingerprints on this at all, even though both Potter and Lomasney admitted to having touched it.

So what was the case against Alf Potter? It is clear that Inspector Fabian had the man in his sights from the start. Soon after the Yard man arrived, he spoke to Lomasney, as the local copper, and learned that the two were on friendly terms. So Fabian told Lomasney to 'keep in close touch' with the farmer and 'without arousing any suspicion, to find out all he could about the latter and his movements on the 14 February'. When I first read Lomasney's account of this, I assumed that it was either an example of a local man not quite knowing where his personal and professional boundaries lay or that Lomasney was bucking for a promotion or commendation. From Fabian's report (April) it was clear that he was only following orders, a phrase which would be on the lips of several ex-Nazis in the months and years ahead. Today, this would be interpreted as police entrapment and a judge would throw out such evidence. The 1940s were different days and Fabian, after all, ran the Flying Squad, the 'Sweeney' that had a reputation for toughness, often beyond the strict letter of the law.

Following the chief inspector's orders, Lomasney visited The Firs at 9.30 on the morning of Sunday, 18 February. Lilian Potter burst into tears with the shock of it all and the bobby calmed her down. 'You know,' she said, between sobs, 'we have never had anything to do with the villagers much and what they will think. They will put it down to Alf. You see, he [Walton] worked for us and it happened on our land, but we can account for where Alf was every bit of the day.'

Out in the yard, Lomasney met Potter himself:

'I think you have been talking to the wife too much about this business; she is worrying about it.' He merely mumbled something inaudible and would not look me in the face. I believe he was on the verge of weeping. As he was not in a talkative mood, I left him.

Still carrying out Fabian's edict, Lomasney revisited the couple on the following Tuesday, 20 February. It was 5.45 p.m. and the inquest had opened in Stratford that day. Potter could not understand why he had not been called. He volunteered the information that 'this was the work of a fascist from the camp'. A slightly bizarre interlude followed when a soldier knocked on the back door and an airman who was visiting the Potters opened it. Outside in the yard, the soldier told Potter that the military police had caught an Italian in possession of a stolen suit. 'The civil police "have taken him away with them", Potter affected greated [sic] glee and his wife became almost hysterical with delight.' It is difficult to see what this reaction was all about. The suit clearly had nothing to do with Walton's murder and a light-fingered prisoner of war was a world away from a vicious killer.

Earlier – and more pertinently – the conversation had turned on possible fingerprints on the murder weapons. 'This had a terrible effect on Mrs Potter,' Lomasney wrote in his statement:

[Potter was] also greatly affected but quickly recovered. 'I have told the Police that I caught one of the tools in my hand to see what had happened; I told them more than once; they knew that.' Lilian shouted at him, 'They will have your fingerprints now and blame you for it, you fool.' He told her not to be so silly.

This was the first time, Lomasney says, that Potter had raised the touching of the weapon but in the same paragraph in his statement contradicts himself. 'Potter also mentioned that I, too, had touched one of the tools and I agreed that I had.' Lomasney believed that he had handled the billhook shaft in such a way as to leave no prints (he still does not mention gloves). Since no prints were found by forensic tests, he was presumably right. And this was not the first time the point had been raised; Constable West wrote it in his statement of events on 15 February.

Lomasney must get full marks for trying. Two days later, Thursday the 22nd, he arrived at The Firs at 8 p.m. and drove with the Potters to the Lygon Arms in Chipping Campden, where L.L. Potter, Alfred's father, was the licensee. On the way home, Potter mentioned that the police had already spoken to his father, as well as the father of labourer Kenneth Workman and Potter seemed concerned over this. There is no paperwork about Workman in any of the police records. The sole mention of him is in Fabian's follow-up report of 30 April, which says that Workman left Potter's employ shortly after the murder. He clearly made a statement to the police, which has not survived, 'but by his demeanour [Fabian's words] I am satisfied that he, too, suspects Potter of having some connection with the murder.' I am not aware that 'demeanour', even when cited by an experienced detective, has any standing in a court of law.

Lomasney dutifully reported all conversations with the Potters to Fabian, who drew various conclusions of his own. In particular, the Yard men talked again to individuals who had had a falling out with Potter. One of these was 'Happy' Batchelor, who effectively gave Potter a pretty solid alibi for Professor Webster's time frame of murder. Batchelor was 'closely interrogated … for a lengthy period'. Given the tactics of the Flying Squad at the time, this was a grilling, with who knew how many legal corners cut in order for the police to get their man.

Police procedure has changed considerably since the 1940s. The Police and Criminal Evidence Act (PACE) of 1984 effectively gave suspects more rights, including the obligatory presence of counsel, who could recommend to their client that 'no comment' might be the most appropriate response to questions. Although tales of police brutality in Fabian's day were no doubt exaggerated by 'villains', there was a tendency for the police version of, say, an interview, to be believed, virtually without question.

Batchelor had a pay grievance with Potter similar to that of George Purnell, but it was actually Potter senior who had refused to budge and Batchelor had found work elsewhere. With an extraordinary leap of logic, Fabian writes, 'I also think it probable that he had been prompted to leave by suspicions he may have regarding his former employer's connection with the death of Charles Walton.'

The fact that Potter had not mentioned returning to the murder scene on 15 February and talking to Constable West, as well as a certain evasiveness about his movements on the day of the murder, convinced Fabian that 'all this is indicative of a very peculiar mentality.' All it actually means is that Potter forgot his chat with West when he was re-interviewed. He could not possibly have claimed that it did not happen in the light of West's testimony. In fact, later in his own statement, Fabian refers to Potter visiting the murder site at 'about half past eight' and talking to a policeman [West]. 'He thought he was the policeman to whom he had mentioned touching the stale of the trouncing-hook.' In other words, all he got wrong was the time. Determined to find all this suspicious, Fabian wrote, 'Potter appeared to remember the incident very clearly', remarking again how 'strange' it was that Potter had not mentioned this in earlier interviews. On the other hand, a careful analysis of Potter's movements on that day, backed up by corroborating evidence of other witnesses, only leave him with an impossible twenty minutes to commit the murder and it is not within Professor Webster's time frame.

Clearly, Fabian was annoyed, by the time he wrote his April report that Webster's tests had failed to find human blood on Potter's trousers, although he no doubt took comfort in the fact that Lilian had let slip that her husband never washed his breeches; so, Fabian ruminated, why do it now? Neither was there any indication of any injuries to Potter as the result of an attack. Enquiries had been made at hospitals and doctors' surgeries regarding anyone who had turned up in mid-February with cuts or other injuries to hands or head, but nothing had been forthcoming.

Fabian wrote:

For the time being, it does not appear that any more can be done in the way of direct enquiries. Wherever possible all persons who could have been in any way implicated in the murder have been interviewed and their movements checked with the result that the only person upon whom the slightest degree of suspicion rests is Potter.

I believe this is why Fabian disliked John Messer, the baker's deliveryman. Lilian Potter made it clear that Messer turned up at The Firs while the farmer and his wife were having a cup of tea after dinner and he joined them for it. Potter then left the house at 'ten or quarter past' two. Messer gave his statement to Albert Webb at Valender's farm on 8 March. The clock on his van dashboard was not working but he guessed the time he saw the Italians at the roadside by the punctuality of another customer, Ernest Cranke, who always left his house to return to work at 1.30 p.m. He got to the Potters at 1.50 or 1.55 and saw the pair in the kitchen. 'I had a cup of tea with them and left just after 2 p.m.' Even if Lilian Potter was lying about her husband's movements, Messer's testimony shaves at least twenty minutes off Professor Webster's murder window when Potter was in his kitchen at The Firs, not out in Hillground hacking Charles Walton to death. For that reason, Fabian had to find Messer untrustworthy; he effectively took away his only suspect.

Chief Constable Kemble wrote to R.M. Howe, Assistant Commissioner CID at the Yard on 10 April:

If anyone had told me two months ago that [the] murder was going to be committed, and that we should still have no real clue, I should have thought it highly improbable. However, we live in hopes that something will turn up. I should like take this opportunity of expressing, through you, to Chief Inspr. R. Fabian, Sgt. A Webb and Sgt. D. Saunders, my very warmest thanks for all their assistance.

They have been indefatigable and I am entirely satisfied that no stone has been left unturned in all their and our endeavours to clear this matter up. Throughout the whole time I have been most happy in knowing that both your officers and men and mine have worked together as a complete team. I am sure that no co-operation could have been more whole-hearted and mutual.

Superintendent T.B. Thompson, senior officer in the Warwickshire constabulary, summed the case up:

The very thorough enquiries made in this case have, so far, uncovered no evidence on which action can be taken. There is suspicion against the farmer Potter, chiefly because of discrepancies in his statements affecting what he says he saw of the murdered man at a time which must have been shortly before the murder. There are, apparently, no finger impressions on the weapons used. The most positive factor, at present, seems to be the missing watch. It may be that the victim's trousers were undone by the murderer searching for a money belt. If robbery is found to be the motive, the offender is likely to be a person with local knowledge, although this may not be so.

I believe it *was* so. I also believe that Charles Walton's killer had been seen, in his shirtsleeves, by Alfred Potter. He may well have been seen, too, by Basil Hall, ploughing on Meon Hill.

Fabian wrote:

And there we had to leave it ... Maybe somebody in that tranquil village off the main road knows who killed Charles Walton, who lies buried among the neat grey tombstones of Lower Quinton churchyard? Maybe, one day, somebody will talk? Not to me, a stranger from London ...

Not to anyone.

Chapter 9

Secrets of the Stones

'But sooth is seyd, go sithen many years,
That "feeld hath eyes and the wode hath ears."'

Geoffrey Chaucer
The Knight's Tale c. 1386

There is nothing about it in the police files. There is no mention of it in contemporary newspaper accounts. Gerard Fairlie, Albert Webb's biographer, makes no reference whatsoever. But in Robert Fabian's account of the Walton murder in *Fabian of the Yard* (1950) he writes:

Anybody can become a witch. All you have to do is to recite an ancient spell that will conjure up the Devil ... When you have become a witch you can put the evil eye on your neighbours, make their cattle die, their crops rot.

You do not believe such nonsense and neither do I, yet in the picturesque Tudor village of Lower Quinton ... they speak of witches with a wry grin and many people will not pass from Bidford down Hillsborough Lane for fear of a headless horseman and a ghostly woman in white. On the hilltops around Lower Quinton are circles of stones where witches are reputed to hold sabbaths ...[14]

By 1968, in a book which we will discuss later in detail, Donald McCormick called his first chapter *Land of the Covens*, implying

---

[14] Fabian, p.124.

that Warwickshire was a focus of witchcraft over several centuries and that echoes of it still existed in 1945 and may have explained the circumstances of Charles Walton's death. The two much earlier works which are always quoted in the case are J. Harvey Bloom's *Folk Lore, Old Customs and Superstitions in Shakespeare Land* (1929) and *Warwickshire* by Clive Holland (1912). These were the books that Fabian implies Superintendent Spooner lent him very early on in their joint enquiries.

Bloom, the son of a vicar, was born in 1860 and became BA at Cambridge at the rather advanced age of 27 and MA four years later. He was ordained as an Anglican priest in Calcutta in 1888 and after various stints as curate around Warwickshire, became headmaster of Long Marston grammar school in the mid-1890s before settling as rector of Whitchurch in the county from 1896 to 1917. He was typical of vicars of his day who took an interest in the folklore of their parishes. Out of such research the folklore book was born. Such books were highly popular in their day and modern guide books still cover essentially the same ground. Anecdotes and tall stories are the stuff of this genre. Antiquarians like Bloom are invaluable for the information they amassed, often from very obscure or now lost sources, but they rarely make good historians.

Clive Holland was the penname of Charles Hankinson, born in Bournemouth six years after Bloom. He attended Mill Hill School and originally intended to go in for law. By the 1890s, however, he was a full-time journalist writing for the *Westminster Gazette,* the *Pall Mall Gazette* and *The Idler* and a number of American papers. He travelled widely with his Japanese wife and wrote three novels, in the science fiction/fantasy genre. Rather like Bloom, he understood what made for a good story, as well as what sold books, but his connection with Charles Walton remains dubious at best. He did not die until 1959 and it would be fascinating to know what, if any, were his views on the case.

It is far from clear how the Bloom and Holland books – and the whole notion of superstition – crept into the mindset of the police. We have already seen that, according to Fabian, Alec Spooner foisted them on him very early on. Sadly, we do not know enough about Spooner to assess his attitude to the whole thing. In McCormick's *Murder by Witchcraft*, the author tells us that 'Inspector [*sic*] Hinksman of the Warwickshire Police Traffic Department had taken out both books from his local library and saw in them a relevance to the enquiries that both men were undertaking ...' In the police record, Hinksman's only role was to interview the local lads snaring foxes and follow up footprint evidence.

But there is, in the Warwickshire Police File, one tantalising glimpse of Alec Spooner's mindset. It is recorded, without mentioning the Spooner connection, by Paul Newman in *Under the Shadow of Meon Hill*. The Warwickshire extract is undated and contains two verses from *The Dream of Eugene Aram*, written by Thomas Hood in 1831.

One that had never done me wrong —
A feeble man, and old;
I led him to a lonely field, —
The moon shone clear and cold:
Now here, said I, this man shall die,
And I will have his gold!

Two sudden blows with a ragged stick,
And one with a heavy stone,
One hurried gash with a hasty knife, —
And then the deed was done:
There was nothing lying at my foot
But lifeless flesh and bone!

Below it, in Spooner's handwriting, is the line 'Sir, almost fits the Quinton murder' and it is signed 'AWS Supt'. It is not clear to whom this was sent or when but the fact the Spooner calls him 'Sir' means that it is either a chief superintendent or, more likely, the chief constable of Warwickshire, E.R.B. Kemble at the time of the murder.

There is of course no witchcraft connection in this eighteenth-century murder but its existence in the Warwickshire Archive implies that Spooner was a policeman with an historic/literary take on things and perhaps this puts the Bloom and Holland books into perspective.

The Eugene Aram case, one of several juicy murders that featured with the usual embellishments in the *Newgate Calendar*, a diary of criminality hugely popular at the time, had almost no connection with Charles Walton's murder. On 1 August 1758, a labourer working in a field near Knaresborough, Yorkshire, stumbled on human remains. Without any actual evidence, a coroner's jury decided that they belonged to Daniel Clark of that parish, who had disappeared on the night of 7 February 1745. Clark was a successful shoemaker and at the time, two men, Eugene Aram and Robert Houseman, were arrested on suspicion, some of Clark's goods having been found in their possession. There was effectively no case to answer, especially with no body, and Aram and Houseman were released.

Eugene Aram was an extraordinarily talented linguist and philologist. Despite his poor working-class background, he taught himself Latin, Greek, Hebrew and Gaelic and became a teacher. After Clark's murder he left the area and lived in London and Middlesex before settling, with his family, in King's Lynn, Norfolk. The later finding of the bones in Thistle Hill, Knaresborough, led to a warrant being served and Aram, Houseman and an innkeeper called Terry were arrested and charged with murder. Houseman turned King's Evidence (a common scam to avoid the gallows in the eighteenth century) and Aram confessed that Clark's body had been hidden, not at Thistle Hill, but in St Robert's Cave, one of the many in the area associated with the prophetess Mother Shipton who is said to have lived there in the sixteenth century.

Aram defended himself at York Assizes in July 1759 but the jury did not buy his argument (actually perfectly plausible) that it could not be proved that the bones were Clark's. After a failed suicide attempt, he was hanged in the Knavesmire at York and his body was hung in chains at Knaresborough as a warning to any other would-be miscreants. His skull is still on display at the Royal College of Surgeons' Museum in London.

There was something about the Aram case that appealed to dramatists, perhaps because of the thirteen-year gap between the murder and the trial. Henry Bulwer Lytton wrote a novel about it and Thomas Hood the poem which Spooner quoted.

All this is a far cry from Fabian's version, which implies that it was Spooner who pointed out the books almost at their first meeting at the murder scene on 17 February.

The fact is, however, that contrary to Donald McCormick and Spooner/Hinksman, Warwickshire is not particularly associated with witchcraft and has no more folkloric tales than any other part of the country. In terms of actual history, the centres of the witch craze of the sixteenth and seventeenth centuries lie in Essex and East Anglia, and establishing a continuous, unbroken chain of such beliefs over the centuries is, as we shall see in the next chapter, far from easy.

Holland's *Warwickshire* is particularly irrelevant and those who claim otherwise have clearly not read it. When it was written, both Quinton villages were across the county line in Gloucestershire. Only Long Compton *just* sneaks in near the Oxfordshire border and the only reference to it in Holland is as a painting by Fred Whitehead commissioned for the book. Long Marston, where the prisoner of war camp stood in 1945, is mentioned in the context of a folk tale of a soldier hiding there after fleeing the battlefield of Worcester in September 1651. The Hillborough that Fabian refers to as 'haunted Hillborough' is in an anonymous rhyme once attributed to Shakespeare, listing various villages in the area. Clive Holland says that the reason for the 'haunted' epithet is 'lost to obscurity'.

Harvey Bloom has far more relevance, although, as we shall see, his book's importance has been blown out of all recognition by recent writers. There is one reference to Quinton, even though it was not yet part of the county, citing an old farmer discussing horse harness. It is Chapter XIV, *Occult Influences*, which may have piqued the interest of the police at the time and has certainly gripped true crime writers since. 'Witchcraft still exists,' Bloom writes, 'or is believed to do so,' at once diluting the impact of the first part of his declamation! We will discuss this in a later chapter.

Of particular importance to Bloom and those who believe that Charles Walton's murder has a supernatural element to it, is the Rollright Stones. This Megalithic circle holds a pre-eminence in folklore, attracting all kinds of nonsense. The stones themselves cannot be counted, the legend runs, because they constantly move.

'The man will never live,' runs the fable, 'who shall count the stones three times and find the number the same.' In fact, there are seventy-two of them, no matter how often you count!

Bloom tells us that the Rollrights lie 700 feet above sea level and the diameter of the circle is about 100 feet. Outside the perimeter stands the Kingstone, with a cluster of smaller stones – the Whispering Knights – to the east. The legend of the stones is that the unnamed king in question (a pagan) believed a legend which said that if he climbed the hill and could see Long Compton, the crown of England would be his. He was baulked in this by a witch, sometimes called Mother Shipton, after the Yorkshire prophetess, who was determined to stop him – 'Rise up hill, stand still stone, King of England thou shall be none. Thou and thy men hoar stones shall be, And I myself an eldern tree.'

The origin of this story may be traced to the repeated Viking invasions of Saxon England from the seventh to the ninth centuries and the creation of the Danelaw. The border between Danish territory and English, constantly fought over, cut diagonally across the Midlands. Bloom, of course, has ongoing supernatural events associated with the stones; long after the Viking time frame, a local farmer could not keep his gates closed on his way to them; another tried to drag one of the stones out of position to bridge a culvert – the team of horses harnessed for the work became terrified and refused to move but the stone was returned easily to its original site by a single animal. The Rollrights were the site of the last alleged appearance of fairies who disappeared beneath them in the eighteenth century. The actual purpose of these stones, clearly placed on the Oxfordshire/Warwickshire border by man, remains obscure, as are all other stone circles scattered throughout Britain. Were they a temple, a calendar, a clock or did they have some other purpose, now forgotten?

Bloom glides effortlessly from tales of witchcraft (see the next chapter) to ghosts, although they are very different phenomena. There were stories of a ubiquitous headless coachman who drove a coach and equally headless horses near Stratford. At Ilmington, a village not far from Lower Quinton, the ghost of the parish clerk, Edmund Golding, wandered the nave of his church long after his death in 1793. The Hillborough Lane referred to by Fabian boasted a ghostly carriage and pair as well as phantom ladies and stags.

Meon Hill itself held a special place in Bloom's quaint ramblings. He was able to buy some of the coin hoard found at the site (he does not specify when or how he came by them) which, he postulates, belonged to 'some Celtic chief of the Bronze Age'. Coin hoards like this are not uncommon and were often a family's wealth buried for later collection in the face of attack or invasion. Alternatively, the Celts of the Iron Age probably used Roman coins as spiritual talismans, rather than currency. Bloom recounts the legend of the Hill's creation, similar to other stories countrywide. When St Egwin built a Benedictine monastery at Evesham in the eighth century, the Devil was so outraged that, watching the building rising from Ilmington Hill, he kicked the ground so violently that he intended the earthquake should engulf the saint and his stonework. The saint, however, was wise to him and prayer made the earth fall short, creating Meon Hill.

In the villages below the hill, Bloom contends, were 'many old folk living' (in 1929) who told stories of 'Hell-hounds, Night-hounds, or Hooter, as they are variously named, that in phantom wise, with hounds and horn, pursue phantom foxes along the hilltops at midnight.' This is a variant of Herne the Hunter, more usually associated with the royal estate at Windsor Great Park and is probably a vague folk-memory of

Cernunnos, the horned god of the Celts who became linked with the Devil by early Christians.

One of the most intriguing stories in Bloom's book, however, concerns a plough-boy from Alveston, a village north-east of Stratford. The boy (no age is given) met a dog on nine consecutive days on his way home from work. He told a carter and a shepherd he worked with about this odd occurrence and they laughed at him. On the ninth day, a headless woman rustled past him – he heard her silk dress distinctly. The next day he heard that his sister had died. So far, so oddly commonplace. Dogs, particularly black ones, feature heavily in British accounts of the supernatural. They have a variety of names – Black Shuck, Old Shuck, Shag-dog and Shriker. The most striking appearance of one took place on Sunday, 4 August 1577 at Bungay in Suffolk when, following a thunderstorm, a huge dog rushed into the church during a service, scorching worshippers with its hot breath. The dog's claw marks can still be seen in the building's stonework and the clock mechanism melted. Neither do dog appearances only occur in the dubious historical record. A dog as death-omen appeared to a Trinity College student in Dublin five years after Charles Walton died. In 1907, a woman saw a dog with huge, glowing eyes at Budsleigh Hill, Somerset. A girl saw a similar animal in Bredon, Worcestershire during the Second World War. Margo Ryan tried to stroke one in County Wicklow and it vanished under her hand.

There are dozens of other sightings, far too numerous to be written off as the ravings of drunks or drug addicts. What is intriguing is the name of that plough-boy at Alveston, Warwickshire who saw the dog on nine consecutive days; it was Charles Walton.

Part of the problem may be linked with William Shakespeare. Today's road signs make it clear – Warwickshire is 'Shakespeare's County' as if no one else ever lived there. And one of the Bard's best-known plays is *The Tragedy of Macbeth* with its unforgettable trio of hags who foretell the hero's rise and fall. If done well, these scenes still have the power to grip us; if done badly, they descend into farce and give rise to giggles.

Macbeth was written in 1606 with the playwright cashing in on the (brief) popularity of the new monarch, James I. In November 1605, a group of Catholic dissidents, dismayed at the king's Puritanism, attempted to blow him up along with most of his parliament. The coup failed and James became the hero of the hour – not least to dramatists because he had doubled their fees for Court performances. James was obsessed with two things – the dangers of the new practice of smoking and the older practice of witchcraft, of which he claimed to have had personal experience. Shakespeare made no secret of the fact that he raided Scottish 'history' (via the *Chronicles* of Ralph Holinshed) to find his Macbeth story; in other words, the weird sisters, worshipping Hecate and dancing widdershins (anti-clockwise) around their cauldron, have nothing to do with Warwickshire at all.

Various writers on the area cannot agree on the significance or age of the settlement at Meon Hill. It was probably a Celtic hill fort like the much grander Maiden Castle in Dorset. Traces of ramparts and ditches for defence bear testimony to this. The invading Romans called these *oppida* (towns) although there was nothing approximating to an actual town in the grid-patterned Roman sense before the Claudian invasion of 43AD. Many sites of this kind remained occupied long after the Roman period and in 1957, archaeologists found a Saxon burial ground on the Hill's slopes. Scattered throughout the area, too, are DMVs (Deserted Medieval Villages) which were abandoned due to epidemic disease or natural disaster. Romano-British finds turn up from time to time on farmland at both Lower and Upper Quinton, and ridge and furrow formations in the fields are evidence that this was an agricultural centre in the Middle Ages before enclosures brought the arrival of the hedges on which Charles Walton worked.

Let us look at the circumstantial spiritualism that hovers around the Walton murder. 'I climbed Meon Hill,' Fabian wrote in *The Anatomy of Crime* a quarter of a century after the event, 'to examine the scene of the crime for myself.' He was walking, although he did not know it, over the bodies of dozens of Saxons who had once been the locals. It may be fanciful, but it is quite possible that he had just finished interviewing their descendants.

> A black dog, a retriever, sat on a nearby wall for a moment. Then it trotted past me. I did not look at it again. Shortly afterwards, a farm boy came along.
>
> 'Looking for your dog?' I asked him.
>
> 'What dog?'
>
> 'A black dog …'
>
> The lad didn't wait to hear any more. He fled down the hill. Instantly, word spread through the village that I had seen the Ghost. Local legend maintained that when Charles Walton was a boy he had seen a black dog nine evenings in succession. On its ninth appearance the dog changed into a headless woman in rustling black silk. Next day, Walton's sister died.
>
> The dog incident caused a total change of attitude towards us in Lower Quinton. No longer did anyone co-operate with our investigation. It was like the pulling down of a shutter. When I walked into a pub [ironically, the Gay Dog!] hoping to chat with the locals, the place suddenly went silent. Then everybody put down their glasses, got up and left.

It was as a result of this, Donald McCormick says, that Sergeant Hinksman decided to show the Bloom and Holland books to Fabian. But that was not what he said at the time of the original enquiry. In his report of April 1945 he wrote, 'The natives of Upper and Lower Quinton and the surrounding district are of a secretive disposition and they do not take easily to strangers.'

There is nothing here about a *sudden* change of reaction, still less one caused by the appearance of a ghostly dog. The locals had clammed up from day one. What we have here is the subtle shift of emphasis that comes with the passage of time. Fabian wrote three books outlining his police career. The first was *Fabian of the Yard* (1950); the second *London After Dark* (1954); and the third *The Anatomy of Crime* (1970). One critic accuses him of 'juicing up' the witchcraft/supernatural angle as time goes on; by 1970, Fabian knew exactly what sold books and what the reading public wanted. To be fair to him, he discusses the theme in all three books and dismisses most of it as nonsense. Even so, he inadvertently falls into its trap himself. The story of the plough-boy Walton and the dog comes from Harvey Bloom, except the Bloom does not specify the *colour* of the headless woman's dress, only its fabric. Black, however, is the colour of death, so Fabian adds it to his version. More importantly, Bloom does not say that the dog *changed* into the woman, merely that the boy saw them at the same time. Above all, who was the plough-boy? Fabian says that he was the same person whose death he was investigating, but this is pure speculation and unlikely to be true. Bloom gives no date for the Alveston incident, so we have no idea when – or if – it happened. Alveston is about 5 miles from Lower Quinton, so the link is feasible. What we are left with is that old shibboleth – that of mere coincidence, in which fictional detectives, at least, are not supposed to believe. The last word on the Walton coincidence is that family records show that the Lower Quinton murder victim had two sisters – Martha and May – and they both survived him, so the omen of the dog and the woman makes no sense at all.

But Fabian would not let the matter drop. 'I realized for certain we were up against witchcraft when the body of a black dog was found hanging from a bush near the spot where Walton died.' All books on the Walton case cite this incident, but if there was any follow-up by the police, no one records it. Was it a practical joke by a local with a warped sense of humour? Was it a threat to Fabian to leave well enough alone? Was it evidence of the existence of a local witch-cult?

For all the Yard man claimed to have 'brought the twentieth century to Lower Quinton like a cold shower-bath', Fabian seems to have left the place as imbued in the hysteria of the occult as the most incredulous ingenue.

When my wife and I visited Lower Quinton, it was not on a cold winter's day, with hints of frosts to come and a cold chill just waiting to touch the backs of our necks. It was a warm, humid August day, the day the heatwave broke in 2022 and there was a light rain just beginning to fall. My wife is an author, mostly of dark and creepy books when writing solo and so I will hand over to her for her opinions of Lower Quinton.

We arrived in the village at around one in the afternoon. The traffic had been horrendous all the way and so our time in the village would be short. We had already checked the website of the College Arms and found it was closed on Wednesday lunchtime, so we headed straight for the church, to retrace the last steps of Charles Walton. As we turned into the parking area, we had to wait to let a lorry past – it came from Darlington, where our family lives. The church was open, which was a pleasant surprise, but on the door was a typed notice to say that a villager had recently died and indeed, there was a team in the churchyard, digging a grave.

We crossed the churchyard and headed for a kissing gate into the next field, following an aerial map from Fabian's 1970 book, but as we were negotiating it, a woman with a dog – we didn't see the dog, just a very long lead and some agitation in the dried grass – appeared and we checked with her where the footpath went. She pointed it out and we turned to follow it. I use a stick and watch the ground carefully so once I was sure I was on flat ground, I looked round to say thank you, but she and the dog were gone. Dogs and Lower Quinton – there really is no escape! I discovered later that the latch of the kissing gate had hit my husband so hard in the side that he had a bruise the size of my hand which lasted for weeks.

The finding of the murder site is a story for elsewhere, but we walked back to the car and, looking across the road, saw that the pub was clearly open. We didn't have much time, but a loo break and a quick drink called, and we went in, to see an empty room except for an untouched but freshly drawn pint of Guinness on the bar. When the landlady returned, we told her that their website said that they were shut on Wednesday and she politely but firmly told us we were wrong – except when she checked, it did indeed say that, to her astonishment.

After a quick drink and bag of crisps (lunch serving having stopped five minutes before we arrived) we got back in the car and, pulling out, had to wait for a van delivering Durham animal feed to go past – we live in Durham when we go to visit our family.

Now, having worked tangentially with Donald McCormick and having read several of his books, I know what he would say about these events and, having typed this book so far, I can imagine what spin Fabian would put on them. The extraordinarily bad traffic was Lower Quinton's way of telling us to go away, to leave the village and its secrets alone. The lorry was underlining the fact that we did not belong there. The grave was telling us that death could follow should we not comply. The disappearing dog walker and her invisible dog was a message sent from beyond, to warn us that we should not go further. The bruise was a portent of what could happen if we didn't leave the village alone. The pint of Guinness – the drink drunk by Alfred Potter in the bar in that very pub the day Walton was killed – was another message to say we were being watched. The website which had 'miraculously' been changed to tell us the pub was closed was a display of computer knowledge that witches have no doubt managed to achieve in these technical days! The van with 'Durham' on the side was to remind us of our bolthole in the city, where we should go and keep quiet, to avoid Lower Quinton's wrath.

Except, Donald and Robert, well-meaning as you probably both were in your quest to make your books a bit creepy and ultimately more readable, that is all a lot of rubbish. Absolutely any occurrence, however normal, can be made to have special significance. To take them in order, the lorry from Darlington was just one of about a dozen lorries which trundled past in the few minutes we took to reach the church door. Although the road through the village is not wide, it has obviously become something of a rat run, especially with the roadworks which seemed to be ringing Stratford at the time. We could have had family almost anywhere and one of the locations would have rung a bell.

The grave digging was not a solitary sexton with a hood shading his eyes – there was a mechanical digger brought from elsewhere on a low loader and two men were working it, their conversation muted in respect for their surroundings but banal as you might expect – something about a car repair, as I recall. The 'phantom' dog walker had clearly just taken one of the other footpaths, the gate being something of a hub. Her 'invisible' dog was just rootling about in a dried ditch, the country being in the grip of a drought at the time. The latch of the gate did not spring out to protect the village – it was because a very polite man stepped back a bit too quickly to give space to a passing lady.

The Guinness which looked so creepy, with the condensation still beaded on the glass, was snatched up by a thirsty pool player seconds later and the last we saw of the landlady, she was planning on ripping her webmaster a new one for having got her opening hours so wrong and consequently losing her business; perhaps he was the only person that day to whom something bad was going to happen.

The van with 'Durham' on the side was not a sign from beyond either – they are a local firm and we saw others as we drove back to the motorway. As a final 'warning', in the loo, three knotholes in the door looked just like a 'grey', an alien straight from any UFO film you care to name – but perhaps even Donald McCormick or Robert Fabian would baulk at blaming little green men from Mars for the death of Charles Walton!

Chapter 10

Enter the Devil

Fabian and Webb had gone home, no doubt frustrated and quite possibly furious that the murder of Charles Walton was still unsolved. Eighty years on, they must both still be spinning in their graves.

As I wrote in *The Hagley Wood Murder* (2023), something odd was happening in Britain soon after the end of the Second World War. Its most obvious manifestation appeared in the United States. On 24 June 1947, Kenneth Arnold, an experienced pilot, was flying over the Cascade Mountains in Washington state. He saw nine objects flying in formation at speeds he estimated at over 1,000mph, faster than anything in the air at the time. 'They flew,' he told reporters, 'like a saucer would if you skipped it across the water.' In a more rational time, these nine anomalies would have been dismissed as cloud formations, flocks of birds, tricks of the sunlight. But the post-war Western world was not a rational time – the whole of Europe and, less directly, America, had been convulsed by nearly six years of war; millions had died; economies had been destroyed; nobody would be the same again. In the Hagley Wood book, I likened it to the recent experience of Covid, with its legacies of anti-vaxxers, Quanon conspiracy theorists and attacks on the Capitol building in Washington DC. So, from 1947, millions around the world accepted the nonsense that 'flying saucers' were real, that alien beings travelled millions of light years to earth just to stick probes up our bottoms!

In 1841, a Scottish academic, Charles McKay, wrote *The Madness of Crowds* which superbly illustrated man's natural ability to embrace the supernatural. Science is a myth; rationalism is nonsense. If the police, even somebody as experienced and talented as Robert Fabian, could not solve the Charles Walton killing, then the answer must lie elsewhere, in the murky realms of the occult.

We have seen where this came from. The folklore books that Alec Spooner or Sergeant Hinksman made available to Fabian hint at all sorts of goings-on. Is that why the drinkers at the Gay Dog downed their pints and left quickly? Is that why Quinton's shutters came down and a wall of silence met Fabian and Webb? Was the area a centre of a witch-cult and was Charles Walton one of its victims?

To answer that, we have to understand what witchcraft is – and there is no simple explanation. Harvey Bloom writes:

> Village folk must have lived in an ever-present dread of evil spells; possibly the terrible picture of Hell and its denizens which adorned the walls of their little church in all the crudity of rude painting, may have helped; in any case, belief in a personal and very active devil and his earthly helpers, witches, was seldom far from their thoughts and to one or both every mischance was blamed.

Far too much credence has been given to the single line in Exodus (22:18) – 'Thou shalt not suffer a witch to live' – as it was written in the 1611 version of the Bible which was still in use in St Swithin's church in Lower Quinton in 1945. But that Bible translation – one of the earliest in English – was the brainchild of a man who today would be sectioned. He was the new king of England, James I, who had written a book on witchcraft – *Daemonologie* – in 1598, claiming to have seen the work of witches up close and personal and to have been targeted by them. The fact that James also ranted against tobacco has given him a positive air today – he was a prophet, a man ahead of his time, an eco-warrior in a ruff. But he was not; he was a mildly deranged bigot who deliberately espoused the radical Puritan faith of his day, advocating the destruction of everything else.

There is a long legal history in Britain relating to witchcraft. In the seventh century, Theodore, Archbishop of Canterbury, wrote *Liber Poenitentalis* (Book of Punishments) in which eating and drinking in a heathen temple was seen as an abomination. Witred, king of Kent, produced a similar edict in 690, fining people who worshipped the Devil. A number of Saxon kings followed suit, underlined by the Laws of Cnut (actually Wulfstan, his spiritual adviser) in the 1020s – 'We earnestly forbid every heathenism; heathenism is, that men worship idols; that is, they worship heathen gods and the sun and the moon, fire or rivers, water – wells or stones, or forest trees of any kind; or love witchcraft ...'

There were a few isolated examples of witchcraft; in 1303, the Bishop of Coventry was accused of paying homage to the Devil. Twenty years later, Dame Alice Kyteler of Kilkenny, Ireland, was found guilty of practising witchcraft. In the next century, Jeanne d'Arc, a probably schizophrenic peasant hijacked by the French government to kick the English out of France, was burned for witchcraft in Rouen market place. But it was the Bull of Pope Innocent VIII in 1484 that kick-started the hysteria that Charles McKay wrote about and that we have seen in the last half century, from flying saucers to Quanon. Two misogynistic monks, Karl Sprenger and Heinrich Kramer, wrote *Malleus Maleficarum* (The Hammer of the Witches) which outlined in prurient detail devil worship in all its Hammer House of Horror glory. Witches were almost always women. They were nymphomaniacs who flew to orgies called sabbats on broomsticks or goats or virtually anything else. They danced widdershins and worshipped the Devil, who was a large black man with horns and a huge, cold penis. In terms of organization, the witches were established in groups of thirteen, in a deliberate mockery of Jesus and his twelve disciples. These covens could be found everywhere, in little villages like Lower Quinton, for example.

Black witches were the evil hags of Shakespeare's *Macbeth*. They produced methods to kill both people and animals, caused storms and the destruction of crops – James I was convinced that a coven of them had tried to kill him and his new Danish bride off the coast of Scotland. They made a compact with the Devil, signing it with their blood. In exchange for super powers, they agreed to obey his every command. For that purpose, he gave them imps or familiars, cats, dogs, mice, toads that fed on the witch's blood via her tit, which felt no pain when stabbed by a witch-finder. White witches practised their art for good; they were the cunning women, often local midwives who attended births and laid out the dead. They also provided love potions to help those anxious to form romantic attachments.

Hard on the heels of *Malleus* and Innocent's Bull came the Reformation. In 1517, an outraged (and surprisingly honest) monk, Martin Luther, condemned his own Catholic church for corruption. His public trial in 1520 convulsed Europe. Rather than burning the man, the traditional penalty for heresy, the Church let Luther live, becoming the unwilling leader of an increasing army of protestors (Protestants) who set up rival churches. All over Europe, two armed camps faced each other: the defensive Catholic faith with its hidebound, centuries-old dogma, its vicious Holy Inquisition and its burning of books; and the Puritans, be they followers of Luther, or Zwingli or Melanchthon, just as rabid and just as bigoted. Thousands of people died in the wars fought over 200 years by these people; thousands more were persecuted for witchcraft.

It was in this melting pot of hysteria and religious mania that the witch craze of the sixteenth and seventeenth centuries was born. Trials were held, with 'evidence' no more compelling than an accusation by a vicious, troublemaking child. Finger-pointing led to infamous examples of miscarriages of justice – Pendle, Lancashire in 1612; Loudon, France, 1632; most damning of all, Salem in Massachusetts sixty years after that, where nineteen people were hanged because of the malice of local teenagers.

Only slowly, with the advent of the scientific Revolution, the Age of Reason and the Enlightenment, did sanity return. In Britain, the Industrial Revolution, with all the horrors of its teething troubles, tended to eclipse everything else. And the twentieth century was dominated by two world wars of unprecedented scale and savagery. Surely, witchcraft had no place in the modern world; it had vanished with the dinosaurs. Not exactly.

'Anybody can become a witch,' Robert Fabian had written in 1950, at a time when, technically at least, witchcraft was still a felony. 'All you have to do,' the detective wrote five years after Charles Walton died, 'is to recite an ancient spell that will conjure up the Devil.' Fabian claimed not to believe in nonsense like this, but he also believed that there were those in Lower Quinton who did. And so did somebody else; her name was Margaret Murray, a respected academic who could be relied upon to add some gravitas to what most people saw as a joke.

Dr Murray was 72 when Charles Walton died. She had long retired from the corridors of academe but still moved in erudite circles as a former lecturer of University College, London. As a young archaeologist and anthropologist, she had worked on numerous Egyptian digs with William Flinders Petrie long before Lord Carnarvon and Howard Carter turned Egyptology into a glorified treasure hunt. She was for many years the only female lecturer in London University and served as a nurse in the First World War, a committed feminist and Suffragette. Always unconventional, Margaret's works became ever more out of sync with the academic world. Montague Summers, another expert in the diabolical field, could not stand her and rubbished her theories in *The History of Witchcraft and Demonology* in 1926. Murray's *The Witch-Cult in Western Europe* appeared in 1921 and was well received, but in comparison with later works by historians, it is rather disappointing. There are swathes of Latin and Medieval French without translation and, unforgivably, no attempt to explain the often bizarre documents that she quotes from witch trials. In some ways, Margaret was the last of the antiquarians rather than an historian. If *The Witch-Cult* was generally well received, *The God of the Witches* (1954) lost her quite a lot of respect. Her thesis here is that all kings of England up to Richard III who died violently were themselves victims of a witch-cult which survived the arrival of Christianity and went underground. Her basic tenet – that witchcraft was the last, twisted version of the Old Religion, based on the seasons and animalism – is more convincing. One of the gods of this ancient faith, practised by the Celts throughout Europe, was Cernunnos, the horned god, symbol of fertility and therefore rampant sexuality. The Christians, with their risen son of God who died for men's sins, would have none of this and the horned god became Satan, Lucifer, the cloven-hoofed fiend responsible for all the evils in the world.

Exactly how Margaret Murray became involved in the Meon Hill murder is not clear. Most books on the case claim that Fabian invited her, but this makes little sense. One of the most successful *fictional* sleuths of the past century is Jane Marple, the dotty old knitter of St Mary Mead (equally fictional). The fact that Jane is 'consulted' by Scotland Yard detectives has as much to do with Agatha Christie's wish to place her amateur creation centre stage as with the writer's woeful lack of awareness of police procedure. In the real world, the police only call in expert witnesses to court who have a tried and tested set of credentials that a jury will believe. How Margaret Murray would have fared in the witness box is anybody's guess, but the role she took on in the Walton case strains credulity.

The story goes that the anthropologist visited Lower Quinton in the summer of 1950, the year that *Fabian of the Yard* appeared. She posed as a water-colourist, wandered the village fete and she told stories to the school children. But it had been five years since Fabian had been there and then, it was only with the express permission of Warwickshire CID. According to Paul Newman, the chief constable by then, Colonel Geoffrey White made the police files on the case available to her. If that was true, then Dr Murray moved in exalted circles indeed. When I asked to see those files some years ago, I was told that Warwickshire Police would review the case themselves at a cost to me of £200. Since their track record in 1945 was not exactly spectacular, I doubted whether a re-run fifty years later would achieve much and I respectfully declined. A second request for the purposes of writing this book led to seventy-eight items being photocopied and sent to me. The dating of these documents runs from the day of the murder (DI Toombs's initial interview with Alfred Potter) to 30 September 1970, after which, I assume, interest in the case had dwindled and there was nothing else to add. Virtually every document has been redacted, including the post-mortem report of Professor Webster, which has been in the public domain and published in various formats for years. By contrast, The National Archives at Kew, essentially the Met files of Fabian and Webb, have no redactions at all.

The earliest reference that I can find to a witchcraft connection with the Meon Hill murder comes from *The News*, a Sunday paper printed on 16 September 1950. Fabian's *Fabian of the Yard* had appeared by then and perhaps journalist Aubrey Thomas took his cue from that. Under a banner headline (and jokey cartoon) 'Those secret black and midnight hags', Thomas churned out the disinformation we have become woefully used to over the years since; Walton's body was found under an oak tree; the billhook was embedded in his heart. The journalist is as disenchanted as Montague Summers regarding Margaret Murray. 'For years, tiny, chubby Dr Murray, standing 4ft 6ins in her flat-heeled shoes and rough tweed suit ... has insisted that witches still exist.' And he quoted her – 'Men as well as women can be witches. It's just that women witches seem to have survived longer than men witches.' None of this sounds remotely like the academic who wrote *God of the Witches* and Thomas's assertion that Dr Murray told him 'the pitchfork is a symbol of man as the broomstick is of female' is pure tosh. In fact, in other discussions of the Walton death, Dr Murray said that she had never come across pitchforks in the witchcraft context.

In November 1951, Margaret Murray spoke to a reporter from the *Sunday Dispatch*:

In other words, if there were no people to believe in them there would be no witches. If, for instance, anyone cursed by a witch just laughed it off and refused to take it seriously ... it would have no efficacy at all. Witches, therefore, are individuals who are believed by those around them to have certain unusual powers either for good or evil. Other people believe them to be witches and in some rural areas even to this day, once that reputation has been acquired, it sticks ... That is how witches are made and maybe always have been made and are still being made; though with the growth of motor travel and the steady penetration of remote rural areas by the outside world, there are fewer with each decade.[15]

Previously, Margaret had given an interview to the *Birmingham Post* (September 1950), a local paper that leapt on any lurid tales to boost sales – 'I think there are still remnants of witchcraft in isolated parts of Great Britain' – ignoring the fact that Quinton was at the heart of the industrial Midlands, only a stone's throw from the conurbation of Birmingham. And the sort of witchcraft that Dr Murray was talking about – a weird survival of a pre-Christian cult – was very different from the type being discussed, and practised, by others.

The Meon Hill murder undoubtedly had an effect on Robert Fabian because of his frequent references to witchcraft in otherwise modern and straightforward accounts of his criminal-catching career. His chapter in *Fabian of the Yard* deals exclusively with the Charles Walton murder, but his other works venture further. In *London After Dark* he wrote: 'the practice of Black Magic – of diabolical rites in the heart of London – is spreading rapidly.' He then weakens this bold statement with 'There is more active Satan-worship today than ever since the Dark Ages, when witches were publicly burned upon Tower Hill.' There was no routine execution of witches between the seventh and tenth centuries; as we have seen, the worst penalty was a fine. And no witches were ever burned in England, on Tower Hill or anywhere else; they were hanged.

---

[15] Margaret Murray's article in the *Sunday Dispatch*, quoted in McCormick, p. 67.

Fabian's account of London's black magic sounds incredible and I seriously doubt whether much of it is true. He claims that books on the subject were found at Helsingfors in Finland when Scotland Yard was called in to assist in the theft of forty corpses from a local mortuary. When the 'wickedest man in England', the self-styled 'Beast', Aleister Crowley, died in 1947, several hundred followers from black magic circles in London, Lewes and Shoreham trooped behind his coffin in a black ritual. Fabian believed that there were secret temples in South Kensington, Bloomsbury and Paddington where devotees stripped and worshipped Satan 'with ritual and sacrifice that would shame an African savage'.

Leaving aside the Africa slur, which today would be unacceptable, Fabian has hit the nail on the head with that one word 'stripped'. 'Others,' he says, 'probably the majority, attend a Black Mass to see a cheap thrill.' It was actually, in the decade before the 'liberation' of the 1960s, all about sex. What concerned Fabian, as it did most policemen at the time, was the luring of the innocent, usually young and female, into cults via the use of hypnotic drugs, long before such things became fashionable and commonplace.

Fabian describes one such temple, a rather sordid basement flat in Lancaster Gate where the occupants, a spiritualist and herbalist, held regular meetings behind locked doors. Black candles dripped on the altar, pentagrams and sigils swirled on the walls, floor and ceiling. The whole place was thick with the smell of incense. This was the site of the 'Mass of Saint Secaire', a parody of the Catholic Mass, including Latin chanting. Teenagers were initiated into the cult and 'sacrificed' on the altar by a high priest (the herbalist himself) having a whale of a time. In Chelsea was the 'Order of St Bridget' that was into flagellation, where 'Inquisitors' laid about them with whips that ten years later would be routinely obtainable over the counter in any number of Soho shops. The police could do little about all this, because they were private clubs and without a complaint, their hands were tied (no pun intended!).

Fabian also believed that witchcraft of this type, liberal London trying to break down taboos and barriers, was spreading into the provinces. Local papers, he noted, carried stories of churches being desecrated. At Yarcombe in Devon, the vicar was horrified to find stone crosses turned upside down, black candles on the altar and the bloody paw of a kitten alongside them.

By the time the detective wrote *The Anatomy of Crime*'s second edition in 1970, the sexual revolution and the devotion to drugs and rock 'n' roll was well and truly underway. Most of the book, while covering tales of wrongdoing, is a sensible how to avoid crime compendium, with practical, useful advice. The last chapter, *Very Black Magic* therefore jars a little and ends with a very brief survey of the Walton murder. He cites a young couple in London lured into witchcraft for a laugh. They were invited to a country house and took part in a Black Mass at which a cat was sacrificed. 'After drinking the blood,' Sylvia told Fabian, 'I was made to gulp a tumbler of gin. I recall the beat of drums. Naked, we danced round in circles, faster and faster. Then the ceremony disintegrated into an orgy.' Which was, of course, the point of the whole thing.

'What exactly are the human failings that Satanists exploit so cruelly? Who in fact *are* the present-day Britons who put back the clock 2,000 years, who prance naked under trees, in attics, basements and garages ... and who prefer their loathsome ceremonies to be conducted by [literally] unfrocked priests?' Fabian asks.

He points out the cynical commercialism of these cults, which he calls 'poppycock'. Love potions were available in London for £1 5s a bottle (the equivalent of £20 in today's money). A jeweller the detective knew sold a ring for £1,000 because he claimed it was a magical device.

The problem for those like Fabian and many of the establishment concerned with the rise of interest in the occult, was that it was given oxygen by intelligent people, some of them only interested in their fifteen minutes of fame. Aleister Crowley made much of his evil and depravity, but his following in Britain was actually quite small. The fact that he was born in Clarendon Square, Leamington Spa, only a stone's throw from Meon Hill, probably passed most people by. The repeal of the 1736 Witchcraft Act in 1951 led Gerald Gardner to create a movement that made the whole thing respectable. He was a retired customs officer whose goatee beard and wild white hair gave him the look of a Renaissance alchemist. He saw sex and flagellation as the heart of magic and his books *Witchcraft Today* and *The Meaning of Witchcraft* became the new Bibles. By the time Fabian wrote his last book, Gardner's excesses had been watered down and Wicca became inextricably jumbled with well-being and feel-good books, probably designed to make the twenty-first-century world less frightening.

So why did the murder of Charles Walton become inextricably linked with the supernatural? Part of it was due to the supposed academic observations of Margaret Murray. To the *Birmingham Post* she said:

I believe Charles Walton was one of the people sacrificed [to witchcraft]. I think this because of the peculiar way in which he had been killed. His throat had been cut and a pitchfork had been used after he was dead to prevent him being moved. The sacrifices are carried out by people who still believe in a religion practised in Britain before Christianity who we call devil-worshippers. They still work Black Magic. The belief is that if life is taken out of the ground it must be replaced by a blood sacrifice. I am not interested in the murder, only in the witches. I think it was a murder without normal motive – no money was missing ...'[16]

The irony of this is that Charles Walton took nothing out of the ground. He was a hedger and ditcher, not an arable farmer, still less a slaughterer of livestock. It made far more sense for Alfred Potter, crop-harvester and animal-castrater, to be a target for sacrifice.

---

[16] *Birmingham Post* September 1951

And the fact that Dr Murray said she was not interested in the murder is very telling. Had she been, she would have known that the use of the pitchfork came *before* the billhook; it was used to stop Walton struggling while he was still alive, not to pin him down once he was dead. If Warwickshire's chief constable had indeed made the police files available to her, as some authorities claim, she would have known that.

Five years later, Dr Murray was still talking to the press:

There was also the significance of the day – the 14th of February. In pre-Christian times, February was a sacrificial month, when the soil was spring-cleaned of the dirt of winter. In the old calendar [changed in 1752] February 2nd was a sacrificial day, but the old calendar was 12 days behind ours, which means that February 14th corresponds to February 2nd. But I found nothing to support my theory beyond that. The pitchfork was never an instrument of sacrifice in this country, though it may have been in Italy – and there were Italian prisoners-of-war in the neighbourhood at the time.

The Celtic religious festival of Imbolc falls on 2 February, which the Christians appropriated as Candlemas. It was a fire festival celebrating the goddess of fertility and the horned god, sometimes equated with the god Pan. It was, as Dr Murray asserts, a tidying up after the death of winter in readiness for the spring sowing. The ritual murder of Charles Walton was symbolic of this sweeping away of the old.

The word 'ritual' has been used by many people in the context of this crime but it is misleading. It has led to the deranged notion of a coven of witches, dancing sky-clad (naked) around the body of a labourer they have just butchered, in the middle of a February day *and no one noticed*! For what we know to be a ritual sacrifice, let us go back, as Fabian would have us do, 2,000 years to find the relevant details.

Peat cutter Andy Mould made a remarkable discovery on 1 August 1984. To the Celts, and to Margaret Murray, the date was significant;

it was the ancient festival of Lughnasadh, long ago appropriated by the Christian church as Lammas. Lugh was the god linked with the harvest, crucial for the survival of man and his symbol was the sun. Traditionally, this was a day when corn dollies or kirn babies were made and distributed. Mould's find, in the peat of Lindow Moss in Cheshire was all the more remarkable as a result. Archaeologists determined that 'Lindow Man' as the discovered body came to be known, was a male in his late twenties or early thirties, suffering (probably like Charles Walton) from mild osteoarthritis. He had been killed with several weapons. A heavy object, perhaps the blunt side of an axe head, had caused deep wounds to his scalp and had been delivered while he was kneeling. Around his neck was a garotte of animal gut, tied with knots to allow a stick to tighten it as a ligature. His airways would have been closed quickly and his spine snapped. Lastly, a sharp blade had been rammed into the jugular vein of his neck. We know from circumstantial evidence surrounding the body – and the fact that it was sunk in sacred water – that this was a sacrificial killing, perhaps to three of the greatest Celtic gods, Taranis, Esus and Teutates.

It is the similarities to the Charles Walton killing that concern us here. The head wounds were similar, though made by the old man's stick, not a metal object. The vicious strangulation equates roughly with the billhook mutilations to the throat, as does the wound to the jugular. There is nothing in the Lindow case that corresponds to the pitchfork, although the jugular wound does have similarities. Lindow Man is one of hundreds of bodies that have been found over the last century in peat bogs across northern Europe. They are often found with wooden stakes criss-crossed over the body, in an attempt to prevent the souls of the dead from escaping from the ground. Was this the purpose of the pitchfork at Hillground? Margaret Murray did not live to witness the finding of Lindow Man, who was probably murdered about 60AD, but she would certainly have found interesting parallels with Charles Walton.

Author Paul Newman makes great play of the pitchfork, citing an earlier murder using the same implement. In his book on Warwickshire folklore, Harvey Bloom writes, 'In 1875 a weak-minded young man killed an old woman named Ann Turner with a hay-fork because he believed she had bewitched him.'

Newman goes on to say that Clive Holland in his *Warwickshire* book refers to the same murder:

> A man named James Hayward, who stabbed to death with a pitchfork an old woman, exclaiming that he would kill all sixteen witches in Long Compton ... his mode of killing was evidently a survival of the ancient Anglo-Saxon custom of dealing with witches by means of 'stacung' or sticking spikes into them.[17]

There are a number of problems with this. First, the above quotation is not from Holland's book and I have no idea where Newman found it. Secondly, the staking practice is much older than the Saxon period and appears to be a distortion of the sticks found in peat-bog burials. Alternatively, it could represent confusion with the vampire tradition of killing the 'undead' which was common to Eastern Europe in the sixteenth to eighteenth centuries.

The Ann Turner murder, however, was real enough, except that her name was Tennant. According to the *Stratford Herald*, James Hayward, described as 'feeble-minded', attacked 79-year-old Ann in Long Compton in broad daylight in full view of appalled bystanders before they could intervene. He was grabbed and arrested by a local bobby and carted off to Shipston-on-Stour to stand trial later at Warwick Assizes. Charged with murder after Ann died of her injuries, Hayward was drunk at his trial and contended that he would kill all sixteen witches living in Long Compton:

> If you knew the number of people who lie in the churchyard, who, if it had not been for them, would have been alive now, you would be surprised. Her was a proper witch. I pinned Ann

---

[17] Paul Newman, *Under the Shadow of Meon Hill* p. 42.

Tennant to the ground before slashing her throat with a billhook
in the form of a cross.

Newman does not give the exact source for this confession, but it is
patently untrue. Hayward did not pin Ann to the ground, nor did he
kill her with a billhook. This overt comparison with the Walton killing
is in somebody's imagination.

The Ann Tennant murder is a fascinating forerunner of Charles
Walton's. Not only is the pitchfork common to both and the ages of
the victims roughly comparable, but the whole taint of witchcraft runs
continuously. Intriguingly, the judge at Warwick Assizes in December
1875 said, after sentencing, that 'he hoped that something could be
done to disabuse the minds of the people of the village of the belief in
witchcraft. It was a most mournful and melancholy state of ignorance.'

The *Illustrated Police News* from the period takes up the theme – 'It
was observed in evidence that fully one-third of the villagers [of Long
Compton] believed in witchcraft.' Unfortunately, the *Police News* had
nothing to do with the police. It was an example of the 'new journalism'
of the 1870s and 1880s where hacks without integrity seized on any
salaciousness they could find and worked up unattributed tittle-tattle
into 'believable' stories.

All this plays into the hands of those who see Warwickshire as a
hell-hole trapped in a Medieval time warp, but I suspect that Mr Justice
Bramwell was reading too much into the hokum he had just heard from
Hayward. The lad's own parents were traditional chapel-goers and the
obsession with witches was in Hayward's mind, nobody else's.

In the event, and perhaps inevitably given the circumstances, James
Hayward was found not guilty of murder, which did not actually reflect
the coroner's verdict at the inquest – 'Wilful murder. Deliberately
stabbed to death by James Hayward with a pitchfork under the delusion
of witchcraft.' He died in Broadmoor in 1890.

But, in the case of Charles Walton, the delusion of witchcraft never
went away.

Chapter 11

Murder by Witchcraft

I n the year that Robert Fabian wrote his last book (1968), author Donald McCormick went into print with the first full book on the killing of Charles Walton, *Murder by Witchcraft*.

I met McCormick years later when my literary agent put us together for a project that, in the end, never came off. He was a dazzling companion, with a sparkling conversation and had an utterly charming (third) wife. At the time, I knew of him as one of the many writers on Jack the Ripper, perpetrator of the most infamous series of unsolved murders in the history of criminology. I also knew that he was not exactly the purest of researchers but I had no idea of the damage he had done to any number of worthy projects.

McCormick gave the impression of being a scholar and a gentleman. He attended Shrewsbury public school but did not, unlike most of his peers, go on to university. He served in the navy during the war and this introduced him to Ian Fleming of Naval Intelligence, the future creator of James Bond. Through Fleming, he got to know anybody who was anybody and specialized in the more lurid stories from history, especially those involving espionage. His supporters – and there were only two well-known ones – claimed that in McCormick's day, sources and careful cross-reference were not the norm, but this is patently untrue. Scholarly academics of his generation, as of ours, positively bury themselves in footnotes and agonize over the reliability of sources. His detractors are legion (one editor calls them his 'victims'), from economist Arthur Pigou to historian E.P. Thompson, who once described McCormick's *The British Constitution* as 'warmed up fourth-rate crap'.

McCormick was a journalist who wrote for *The Times*, the *Spectator* and *Encounter* and his books spanned a whole range of topics from 1934 to the aptly titled *Taken for a Ride: the History of Cons and Conmen* in 1976. In the 1950s and 1960s, he was concentrating on murder (hence *The Identity of Jack the Ripper* 1959) in which most of his source material came via the *News of the World*, a now defunct scandal sheet. One critic has described him as 'the fantasy historian'.

Why does all this matter? Because McCormick's was the *first* book on the Meon Hill murder and because others have blindly followed him without checking his credentials. Paul Newman has clearly got the man's measure and warns against him, but others have fallen into the trap. The one good piece of news is that *Murder by Witchcraft* is no longer in print.

The very first line is wrong. 'Dusk was creeping slowly and mistily across the Warwickshire fields on St Valentine's Day 1945, when the body of Charles Walton ... was found.'[18] No, it was not. It was well and truly dark, hence the torches carried by the little search party. Sunset that day was at eighteen minutes past six.

'Charles Walton has [*sic*] been pinned to the ground by his own hay-fork. Across his throat a rough but unmistakeable sign of the Cross had been savagely slashed.' No, it had not. Professor Webster's post-mortem notes refer to multiple slashes to the throat, but the Cross, with its capital letter and good v. evil symbolism, is pure McCormick.

'"Witchcraft" whispered the villagers.' No, they did not. Nowhere in the contemporary police accounts of Warwickshire or the Met is there any mention of the occult. It was at least five years later that this sort of speculation began.

'This part of Warwickshire had been notorious as "the land of the covens", the one part of England said to suffer from a superfluity of witches.' No, it had not. Despite folkloric mentions of witches in Long Compton by Harvey Bloom via the Ann Tennant murder, the county

---

[18] All quotations are from Donald McCormick unless otherwise stated.

seems particularly devoid of actual witchcraft. In her *The Witch-Cult in Western Europe*, Margaret Murray cites seventeen high-profile witch-craze trials across Britain from the fifteenth to the seventeenth centuries and not one of them is in Warwickshire or anywhere near it.

McCormick visited Lower Quinton as part of the research for his book and he is even able to see spooky architecture in St Swithin's church – 'For over the chancel arch was carved a sixteenth-century coat of arms, comprising a unicorn raging at a winged dragon with ferocious jaws and hideous claws, all in red and yellow and black.' This was the royal arms of the Tudors, to be found in every church in the land at the time and the ferocity of the beasts is purely in the eye of the beholder. 'It was an oddly sinister touch to find in a country church'; wrong again. When my wife and I visited the church in preparation for this book, we were struck by McCormick's exaggeration. The only easily visible part of the heraldry is the motto 'God Save Our Noble Queen Elizabeth'. The rest is a partly obliterated outline and was clearly neither 'ferocious' nor 'hideous'; neither was it in red, yellow and black. Even allowing for the passage of time between 1968 and today, essentially what we saw was what McCormick would have seen – the rest he simply made up.

McCormick sat in both village pubs, the College Arms and the Gay Dog, chatting to locals. Perhaps they were newcomers (which seems unlikely as they told old legends and stories) or they were not as fazed by the writer as they had been twenty-three years earlier by Fabian and Webb. According to McCormick, he had told no one why he was in the village, yet supernatural goings-on cropped up almost at once in conversation and the writer was able to record these ingle-side chats with total recall (and, one assumes, no clunky 1968 reel-to-reel tape recorder). One local told him of the tale of the widow of Sir William Clopton buried in the church who became, not a nun, as folklore maintained, but a witch. The tomb of Joanna Clopton is very specific in terms of the vows she took on widowhood. Anyone with even a suspicion of witchcraft against her would never have been buried in consecrated ground, still less given such a lavish tomb. Her death coincided with that of Jeanne d'Arc, accused by both the French and English chroniclers of devil worship and burned alive in Rouen marketplace in 1431.

When McCormick raised the 1945 murder, it created a sense of unease. 'There was a lot of nasty talk about it in the village then,' someone told him, 'and it wasn't very nice.' Things that are 'nasty' are rarely 'nice' in the scheme of things!

Three locals, however, believed that witchcraft was involved and witches still lived in the area. Two of these locals had lived in Quinton for eighteen years, in other words, arriving after the Walton murder, but the third, a genuine local, suggested that McCormick visit Long Compton and the Rollright Stones '"for that's where the witches make their homes".' For six pages, the journalist sleuth regales us with the usual legends of the Rollrights, most of it lifted (with acknowledgements, to be fair) from Harvey Bloom. McCormick reminds us that the tall tales of witchcraft collected by Bloom were not jolly party pieces, but 'seriously told, after much persuasion and with fear of consequences, in 1912'.[19]

McCormick also refers to Cecil Williamson, a man obsessed with the murder of Charles Walton, according to author Paul Newman. Williamson had an unrivalled collection of witchcraft artefacts, such as poppets, goat masks and ritual paraphernalia which he put on display for a ghoulish, fee-paying public at Castleton in the Isle of Man. Some of the locals found this disturbing and he moved his collection to Bourton-on-the-Water in the Cotswolds (which I visited as a 12-year-old). Part of it was burned down by locals claiming to be Christians and it moved again, via Polperro in Cornwall to Boscastle where it narrowly escaped a flash flood in 2004.

As a boy, Williamson attended Malvern College in Worcestershire (Aleister Crowley, the 'great beast' was another alumnus) and, through holidays in France and an attempted farming career in Rhodesia

---

[19] Bloom, p. 96.

(now Zimbabwe) he picked up clairvoyance, divination and Voodoo. From 1930 onwards, he worked as a film maker but never lost his interest in the supernatural, becoming a friend of Montague Summers, the renegade Catholic priest, and Margaret Murray, who, as we have seen, had her own view on the Meon Hill murder.

The problem with Cecil Williamson is that he was a man after Donald McCormick's heart, given to tall stories and dark hints because of his work with the Secret Service during the war. In a letter to a supernatural magazine, *The Cauldron*, he wrote:

> I can still recall the events of that February in 1945. The War was drawing to its close [no one *at the time* could be sure of that, of course]. The US troops had broken through the Siegfried Line and the Russians had taken Stettin. I was back at my MI6 base at Whaddon Hill close to Bletchley Park. Just before going into lunch, Brigadier Gambier Parry stopped me and said 'Oh, Bill, here's a bit of news that should be of interest to you. There's a report out of a witchcraft-style killing of some person, not so far away from here and I thought you might like to look into it.'[20]

When Williamson reached Lower Quinton, he claimed to find the place swarming with reporters and the locals hiding behind their front doors.

It is difficult to know where to begin to unravel this nonsense. No news at the time tied the murder of Charles Walton with witchcraft; not until 1950 would that suggestion be made. And if there were journalists all over the place, what happened to their stories? We have seen how little space there was in the press for detailed reporting. The nationals seem to have ignored or missed the story entirely and in the local papers, which could be expected to provide more coverage, the best that the Walton case could muster was a mediocre page four.

---

[20] Quoted in Newman, p. 130.

Williamson's role, according to him, was to work for MI6's black propaganda department, specifically investigating the Nazi high command's obsession with the occult. Heinrich Himmler certainly believed in clairvoyance. So too did Hitler's deputy, Rudolf Hess, who had flown on an abortive peace mission to Britain four years before Charles Walton died. Since Williamson spent most of his time during the war broadcasting misinformation to German U-boats in the North Sea, it is difficult to know how an obscure murder in a Warwickshire village could have any relevance to that.

After the war was a different matter and Williamson was approached at his Bourton-on-the-Water museum by someone who claimed to have arcane knowledge of the murder. Paul Newman, who covers all this, does not give dates but we can assume that this incident, if it occurred at all, happened in the 1960s. The importance of this anonymous visitor will be discussed in Chapter 11.

Just as Donald McCormick was convinced that the royal coat of arms in St Swithin's were horrific and demonic, he also finds sinister the fact that so many pubs in the area have animalistic names – cats, dogs, bears and so on – conveniently ignoring the scores of horseshoes, roses and crowns and queen's heads that also litter the countryside.

The writer takes up the theme expressed by Fabian as to the prevalence of witchcraft in modern Britain. Joan Westcott in *New Society* (1964) claimed that there were about 400 practising witches around the country, largely centred in the big cities and totally independent of each other. Most of the practitioners were middle-class professionals, not the peasants of the Middle Ages and most of them aspired to the positives of white witchcraft, promoting the Life Force. The word 'Wicca' wasn't used in 1968, but its essence is there.

The kind of witchcraft that McCormick claims to have been faced with in Warwickshire was not of this liberal, drug-related, urban sort, but something altogether older and more violent. 'Here,' he wrote, 'more than elsewhere, the tradition of hate, jealousy and fear in witchcraft has lasted longer than anywhere else ... remoteness breeds suspicion of strangers.' There is, of course, no evidence for this and we have already noted that Warwickshire in 1945 was hardly pre-industrial Brontë country, with its windswept, romantic loneliness.

After setting the scene on the 'land of the covens' (which does not really exist), McCormick has prepared his readers for anything spooky and he launches into the murder itself. He is right about the weather, but after that, things go a little awry. According to the writer's memories of what the locals told him, Charles Walton was a cross between a madman and Francis of Assisi. He talked to birds, sang like them and knew every call by heart. He 'lived all his life in Quinton', apart, that is, from a possible eighteen years in Offchurch. He was 'half-crippled' with rheumatism. No, he was not. Nobody as disabled as that could spend an entire day hedging.

People's opinions of Walton varied. To some he was a curmudgeonly recluse, more interested in birds and animals than people. To others, he was cheerful and friendly. Unusually for his generation, he did not smoke or drink in the pubs, but he was reported to buy cider and to drink at home. One villager told McCormick:

> Always drank alone, never in company. Wouldn't stand a round like the others. Sometimes he pretended never to drink. But he drank all right. Paid cash for twelve gallons [96 pints] of cider at a time ... sometimes it would be delivered but I have known him wheel it back on his own on a barrow.

According to McCormick, Edith Walton worked in a factory rather than at the Society of Arts, so clearly he had not talked to her. Neither did he have access to the police files; they were gathering dust at the CID headquarters in Stratford, despite apparently having been made available to Margaret Murray eighteen years earlier.

As to the finding of the corpse itself, McCormick is all over the place. On page 1 Walton lay under an oak tree; on page 35, it has become a willow. There was a 'contorted look of horror on his face'. Not according to Professor Webster, who actually saw it, there wasn't! And, of course, we have the 'unmistakable shape' of the cross at his throat, which has been repeated by almost everybody. There is no mention in McCormick of the most vital piece of evidence of all, the fact that the dead man's trousers were undone and partially rolled down.

The first part of Fabian's enquires is recreated by McCormick as a work of fiction. It relates to the curious incident of the dog that ran past the detective on Meon Hill. McCormick's animal is, of course, black because that fits the legendary creature of doom found in various parts of the country. In Fabian's version, Superintendent Spooner was with him and he trots out the story of the headless woman and 'a local legend of a man' whose sister died the next day. 'His name was Charles Walton.' We have already dismissed this coincidence, but McCormick plays it up. The Meon Hill victim would have been 15 at the time of this alleged canine occurrence, but, like so many other examples of McCormick's work, only he gives the date of 1885. Fabian does not mention it; neither does Harvey Bloom.

McCormick elaborates with a local at the pub that night regaling Fabian with the original ghost story (again, the total recall of a casual chat) of the silent dog with strange eyes that appeared to 'a young farm lad on Meon Hill'. The journalist underlines Fabian's belief that the mood of the village changed after this and McCormick concludes that 'no longer were orthodox methods of crime detection applicable. The murder of Charles Walton suddenly belonged to the readers of fantasy' – which is an accusation that might be levelled at most of McCormick's work.

According to him, police investigation revealed that Warwickshire was awash with stories of witchcraft (although the files make no mention of it) and quotes the trial of John Haywood [*sic*] for the murder of Ann Turner [*sic*] in 1875. In one sentence, McCormick makes two crucial mistakes; he also attributes his source to Clive Holland, whereas it is Harvey Bloom, who also gets Ann's surname wrong. McCormick, of course, gleefully cites Bloom's folk tales of nineteenth-century witches at Honington and Ilmington, shape-shifters who terrorized the neighbourhood. All this spurious nonsense from a folklorist is adduced as fact by a journalist who claims not to believe any of it, but throws it into the melting pot because he knows it sells books.

According to McCormick, Warwickshire CID were bombarded with 'helpful' letters from the public. Some suggested Margaret Murray's theory that Walton was a sacrifice in the Old Religion tradition to replenish the soil. Others suggested that the old man was a witch himself and that the birds he spoke to were his familiars, creatures of the Devil. The only letter in The National Archive files today relates to the anonymous author from Birmingham in 1950 who wondered whether escaped 'mentals' might be responsible. The rest is silence.

The Warwickshire files are not much more forthcoming and certainly do not add up to McCormick's 'bombardment'. One letter that *is* there, typewritten and with all names redacted is dated 15 November 1956. The letterhead is SOUTH STAFFS METAPHYSICAL SOCIETY, founded the previous year, the object of which was 'research into the unknown'. The correspondent wrote to Spooner, referring to a 'thousand to one shot' in the Charles Walton murder. In a classic piece of metaphysical psychobabble, he/she writes, 'If you can let me have the following information I can try and piece together what is in my mind, a vague clue with even less details, if your answers make sense to me, the puzzle may be solved.' He asks Spooner to confirm whether a (redacted) couple were still living (presumably in the Quintons) or had left and returned, even though, apparently, they had no connection with the crime. Across the top, in handwriting, Spooner understandably passes the buck – 'Supt Wardman, can you help please? (In confidence of course).'

In what may be a follow-up letter eight days later, a redacted constable, No. 140, had chased up this couple who had always lived at Long Marston. The man seems to have been a retired labourer who still did a bit of hedging and ditching in the area. The significance of all this, even without redaction, escapes me, as no doubt it did the police, who would have been within their rights to shove it in the Wasting Police Time bin.

Another letter, dated 14 February 1960, exactly fifteen years after the murder, has been so heavily redacted as to be worthless. The writer had been living in Lower Quinton in 1945, though clearly not a villager, and was questioned by the police along with everybody else. The letter spoke of a strange incident involving a man who spent a great deal of time on Meon Hill and had frequent clashes with farmers and landowners. The inference seems to be that this man was a poacher, caught in the act by Walton who 'defended himself with his slash hook'. The last line, cryptically, reads, 'Why the stolen watch'.

Apart from the odd Italian, the only person connected with poaching was Camp 685's rat-catcher, Private Davies of the Pioneer Corps. Fabian describes him as 'unreliable' but there is no hint of a short temper or any use of violence. In what appears to be a follow-up report, the superintendent's office in Oswestry filled Spooner in on Davies's record after demobilisation. The actual crimes have been redacted, but he had three convictions between 1956 and 1959 and was fined in each case. He is described as a nuisance and heavy drinker but not violent and he was separated from his wife.

The Chief Features Writer (name redacted) of the *Empire News and Sunday Chronicle*, a London paper operating out of Grey's Inn Road, contacted Spooner in February 1960. The *News* had published an article on the murder, undoubtedly on the crime's fifteenth anniversary and had offered a £1,000 reward. As in the Hagley Wood case (see Chapter 10) where a local paper also offered a reward, it acts as a green light to any number of greedy and/or deranged individuals to leap into print. The *News* had received a number of letters from 'armchair detectives'. Most of these merely commented on the various themes in the paper, but two stood out and the features writer enclosed them in his letter to Spooner. They are no longer in the file. It is clear from this letter that Spooner had worked with the journalist before, at Nuneaton in the previous December, and the superintendent's cryptic pencilled comment reads, 'Not acted'.

There is only one reference to the supernatural in the entire Warwickshire file. A letter written to the constabulary in April 1970 (by which time both Fabian and McCormick were in print) came from a soldier stationed at Long Marston in 1945. 'The people around there can forget about any black magic.' The writer assured the police that he was not a 'crank of some sort' and that a recent article in the *Daily Mirror* had brought the case back to him. The *Mirror* article was one of many linking Walton and witchcraft which the Warwickshire police put down, quite rightly, to the ghoulishness of journalists. There was no record of the soldier having been interviewed at all. Whoever this man was, he was interviewed by Lancashire police on 11 May. He admitted he had never been interviewed at the time of the murder and recalled that he had suspicions of:

a man who had complete freedom of the camp and the surrounding area and could come and go as he pleased. He was a person with whom no other man on the camp would associate and a man with a violent nature. He had once seen this man hit somebody else with a gin trap because he believed he was stealing from him.

This had to be Davies the rat-catcher, but the police had already exonerated him in 1945 and 1960 and they were no further forward.

Fabian mentions, in *The Anatomy of Crime*, but nowhere else, a dog-related incident. 'I realized for certain we were up against witchcraft when the body of a black dog was found hanging from a bush near the spot where Walton died.' There was no explanation for this and neither Fabian nor McCormick gives us a definitive date for the incident. Other animal fatalities which McCormick throws into the mix include yet another black dog being run over by a police car and a heifer dying 'the next day' – the 'cause of death could not be determined'. This is almost certainly the heifer in the Doomsday ditch on Alfred Potter's farm, retrieved on the day of Walton's death. Cars kill animals on narrow country lanes all the time and the lack of cause of death for the cow can be attributed to a very common situation – the incompetence of the local vet. There are various references in farming lore that sick animals commit suicide but the Doomsday area was flooded in February 1945 and the heifer almost certainly died of accidental drowning.

In *Murder by Witchcraft*, McCormick devotes an entire chapter to Margaret Murray (who appears nowhere in any police files). We have already heard her views on witchcraft as expressed to local and national papers. The press, as ever, were anxious to paint as juicy a picture of anything, even the most improbable theories and depict them as fact. So, Lower and Upper Quinton became a 'village of devil-worshippers', which Dr Murray had certainly never said. Various locals, McCormick tells us, were indignant at the suggestion. An unnamed farmer scoffed 'Witchcraft? Don't make me laugh!' Arthur Dobson, who had run the village school for forty years, was furious. 'Since I first heard of this witchcraft nonsense, I have wanted to make a public protest on behalf of the villagers. When the police asked me what I thought of the story, I told them "Tripe".' St Swithin's vicar, the Reverend J. Stone, agreed.

By the time McCormick wrote, Margaret Murray was dead and we have no way of knowing whether she talked to McCormick or wrote to him. He regretted the fact that he was unaware of any dossier the anthropologist may have compiled on the case; she certainly does not mention it in her autobiography, *My First Hundred Years*. McCormick nevertheless quotes her – 'What was interesting, psychologically speaking, in the case of Lower Quinton people was that they appeared to be afraid of being got at. That was an unusual reaction and it suggested there were some guilty feelings somewhere.' McCormick/Murray quote one local who said, 'Of course it isn't wise to pry too deeply into other people's affairs. There may be things that I don't know of and it's better I don't. It was a funny case. Funny the thing could be done and nothing found out.'

In the middle of *Murder by Witchcraft*, Donald McCormick suddenly changes tack. To be fair, he tried to prepare us for this with the book's subtitle, *A Study of Lower Quinton and Hagley Wood Murders*, and in doing that, McCormick not only muddied the waters in both cases but established a link between the two which is actually non-existent. Later writers blindly followed his lead; in 2009, Paul Newman again lumped them together in *Under the Shadow of Meon Hill*.

I have dealt with the Hagley Wood case in the companion volume to this book,[21] but for reasons of clarity, it must be summarized here. In April 1943, four teenaged boys looking for birds' nests in Hagley Wood near the village of Hagley on the Birmingham–Kidderminster road, found human bones jumbled in the hollow bole of a wych elm. The police were called and the pathologist on the scene was the same Professor James Webster who would carry out a post-mortem on Charles Walton nearly two years later. The files on the Hagley Wood case in the Worcester Archive are notoriously scanty, but the essence of the enquiry can still be worked out.

The wych elm body was that of a woman in her late twenties or early thirties. She was barely 5ft tall; what remained of her clothing was poor and she had very distinctive protruding front teeth. Unlike the Warwickshire force, Worcestershire CID did not call in the Yard but pursued their enquiries alone where the leading investigator was DI Thomas Williams. Promising leads, of the dead woman's shoes and dentition, led nowhere. No cobblers or dentists came forward with a positive identification. The inquest (the record of which no longer exists) decided on the usual safety valve of 'murder by person or persons unknown'. The macabre disposal of the corpse, stuffed into a hollow tree, has no known parallels in criminal history.

Within six months of the body being found, a series of wall writings, usually in chalk, appeared all over the Midlands. Although the actual words varied, in essence they all posed the same question – 'Who put

---

[21] *The Hagley Wood Murder,* Pen and Sword, 2023.

Bella in the wych elm, Hagley Wood?' About a third of the surviving documents at the Worcester Archive relate to a fruitless search for the author(s) of this graffiti. The whole task was pointless. Rather like the plethora of 'Mr Chads' that appeared everywhere and the American equivalent, 'Kilroy Was Here', the 'Bella' graffiti was simply a harmless, if annoying, example of the madness of crowds which raises its head with monotonous regularity. Even if the Worcestershire police had been able to track down the author(s), there was no evidence that he/ they were Bella's killer(s).

Nevertheless, the name Bella stuck; even the police used it and the dead woman's fictional name became part of folklore, as surely as witchcraft did in the case of Charles Walton. Because the woman's real identity could not be discovered, the possibility arose that she was not British at all, but a spy, parachuted in at dead of night to sabotage or report on the military centres and munitions factories dotted in and around Birmingham. Later researchers, including McCormick, speculated wildly on this and drew all kinds of fanciful conclusions which could not, and cannot, be verified. Because, at some point, badgers or foxes in Hagley Wood disturbed the corpse and Bella's right hand had become separated from the rest of her, the possibility arose that she, like Charles Walton, was part of a witch-cult, the 'hand of glory' being a magic talisman associated with the dead. McCormick's garbled account of the Hagley Wood murder is as wide of the mark and vague as his version of Walton's death. The *only* similarity between the two is the possible witchcraft connection, which, in both cases, is highly spurious. The bodies were found 40 miles apart. Walton was killed in February 1945; Bella probably died in the summer or autumn of 1941. They were of different sexes and separated in age by at least forty years. Walton was bludgeoned and hacked to death; there were no signs of violence on Bella's bones and Professor Webster speculated that she had been suffocated. Whereas the killer merely left Walton where he lay, somebody went to great lengths to conceal Bella's body inside a tree, which must have been a difficult and gruesome task.

I fervently hope that now I have written two different books on these very different cases, the crime-writing and -reading fraternity will stop equating the two.

In the 1960s, Margaret Murray would not leave it alone. 'I believe the dead woman here [Bella] was another victim of the devil-worshippers. Like Walton, her body was found in an isolated place.' Actually, the wych elm was only yards from a main road, and, at the time, Hagley was as full of war refugees, regular troops and the Home Guard as was Quinton.

But, human nature being what it is, it is the McCormick/Murray angle that fascinates everybody. We *like* being frightened. We *like* things that go bump in the night because science and technology has made our lives so banal and predictable. And if the murder of Charles Walton could not be solved by the rational and the here and now, was there another way?

Chapter 12

Séance on a Snowy Evening

W e have already seen the rise of interest in the occult in the 1950s. Margaret Murray spearheaded it from the academic point of view; Gerald Gardner from the practising end. The tabloids of the day ate it all up, with hints of an elite group of the great and powerful who were up to their old school ties in diabolism. We have seen an outbreak of this kind of hysteria recently in which fantasist Carl Beech made ludicrous claims of child molestation and murder against famous personalities; bizarrely, Robert Fabian's old force found this 'credible and true'.

The unsolved murder of Charles Walton was meat and drink to the sensation seekers and people descended on the Quintons, quizzing locals about what *really* happened in February 1945. On 12 May 1949, papers carried the story that a witches' sabbat was held in the circle of the Rollright Stones – 'the night of the full moon', as McCormick describes it, 'nearest to Walpurgis Night, which was May Eve in the old calendar and a very special date for the holding of a witch's sabbat'. *Walpurgisnacht* was the German phrase for the Celtic festival of Beltane (allowing, once again, for the change of calendar) which venerated the marriage of Walpurga and the horned god, a rebirth of the sun and the end of winter. It survived into the Christian period with bonfires and dancing around the maypole, a phallic symbol which appalled the Puritans of the seventeenth century.

Typically, McCormick has two anonymous witnesses to this sabbat, a man and a woman. She lasted only half a minute as an observer before she lost her nerve and ran, but not before she had seen 'shadowy figures dancing in a queer fashion and bouncing up and down as though they were on pogo-sticks'.[22] If this sounds a little modern for 1949, the children's toy was patented in Germany in 1920; it reached its widest popularity across the world in the 1970s. The male observer counted half a dozen participants, so it was clearly not a conventional coven. The dancers were male and female, performing some sort of rite around the King Stone, dancing back to back. Reports to the police led nowhere, almost certainly because the police had better things to do with their time. The *Weekend Telegraph*'s Andrew Duncan wrote that 'witches are more security conscious, because they feel spells are weakened by unsympathetic witnesses.' McCormick claimed to have traced a witness of the sabbat, J.F. Rogers of Banbury, drawn to the site by rumours. He watched from behind one of the stones on the clear, moonlit night and heard a mumbling, 'just mumbo-jumbo'. The leader of the group wore a goat's head mask. The *Sunday Mercury* of 6 September 1953 regurgitated the story, using the old witchcraft word for dancing, 'widdershins'.

To McCormick and many others, the 1949 sabbat not only happened and was in accordance with historical accounts of similar pagan festivities, it was also proof that witchcraft was alive and well in Warwickshire in the middle of the twentieth century. None of this, of course, had anything to do with Charles Walton.

But what happened on 2 February did; or was supposed to. The links between witchcraft and spiritualism are complicated, but the notion that the spirits of the dead never actually leave the earth, at least for long, are ancient and held all over the world. When two teenaged girls, the Fox sisters, claimed to be able to contact the spirit of a murdered drummer (travelling salesman) in Hydesville, New York, in 1848, a belief system and an entire industry were born. Never mind that the girls were almost immediately exposed as frauds (they could dislocate their knees to make the 'knocking' sounds of the ghost) the idea caught on, spreading first to France and then to Britain. Talking

---

[22] McCormick p. 109.

to dead people became a Victorian parlour game and in 1851 the Ghost Club of Cambridge University assembled an elite group of academics to prove or disprove the existence of spirits. From this emerged the Society for Psychical Research, using ever more advanced technology to outwit the army of fraudulent mediums who were making money out of gullible people.

Despite little headway, the Society was still operating in 1952 and the Birmingham branch decided to visit Meon Hill on Candlemas Day of that year. This was not their only target. According to McCormick, they sent groups to Warley Abbey in Smethwick and to a haunted golf course at Mucklow Hill near Halesowen. In the event, the Meon Hill venture had to be called off because no one could find a medium willing to do it. There was much talk of negative energy, as if the wrathful wraith of old Charlie Walton would be too much to handle. But they tried again.

Tony Mills was president of the Staffordshire Metaphysical Society, and a parish councillor of Moreton Morrell in Warwickshire. Was he, we are entitled to ask, the author of the redacted letter to Spooner, offering his services in solving the murder? McCormick gives his name as Alfred and he had already visited Lower Quinton to snoop around. As with Fabian, he found the locals tight-lipped. He told reporters:

I must say that in my subsequent research into the Walton murder, I had an uncanny sense of evil. For instance I took a sample of the soil from the ground where Walton was murdered. I had it analysed and it was ordinary enough. But from the day on which I brought that ordinary little bottle into my home, I had an extraordinary run of misfortune. My little girl took pneumonia three times in succession. I broke my ankle. Of my sixty chickens, forty-five died unexpectedly and inexplicably. The cattle sickened ... Of course, I had considered the possibility of the soil being the malignant influence, but it seemed too absurd for words. Nevertheless, the day I took the bottle and hurled it far away as I could, these odd mishaps stopped.[23]

The re-convened séance took place on Thursday, 27 November, Tony Mills having thrown in his lot with the Birmingham SPR. A *Birmingham Post* journalist was with them to record events:

The party tramped for an hour across ploughed fields, barbed wire fences, muddy ditches and puddles of icy water. It was snowing hard and dark and the combination of darkness and weather defeated the team; they were lost. A few of the sixteen knew where Charles Walton died and decided to hold the séance where they stood. Their medium was Mrs Hinkinbottom from Birmingham who obligingly went into a trance. She spoke with a man's voice, [straight out of the yet-to-be made *Exorcist*] – 'I forgive. I forgive. I deserved what was coming to me, but not in such a brutal way.'

Mrs Hinkinbottom mumbled something else and then came out of her trance. Mills had now found the white gate close to where the body was found under an old willow tree. 'The party,' wrote McCormick, 'then turned for the two-mile trudge back to their cars in the village.' How much this is McCormick and how much the *Birmingham Post* is not clear because the author does not give his sources. But the aerial photographs used by Fabian in 1945 clearly show the murder site less than half a mile from Walton's cottage and the search party's starting point of the College Arms.

As my wife and I discovered on our visit, the murder site, using Fabian's aerial photograph from *The Anatomy of Crime* is not difficult to find. The white gates have been replaced by metal 'kissing gates' now, but the public footpath that leads to Meon Hill en route to the Heart of

---

[23] Quoted in Newman, pp. 63–4.

England Way leads right past Walton's last hedge and the place where he died.

I suspect that too many researchers have been seduced by the lure of Meon Hill. 'Under the shadow' of the place is Fabian's phrase and it gives a totally false impression. The photograph of it in this book was taken from the murder site; the hill is at least 2 miles away and does not 'loom' at all; in fact, it is something of a disappointment.

During daylight, Mills had taken a photograph of the corner of the field where Walton died. It revealed a mysterious white shape in the form of a hideous female face. Alternatively, it could have been the random light shining through the equally random pattern of the hedge. There is a similar photograph in this book; how many spooky faces can *you* see?

According to McCormick (how often have I written *that* phrase in this book?) the medium mentioned two names in her Walton persona – 'They meant nothing to us at the time,' Tony Mills told the *Empire News*, 'but when we checked up, we discovered that these were Christian names of people in whom the police had been interested at the time of the murder.' We all know that leaks happen; local bobbies like Michael Lomasney, who knew everybody on his patch, may not have been able to keep their mouths shut. But *officially*, neither Tony Mills nor anyone else would have been able to have found this information from the police files. McCormick, of course, with his tendency to have inside information on *everything*, had an (unnamed) police confidant who told him that there was indeed a suspect with that particular Christian name. 'We are convinced,' the detective told McCormick, 'that old Charles had been up to something rather queer.'

How right he was.

By 1952, we have come a very long way from the realities of 14 February seven years earlier. In America, Senator Joe McCarthy of Wisconsin was leading his anti-witch campaign in the hysterical hunt for Communists; Arthur Miller countered it with *The Crucible*, which exposed the cruelty and bigotry of the original witch-hunting craze in Salem, Massachusetts in 1692. And by the 1950s, the world was ready again for the occult in all its various guises. The *Sunday Pictorial* ran a story on 19 February 1956 under the headline 'Black Magic Killer – Woman Talks'. It read like a tag-line from a Hollywood B-feature horror flick which would soon find its British counterpart at the Bray studios of the Hammer corporation:

> A terrified woman, driven grey-haired by some of the most evil men in Britain, offered last night to help solve the murder of Charles Walton, who was impaled with a pitchfork in a lonely Warwickshire field on St Valentine's Day 1945. She will give the name of the alleged murderer to Det. Supt. A.W. Spooner, Chief of the Warwickshire CID. This woman, who begged me not to reveal her name, has offered to tell Det. Supt. Spooner everything – provided she is protected from the vengeance of Britain's black magic cults. For twelve frightful years she took part with other members of the cults in grotesque rites that stem from Britain's mysterious past. Now she wants the police to stamp out these evil practices. And she wants them to solve the 11-year-old crime she claims was a ritual murder.

There was actually a precedent for this. Three years earlier, an equally anonymous woman calling herself Anna from Claverley in Worcestershire claimed to know what happened to Bella, the corpse in the wych elm at Hagley Wood. She wrote to Wilfred Byford-Jones of the Wolverhampton *Express and Star* who, delighted to have such a scoop handed to him on a plate, set up a clandestine meeting between Anna, himself and DI Thomas Williams, in charge of the ongoing case. Research has shown that Anna was actually Una Mossop, a local housewife and her claims were utterly baseless. What motivated her to waste police time remains unknown, but the Mossops were a dysfunctional family. Anna's husband died in a hospital for the mentally ill and her son was wanted by the police on a variety of charges. The fact that Byford-Jones had offered £100 for information relevant to the Hagley Wood case might also have had a bearing. So, too, in the murder of Charles Walton. If the anonymous 'terrified' woman had any real evidence regarding the Meon Hill murder, why not to go to the police direct, rather than involving a journalist? If she really feared the vengeance of a cult, a newspaper was hardly the safest hiding place. She had been inveigled into a cult by her husband, she said, and the Walton murder was carried out as part of an internal coup among covens. The *Pictorial* trotted out the usual nonsense of the 'identical' killing of Ann Tennant in 1875. The actual killer was not a member of a local cult, based in Birmingham, she said, but a woman brought in by car from elsewhere. The savagery of the killing hardly fits a woman's modus operandi; women prefer to do their killing at a distance. A strange car in a small village in 1945 may not have attracted *too* much attention, giving the comings and goings of outsiders at the time, but a *woman* who was not a Land Girl tramping the fields at lunchtime on 14 February would surely have attracted attention of all sorts. Although female eyewitnesses were interviewed by the police at the time, the only people seen walking about in the Quintons that day were men.

The following day the paper ran the story – 'Murder at Black Mass, says Woman'. The facts had by now changed beyond all recognition. Charles Walton had become a shepherd (which he never was) and was murdered at midnight during a Black Mass. Professor Webster's murder time frame of between 1 and 2 p.m. had slid forwards (or back) by thirteen hours or twelve, depending on which midnight the paper is referring to. A Black Mass implies *people*, not a solitary killer, with candles, dancing and the usual mumbo-jumbo. Was *anybody* supposed to believe this? But it got better. Walton was killed in the centre of a circle of stones in a field at Lower Quinton, which, of course, did not exist. Inevitably, by this time, his throat was slashed in the form of a cross and 'villagers said it was a ritual murder'. The anonymous woman was due to be interviewed by Warwickshire CID later that week. Needless to say, there is nothing in the Warwickshire police files on this.

By the devious means known only to journalists, another paper – *Reynolds News* – tracked the woman down to Wolverhampton and she happily added more detail. How much is from her and how much journalese the reader can judge for him or herself. Thirteen people took part in the Mass (naturally). One of them knew Walton; the others were strangers. The old man was working 'well away from houses' (300 yards in fact) and three of them approached him and struck him down. 'It was exactly midday.' So, from the midnight Mass, we have swung across half a day's time frame to more or less the correct window of opportunity. 'Rapidly they mutilated his body, soaked some robes in his blood, drove in the pitchfork and danced round the body.'

Gerald Gardner, the leading practising witch in the country at the time, could not remain silent at this rubbish. He wrote in a letter to the press:

> I shall be greatly obliged if anyone could explain to me how thirteen people could dance round the body of a man which, according to the evidence given at the inquest by one of the three people who found it, was lying close against the hedge in a bit of a ditch.

To point up the terror the cult whistle-blower felt, she told reporters that a 'circle of silence' made of twigs and graveyard clippings appeared on her doorstep as a warning. That night, on her way home, she was 'grabbed and scalped, a circle of hair and skin sliced off using a doctor's scalpel.' The woman went on to describe the 'diabolical' rites of Mass ceremonies generally, which was straight out of the Hammer Studios rent-a-coven.

Paul Newman traced Gerald Gardner's contention that in 1956 we had heard all this before. A year previously, Mrs Shari-i-jay Jones, a Spanish lady who spoke Romany, visited various cults in Birmingham with her husband, Peter Jackson. Some of these were situated in premises belonging to the Heslaw Press in the city. Mrs Jones contacted journalist Peter Hawkins of the *Sunday Pictorial* who followed up on the name of Walton's killer as given to him by Mrs Jones. She was Patricia McAlpine née Doherty, of Newlyn, Cornwall. What this was all about was a sort of turf war between cults. Charles Walton was an irrelevance, but this murder and the witchcraft nonsense associated with it gave Jones a chance to libel Gerald Gardner. Dierdre Patricia Doherty was one of the many mistresses of Aleister Crowley, the great beast, and in 1937 gave birth to his son, Randall Gair, whom he called Ataturk, presumably after the hero and moderniser of Turkey, Kemal Ataturk. Gardner, Mrs Jones contended, had been present at various occult meetings but the last thing Gardner wanted was to have his infant Wicca movement linked with ritual murder. As writer Paul Newman says, 'Even journalists realized it was unlikely a dead ditcher would be of any use to a sophisticated occultist who confined his ceremonies to flats and hideouts in London, but such objections hardly mattered when millions awaited the latest dish of devilment.'[24]

So, in the febrile 'witchy' atmosphere of 1950s media, Charles Walton developed a back story that went far beyond an old countryman who recognized birdsong and knew how to lay a hedge. There were still hundreds, perhaps thousands, like him all over the country, but they had not met a grisly death at the wrong end of a pitchfork and billhook. Walton became a full-blown witch, a horse-whisperer and breeder of natterjack toads.

A number of these animals had allegedly been found behind Walton's cottage during a police search of the premises, and devotees of witchcraft recognized the significance at once – the toad was a typical familiar of sixteenth- and seventeenth-century witches, a creature sent by the Devil to do the witch's bidding. Lynn Picknett, in *The Encyclopaedia of the Paranormal*, devotes two pages to toad magic, beginning with the Walton

---

[24] Ibid p. 70.

link. Toads are not actually poisonous, but they do produce bactericides and the hallucinogen bufotenine. If swallowed or rubbed on the skin, this can give a sensation of flight, with its inevitable suggestion of witches, broomsticks and transport to the local sabbat. The fourteenth-century heretic cult, the Waldensians, based in Turin, admitted (albeit under the torture of the Inquisition) that they worshipped the toad that they equated with the Great Dragon of the Book of Revelations. Covens were believed to kiss the *occulum infame* (arse) of a toad in lieu of the actual Devil, who may have been busy elsewhere at the time. Aleister Crowley allegedly baptized a toad before crucifying it in a weird parody of Christ. Some believed that toads had a precious gem in their brains, but the most ludicrous story came from navvies working on the London to Birmingham railway in 1835. One of them crushed a stone and a toad fell out, still alive after incarceration without oxygen and its colour changed from brown to black. It died four days later. Nobody seemed to notice that the navvies were well-known pranksters, several of them dying in a game of 'follow my leader' when they fell down a deep shaft at the construction of the Blisworth Tunnel in Northamptonshire. Some of them sold their common-law wives for cider and it was their drunkenness that made them feared in local communities where track was being laid; elsewhere, they were figures of fun.

The natterjack toad (*bufo calamita*), known in various places as the golden-back, is distinctive, not only for its yellow markings but the fact that it runs rather than leaps like other sub-species. The male has an unusual call, like that of a nightjar. Stories began to circulate – it is difficult to pinpoint when – that Walton harnessed these creatures to a toy plough he had made, although exactly what the purpose of this was is not clear. There are a number of references to toad familiars in the accounts of witch trials. In 1579, Mother Dutton of Cleworthe near Windsor 'keepeth a spirite or feende in the likeness of a toad'. She fed it with herbs and blood 'from her own flancke'. Three years later, Ursley (Ursula) Kemp had a number of familiars, one of which was a black toad called Pygine. In 1588, an anonymous English witch had three familiars – the cat killed cattle, the weasel killed horses and 'the Toad would plague men in their bodies' (whatever that meant).

The reference to the toad and the plough comes straight out of a witch trial held more than 200 years before Charles Walton was born. Isobel Gowdie was at the heart of a coven at Aldearne in Fyfeshire in 1662. Scottish witchcraft has always had a high profile because of James I's obsession with it and the Highland setting of *Macbeth*. Unlike the English penalty of hanging for witchcraft, in Scotland they followed the European fashion of burning at the stake. Even though illiterate Gowdie's confession is the most detailed of all British witches and appears to have been given freely without torture, we do not know what happened to her. In one of three confessions, she explained that she and her sister harnessed toads to little ploughs and let them go across fields to make the soil sterile. A couple of poor harvests in the Midlands in the mid-1940s were believed to be evidence of the same spell (although 1943 was a bumper year for crops).

But toads were not the only things found on Charles Walton's premises (if indeed they were); the other thing was his watch. Because there was a dispute over how much money the old man had on him on 14 February 1945, the only thing *known* to have gone was his pocket watch. I believe his knapsack was also taken, but since only one eyewitness (Charlotte Byway) mentioned this, the fact seems to have been overlooked. I think the missing knapsack was of vital importance in what happened.

At the inquest, Edith Walton told the coroner, 'Every night he used to wind it up before he went to bed and place it on the wash-stand beside his bed. I have never known him go about without his watch.' Fast forward fifteen years. In 1960, workmen demolishing outhouses behind Walton's cottage came across a pocket watch in the rubble. It was handed in and the maker's name – Edgar Jones, Stratford-upon-Avon – was identical to the one the old man habitually carried. Police enquiries were re-opened. There were various marks inside the case, but Jones was long dead and actual verification could not be made.

All this was too good for Donald McCormick to pass up. He devotes half a chapter to 'The Puzzle of Charles Walton's Watch' and of course found an obliging local who filled him in on its significance. As usual, using casual (and unlikely) dialogue, the local told the journalist that Walton had kept a piece of glass inside the watch case that brought him luck. That led McCormick into a welter of speculation over why, uniquely, the watch had been taken in the first place. He ignores the obvious reason, that the killer might have believed it to be valuable, despite its being a cheap tin version. He then speculates that a devious murderer would have taken it so that if the hands were stopped by damage during the struggle, the experts would not be able to pinpoint the exact time of death. But what, McCormick wonders, if the watch had another significance? Could the black glass inside be a witch's scrying mirror, used for fortune-telling, like the one allegedly carried by Elizabeth I's magus, Dr John Dee? Only McCormick has the tale of the dark glass. Only McCormick once knew the name of the local who provided the information. Like much else passed on by the 'fantasy historian', it should be taken with a huge pinch of salt.

Someone else who has the dark glass story is Cecil Williamson. The mysterious visitor who called into his witchcraft museum in Bourton-on-the-Water (see previous chapter) told the former black propagandist to talk to a chemist in Shipston-on-Stour, not far away. Naturally, the chemist is anonymous, as is a fruiterer who was involved in a witch-cult in the Vale of Evesham in the 1930s. They devoted themselves to furthering the occult work of John Dee and acquired a scrying stone. The war, Williamson claimed, forced them to close the group down and the stone was given to Charles Walton, because of his ability to charm birds, whisper to horses and talk to toads. 'A spiritual keeper was required,' Williamson wrote, 'and Charles Walton was selected for the job of Keeper of the Stone, being the key to the door between the two worlds of here and Hereafter.'[25]

---

[25] Quoted in Newman, p. 132.

The fruiterer was dead by 1944 but two female members of the coven took it upon themselves to reorganize. To do that, they needed Walton's stone and Walton was not playing ball. He refused to hand it over, so he had to die. The date was deliberately chosen; so was the murder method. What Williamson does not explain, of course, is the fact that the stone was not found (if indeed it was) until 1960. It was not on Walton's body when it was found and why should the two unnamed witches bother to return the watch after the event?

A far more interesting question is how the watch turned up where it did, when it did. Various commentators have wondered why the killer should take the watch in the first place and then risk everything by returning it; why not simply throw it away once he found it to be worthless? A far more likely explanation is that Walton did not have the watch with him on the day he died. Perhaps it was faulty and he took it to his outhouse planning to work on it when he got home. Perhaps he slipped it for safe-keeping into a hidey-hole in what must have been very much *his* domain. Except that Charles Walton did not come home and Edith assumed the watch had been stolen during the attack. As for the police search, how thorough was that? We know, in a different context, that they missed Charles Walton's second stick because it was made from hedgewood and umpteen big-footed coppers tramped past it before it was identified by Alfred Potter. Once the search of the outhouse was over (the work of an hour?) why would they look again? Note that all accounts describe the watch as being found in a pile of rubble. In my wife's grandparents' house, in a Warwickshire village not unlike Lower Quinton, there was a loose brick in the chimney breast where valuables could be stored. Only certain members of the family knew about that.

According to McCormick (!) *Reynolds News* carried a relevant witchcraft story a week after Shari-i-jay Jones had told her all. The writer was Irene Layton, from London, and gave the police a 25,000-word dossier on a cult in the capital which had been set up at least fifteen years before. From this group, Mrs Layton learned that a female Austrian doctor had died mysteriously after retiring from the Midlands where she had been investigating Walton's murder. McCormick offers no more information but veers off into a six-page description of coven/Black mass rituals which have nothing to do with Warwickshire, still less Charles Walton. As though suddenly reminded that he is still nominally in the chapter about the old man's watch, he veers back to the Austrian doctor – 'it seemed just possible that the woman doctor might have had a relative at the prisoner-of-war camp at Long Marston', especially if said relative was on the police suspect list. As so often, the journalist dismisses an impossible piece of research with a single line. 'I could, however, find no Austrian on the list.' How did he obtain such a roll? Information like this remained classified for years after the war and McCormick had not seen the police file which *does* contain a list, at least of Italians. In any case, by the time Walton died, there were many Germans at Long Marston; how was it possible to tell a German name from an Austrian one?

As usual, McCormick had an obliging local to help him out. Those who were reticent to the point of sullen silence in 1945 were suddenly falling over themselves to provide information twenty years later. This particular local remembered a woman with a 'foreign accent' several years before. She had not mentioned Walton but wanted to know about 'some chappie from the POW camp'. Armed with this, McCormick took himself off to Long Marston and 'this time I was luckier'. It is very difficult to see in what way. By the time McCormick got there, Long Marston was a Polish resettlement camp and remained so until its closure in the 1970s. The information that McCormick says he was given concerned an Austrian doctor who was specifically looking for a Hungarian astrologer who had been an inmate of the camp during the war. 'I seemed to be going round in circles,' McCormick wrote, whereas in fact, his reach into the realms of astrologers brought him neatly back to Bella in the wych elm with the spurious espionage/astrology links associated with that case. The Long Marston people told him that they knew nothing about the Meon Hill murder, but McCormick's book was about that *and* Bella and the link was just too good (and improbable) to pass up. With astonishing chutzpah, having ploughed through 157 pages on the two cases, McCormick claims that 'there is no link whatsoever, not even a remote one, between the Hagley Wood and Lower Quinton crimes.' It is a pity he did not make this statement on page 1 and save everybody the hassle of wrestling with them both. Even that statement is, however, disingenuous, as the 'fantasy historian' goes on to illustrate the 'many parallels' between the murders.

Having written off superstition and witchcraft earlier in the book, McCormick outlines how the motivation for Walton's murder could be attributed to any of the following:

1. A sacrificial killing in connection with fertility rites, ordained by a coven or carried out by a lone warlock.

The author hints at crop failure, which would have to refer to the harvest of 1944 and earlier. The summer of 1943 in particular had been long and hot and produced a record harvest. In comparison with that, 1944 probably disappointed, but it was not a *sustained* problem; and in February 1945, the harvest lay months in the future. To feed the population, the government insisted on pasture land being ploughed up and planted. This was happening all over the Midlands, no doubt on the farms of Alfred Potter and Joseph Stanley and Frederick Frost, as on many others. By 1944, there were 5.75 million more acres under crops than at the start of the war. As a whole, farmers did better out of the war than any other single economic group. It is difficult to see much of a motive in all this for McCormick's first premise, but at least he was probably right in his assertion that the killer was a warlock (male) rather than a witch (female); women do not kill like that.

2. A killing ordained as a 'sanction of the Devil' – i.e., a killing aimed at appeasing the Devil and carrying out his wishes.

Here we are in the unknowable world of the witch hysteria of the sixteenth and seventeenth centuries. Much of the testimony relating to this – the Devil spreading evil and destruction in the world – came as a result of torture. The rare examples of such information – as with Isabel Gowdie – being given *without* torture, we can safely put down to the mentally ill and plain deranged. The belief that ergotism, which was caused by eating infected corn and produced hallucinations, was behind at least some of this, is a distinct possibility as an explanation.

3. A killing carried out to silence an enemy of the witches or to silence Walton for having learned too much about witchcraft activities.

This one is based on the rumour, unattributable as fact, that Walton as a lad had watched sabbats taking place at various sacred sites, including the Rollright Stones. It is worth noting that his niece Edith, who had lived with the man for thirty years, never once mentioned any such story relating to her uncle.

4. A killing carried out because Walton himself was suspected of witchcraft and because the killer was superstitious and feared him.

Here we have a surreptitious 'witch-finder' figure, identifying witches and killing them for the good of society. In 1640s East Anglia, the self-styled Witch-finder General, the lawyer Matthew Hopkins, filled this role, hunting down an estimated 200 witches, always for money and invariably using torture. Such was the temper of the times, after nearly five years of civil war and the collapse of society, that men like Hopkins could assume an air of authority. That was not possible in the 1940s, so the killer had to work alone and in secret. The question must be asked – why then? Why in broad daylight with the potential to be caught? Any local would probably know that the old man did not venture out when the weather was bad, but that Edith did, five days a week. Why not choose such a day, and kill him in his home, with relative seclusion?

5. A kind of power game, between rival witches in which jealousy played the chief part.

This one is straight out of the Pendle playlist of 1612, when two old women – Mother Chattox and Mother Demdike – sucked a number of others into their vicious world, leading to eleven hangings and the death of a twelfth in prison. The verbal spats between Gerald Gardner and Shari-i-Jay Jones ten years after Walton's death fall very far short of murder.

McCormick plumped for a combination of numbers 1 and 4:

I think [the killer] was secretly obsessed by ancient fears of witchcraft and the feeling that witchcraft in the district was directed at crops and livestock. For that reason I believe the killer was a countryman whose life and financial interests were tied to these things. I also think that he suspected Walton of being mixed up in witchcraft and of being a malign influence. For this reason, he was afraid of the man. He had tried to appease him, to shake off his fears, but had failed. Then, when crops began to show inexplicable signs of failure and cattle became sick for no apparent reason, fear turned to blind hatred and one day he decided to kill the old hedger.

We know that the sudden crop failure is nonsense and that heifers die in ditches from time to time as part of the natural order of things.

Naturally, McCormick's view is backed up by a woman 'who declines to be named' but is the high priestess of a local coven. This woman, if she is anything more than a figment of the imagination of the 'fantasy historian', at least gets it right in one respect. McCormick quotes her at length – 'I assure you the modern practitioners of witchcraft, inside or outside of covens, are not to be found among hedgers and farm labourers. They come mainly from the professional classes and this would have been just as true during the war as today [1968].'

In 1971, the BBC produced a curious little documentary called *The Power of the Witch*. Watching it today on YouTube, it strikes an artificial chord which is almost laughable. As titillation, it is a disaster; a group of middle-aged men and women dance naked in a circle (going the *wrong* way for witches) and everybody interviewed is extraordinarily well spoken and middle class. An officer of the Church Army warns of young people being seduced into cults and two former members of such cults are anxious to atone for their previous involvement. The programme is fascinating, however, for two reasons. The first is that Cecil Williamson appears as a harmless and rational old man (which I do not believe he was) and the second is the banal arrival in front of the camera of a middle-aged woman called Edith Goode. We know her as Edith Walton ...

Michael Bakewell, the presenter, complete with flares and long hair, stands *far* too near to the summit of Meon Hill to be anywhere near the murder site. He trots out the usual nonsense about the cross carved into the dead man's throat and that the police *at the time* took the witchcraft angle seriously. His bubble must have been seriously burst when Edith appeared on camera, denying that her uncle had anything to do with witchcraft or that he had ever mentioned the subject in his life.

McCormick is not in the programme, but in *Murder by Witchcraft*, his high priestess drops a little bombshell which most later writers have missed or ignored. She met Margaret Murray (when is unrecorded) who told her that she believed the killer thought that Walton had, presumably through black magic, made him impotent. This deeply personal motive would go a long way to explain the savagery of the attack. Dr Murray had found a similar motive in the case of Jonet Clark in Edinburgh in 1590. According to Joseph Glanvil, writing a century later,[26] she was hanged for 'gewing and taking of power fra sundrie mennis memberis' (destroying many men's reproductive powers). Rather bizarrely, the high priestess told McCormick that Margaret Murray looked all this up in a library copy of her book (why would she do that when she surely had a copy of her own?) and found a pencilled comment alongside this paragraph – 'it happens today'.

With a high degree of self-satisfaction, Donald McCormick ends his *Murder by Witchcraft* with, 'As to the crime at Lower Quinton I am convinced that witchcraft was a motive, though the murderer was neither a witch, nor a warlock. I do not pretend to have solved the crime, but I think I know who did it.'

A very similar line can be found in Robert Fabian's *The Anatomy of Crime* – 'I have never said this publicly before, but I *think* I know who did it.' In this case, it is fairly obvious that Fabian was thinking of Alfred Potter, who had been in the Yard man's sights from the start. According to some sources, the detective had confided as much, shortly before his death in 1978, to crime writer Richard Whittington-Egan.

But McCormick and Fabian were both wrong.

---

[26] Joseph Glanvil, *Sadducismus Triumphatus*, London 1681.

Chapter 13

The Crime That Dare Not Speak Its Name

Robert Fabian always believed that the motive for Charles Walton's death was financial. There was no money found in the money belt on his body, so why carry it, unless the murderer had helped himself to its contents? Walton's expenses were few, yet the large inheritance from his wife had disappeared. Had he lent it to Alfred Potter and did he remind Potter of the debt on 14 February, which led to an altercation and murder? Or was there another reason for its disappearance?

Initially, the detective's mind was more open. Standing at the murder scene two days after Walton died, he put a question to Spooner and Webb, standing with him. '"What motive?" I inquired briskly. "Robbery – revenge – a quarrel?"' I believe that if Fabian had dropped the first idea and gone with the other two, he might have caught his man. As it was, in his initial 5 April report, Fabian can only lament that 'one of the most extraordinary features has been the entire absence of motive'.

Either Margaret Murray or Donald McCormick speaking for her, quoted a Lower Quinton local as saying 'Of course, it isn't wise to pry too deeply into other people's affairs. There may be things that I don't know of and it's better I don't. It was a funny case. Funny the thing could be done and nothing found out.' And this attitude has never *quite* gone away. In 2014, a BBC journalist called Faye visited Lower Quinton and found a population with a prepared community response. They were 'friendly, but impenetrably tight-lipped'. Toni Smith, who ran the College Arms, told her 'There are some things we don't talk about.'

And, whether you believe in the results of séances or not, the 'Walton' spirit conjured up by one on 27 November 1952 had said,

'I forgive. I forgive. I deserved what was coming to me, but not in such a brutal way.' Donald McCormick's anonymous police informant told him, 'We are convinced that old Charles had been up to something rather queer.'

If not witchcraft, what? What could have led someone to hack an old man so brutally to death? What spurred him to do it in the open in broad daylight with the huge risk of being caught? What could make an entire community clam up and be of so little help to the police? I believe there is only one answer; revenge in the context of 'the love that dare not speak its name', as Lord Alfred Douglas described homosexuality in his poem *Two Loves*.

Attitudes to same-sex relationships vary widely all over the world. Today there is such a degree of tolerance in the West that the world I am describing in this chapter will be unrecognizable to many people. No one under 50 can remember the contempt that society once had for homosexuals in Britain, where a lack of sexual conformity was equated with the most abhorrent of crimes, such as murder and treason. Yet, depressingly, over the last two years in Britain, 'queer-bashing', physical assaults on homosexuals, has increased once again.

In the ancient world, the Greeks believed homosexual love to be on an altogether higher, more spiritual plane than heterosexual relationships. Spartan warriors fought in pairs, one lover protecting the other, and they were the most formidable military power in the world. The Romans were ambivalent about it. Male brothels stood alongside female ones in Rome, Pompeii and other civilized cities. A number of emperors were bisexual, like Tiberius, Caligula, Nero and the emperor-wannabe, Julius Caesar. Various scrawled examples of graffiti, from Pompeii and Herculaneum, are homosexually referenced.

Then the Christian church stepped in, with its hard-line dogma and its own rigid interpretation of Hebrew texts translated via Greek into Latin. Homosexuality was thought to be unclean and unnatural, as it remains in much of the Middle East today. Practitioners of it were beyond the pale, barbarians whose backwardness was the cause of aberrant and abhorrent behaviour. According to some sources, the term buggery (the legal term for homosexual acts for centuries) comes from the Bulgarians, who remained pagan long after most of Europe took the cross. 'Hunnish practices' was a euphemism for same-sex for years. And Biblical scholars and vicars alike pointed to one of the cities of the plain in the Old Testament, Sodom, to create another legal term that rang down the centuries – sodomy. It was said to be particularly prevalent in the armed forces, especially the navy, where men were cooped up together without female companionship for weeks on end. Winston Churchill allegedly described life in Nelson's navy as one of 'rum, sodomy and the lash', even though sodomy itself carried the death penalty.

Morality, throughout the Middle Ages and well into the modern era, was the responsibility of the Church, be it Catholic or Protestant, but many of the bigoted views of Christianity were carried over wholesale into the realm of law. One high-profile figure who was probably homosexual was the Tudor playwright Christopher Marlowe, criticizing conventional people who 'loved not boys and tobacco'. One of his best-known plays was *Edward II*, about a bisexual ruler whose affection for one of his courtiers, Piers Gaveston, brought about his downfall and eventual death. In Marlowe's day (he himself was killed in 1593) homosexuality was a hanging offence, but interestingly, in the 100 years between 1525 and 1625, only four men were convicted of it in England. Two were hanged, one lost his job and one, Nicholas Udall, not only continued in his role as headmaster of Eton, but did not even bother to turn up to court for his trial!

The problem with examining the extent and type of homosexuality is that references to it are few and almost always confined to cities, especially London. Mention of it in rural areas is virtually non-existent. There were male brothels known as 'Mollie houses' in London as early as 1700 when City businessmen picked up rent boys at the Fountain, the Bull and Butcher and the Sun. And it was not until Labouchere's

Bill exposed Oscar Wilde that the country was suddenly made aware of a dark side of human behaviour that most people had no idea existed. Male brothels were discovered in Little College Street, Westminster and a far more notorious one in Cleveland Street where post office boys and peers of the realm met for secret assignations. The last two men to be hanged for buggery were John Smith and James Pratt in 1835 and the death penalty for the crime was abolished in 1861.

It is difficult for us to understand the shame that surrounded homosexuality. In 1707, nearly forty men were arrested at the Sodomites Club in the City. Cheapside mercer Jacob Ecclestone committed suicide in Newgate prison; as did draper William Grant and Mr Jermain, curate of St Dunstan's-in-the-East who cut his throat with a razor. In 1764, *The Public Advertiser* described the punishment meted out to 'a bugger aged sixty [who] was put in the Cheapside Pillory ... the Mob tore off his clothes, pelted him with filth, whipt him almost to death ...'

At a trial in 1726, an eyewitness to goings-on at Mother Clap's house of ill repute in Holborn, told the court what he saw. About forty men were taking part in an orgy, sitting on each other's laps, kissing and 'using their hands indecently'. They also danced and mimicked male-female courtship rituals – 'Eh, you dear little toad! Come, buss [kiss me].' At the White Swan near Oxford Street, mock marriages took place, involving (which made the scandal all the more salacious) 'men of rank and respectable situations in life'. In 1810, the Swan was raided by the Bow Street runners, who arrested twenty-three men, who were punished with the pillory and one to three years' imprisonment. In every case where public punishment was carried out, the ferocity of the mob was extraordinary, most of it coming from women.

Ernest Bolton and William Park got away with cross-dressing in 1871 (when Charles Walton was still a baby) because, essentially, they had broken no law. The evidence suggests that they were soliciting, but the jury did not see it that way and gave them the benefit of the doubt.

Homosexuality came under the microscope once more in Nazi Germany, perhaps as a response to the libertarian reputation of Berlin under the Weimar government in the 1920s. Heinrich Himmler, head of the SS, wrote:

> We must exterminate these people root and branch. Just think how many people will never be born because of this and how a people can be broken in nerve and spirit when such a plague gets hold of it … We can't permit such danger to the country; the homosexual must be entirely eliminated.[27]

Thousands of them were rounded up and placed in concentration camps along with Jews, Socialists and gypsies. They were forced to wear pink triangles on their clothes to identify them.

Clearly, nothing like this happened in Britain, where there was greater tolerance about everything. Even so, society generally was antipathetic, especially in the more rural areas away from the bright lights and urban sophistication. Between 1900 and 1940, eleven men were hanged for murders which had a homosexual dimension. Of these cases, seven victims were children, which almost always pressured juries into findings of guilt.

The Age of Reason had seen an altogether more tolerant approach, but Victorian England had become almost paranoically worried about its morality. At the same time that drunkenness was become a national problem, so too, some believed, was homosexuality. Into the limelight had stepped Henry Labouchere, a crusading journalist and Liberal MP who wanted to clean up what he saw as the cesspit of London. 'Labby's' Civil Law Amendment Act of 1885 had come down hard on homosexuals and would have targeted lesbians too had not Victoria intervened to use the royal veto. She had claimed that lesbians did not exist (despite a wealth of evidence to the contrary) and so British law has never had any legislation regarding female-female sexual relationships. Tellingly, in the context of what I believe happened below Meon Hill in

---

[27] Heinrich Himmler to Dr Felix Kersten, *The Kersten Memoirs*, 1957.

1945, Labouchere's Bill came to be known as the 'blackmailer's charter' because it made homosexuals, especially with a public reputation to uphold, particularly vulnerable.

Attitudes to the situation in the days of Charles Walton are obvious, but references are few. Of the Yard detectives who wrote their memoirs or had memoirs written about them, very few refer to the problem at all. One who does, tangentially, is Robert Fabian, probably because he ran the Met's Vice Squad for several years. In *London After Dark* (1954) he has a chapter called 'Problem of the Perverts' in which he quotes various advertisements on display in shop windows in Leicester Square and Shepherd's Market, such as 'Young man, artistic type, in need of strict discipline, seeks companion, preferably older, of dominant personality and habits' and 'Bachelor (45) seeks young man, artistic and understanding disposition, to share flat. Nominal rent to right kind of personality'. Vice squad officers took such advertisements down.

Fabian wrote:

The one type of perversion that the law vaguely recognizes is that of homosexuality. This is an offence against decency and is punishable by heavy imprisonment [as opposed to female prostitutes who invariably got off with a £2 fine]. As a law-breaking act it is a parallel with robbery with violence ... there is not one night in London when – if you go to the right places – you will fail to see an example of persons soliciting to commit the offence of homosexuality.

The underworld term for these men is 'Queers'. The puzzling thing is that they are usually normal in appearance and manner. The cheap antics of stage comedians have made most people think of the 'pansy' as a lisping, mincing creature who uses perfume and nail varnish. This is not correct. Of all the men I have convicted for offences of homosexuality, I would defy anybody to pick nine out of ten of them from any ordinary assembly of men. Quite a number of them are married.

Men, perhaps, like Charles Walton.

In *Murder by Witchcraft*, Donald McCormick concludes that neither Fabian nor Spooner had much in the way of a suspect shortlist for the murder of Charles Walton. 'But there were three men against whom a large question mark remained.' This is not obvious from the police files. The only man suspected, clearly, was Alfred Potter. His behaviour on the day had seemed odd, at least to Constable Lomasney, and his detailed movements seemed to shift as time went on. Fabian's references to 'huge discrepancies' in Potter's timing on the day in question are in fact minimal. While the Yard man was prepared to write off the wrong timings of Charlotte Byway who had seen Walton leave for work on the day of the murder, a ten-minute discrepancy from Potter makes him a likely murderer. That said, there was nothing to point to him as a killer. Some workers did not like him; others did. There were doubts about his financial integrity, but alongside that, he was a sidesman at St Swithin's and a member of the Chipping Camden branch of the British Legion. His interests were nothing more alarming than cricket and an occasional flutter on the horses. Some said that he liked a drink and was short tempered; others had never seen this side of him.

A second person of interest, McCormick says, was the rat-catcher stationed at Long Marston. 'It was generally known ... that he set rabbit snares in the fields around Lower Quinton. Some villagers thought he might have been caught on poaching expeditions by old Charles.' This, of course, although McCormick does not name him, was Private Thomas Davies of the Pioneer Corps, regarded as an 'unscrupulous type' who nevertheless had an alibi for the day of the murder; five comrades at Long Marston and fellow drinkers at the Leg of Mutton pub vouched for him. Unless Davies was unusually violent, not to say psychotic, it is most unlikely that a poacher would hack a man in the way someone killed Walton over an offence so trivial. The days of farmers emptying their shotguns on poachers or using mantraps to shatter their ankles had long gone. In fact, the West Yorkshire Police Training Manual of

1938 does not mention poaching at all, even though, technically, it was still a criminal offence.

It is McCormick's third 'suspect' that I find most interesting. He was, the author says:

> A young man named Smith [!] who lived in Upper Quinton, notorious for his violent temper and who had been involved in an incident in which a man and his wife were beaten up in their garage not far from Lower Quinton. A few weeks after the Walton murder, Smith left home. Later, his body was found. He had gassed himself and a verdict of suicide was returned.

Fabian, annoyed that locals had closed ranks, had written:

> The natives of Upper and Lower Quinton and the surrounding district are of a secretive disposition and they do not take easily to strangers. Therefore I have borne in mind the possibility of there being some local history attached to the murdered man or his neighbours which we have not yet touched upon and which may have a direct bearing on the murder. The local police officers are keeping in close touch with the inhabitants of the district in the hope of bringing to light any such matter as would open a fresh line of enquiry. If, as I believe, this murder was committed by a local person, I do not think it possible for the matter to end without there being some repercussion which will give rise to an opportunity for us to take such action as may solve the mystery and bring the murderer to justice.

Superintendent Spooner agreed, which is why, on 14 February for the next twenty years, he revisited Lower Quinton, holding a minute's silence by the willow tree – 'Spooner's Willow' as some writers term it – which marked the murder site. He wrote:

The villagers are frightened to talk. That was our trouble right through the investigations. I go to the village. I talk to people. I let myself be seen. If the murderer is about, he wants the crime forgotten. My return shows him that it has not been forgotten and this may wear him down. I don't need the file. Every date and every detail is in my mind.

The problem, I believe, was that it was all too late. Spooner's dramatic returns to the murder scene, every year until his retirement in 1965, were largely a waste of time. I believe that there were, indeed, people who knew that the enigmatic Smith had killed Walton and they knew why. But now that both men were dead, why rake up unpleasant facts everybody would rather forget?

But Alec Spooner did not confine himself to a histrionic walk around the village. In the police file there is a letter addressed to the Superintendent, County Police Office, Skegness. It is dated 28 August 1948 referring to articles about Walton in the *Police Gazette* in February and March three years earlier. Spooner had uncovered the fact that Lincolnshire Constabulary were holding Ernest Roy Smith for trial at the next assizes on a joint charge of burglary. The property stolen amounted to £777 1s 0d and the robbery had been armed. Smith had given his home address as Quinton. There was no evidence linking the burglar with the death of Charles Walton (the date of the burglary is not given) but Spooner wanted the Lincolnshire police to interview Smith to find out exactly where he was on 14 February 1945. He also hoped that the local force would turn up Walton's watch as evidence of a connection, whereas, of course, in all probability it was still waiting to be found in Walton's outhouse where the old man had left it on 14 February. Sadly, there is no reply in The National Archive file to Spooner's letter but there is in the Warwickshire Archive. On 9 September, a redacted DS rang Spooner with the news that he was dealing with the enquiry. A week later, another promising lead closed. Superintendent Barnes of the Lincolnshire police reported that Smith had an alibi for 14 February 1945; he was driving a redacted vehicle 'almost continuously between the hours of 10.30 a.m. and 9 p.m. – it would therefore appear certain that he had no connection with the murder referred to.'

Smith is, of course, the most common of English surnames – there were probably 300,000 of them in Britain in 1945 – and I believe that McCormick has conflated two people in his quest, however half-hearted, for the killer of Charles Walton. Ernest Roy Smith may well have been the man who attacked a couple in a garage, perhaps even doing the commission of the burglary on which Lincolnshire held him, but we have no idea when he left the area and, generally speaking, such hard men do not commit suicide. He certainly had not by 1948.

The commonness of the surname and the fact that burglary, even with violence, is a relatively minor crime, means that I have been unable to trace Ernest Smith. I do not know where or when his case came to trial or what became of him. The savagery of the Walton murder would certainly fit a violent man looking for money, but once again, we have to face the fact that Charles Walton was not known to carry any. No one, surely, would have assumed that an old hedger, toiling away in scruffy clothes for someone else, would be a walking goldmine? It is true that, today, people can be killed for a pair of trainers, but this sort of crime belongs to street gangs and urban environments. Charlie Walton and Lower Quinton hardly fit the pattern.

Fast forward more than fifty years. In 1999, everybody was looking forward to the Millennium. It was time to put the twentieth century to bed. The generation that fought the Second World War had all but gone. The geopolitics that had seen the outbreak of that war had changed out of all recognition. The European Union rode roughshod over older national identities in a bid to create a new superstate to balance the East-West giants of the USA and Russia. The Cold War was over; the Berlin Wall, symbol of all that divided East and West, had gone. It was a brave new world, happy to leave the old divisions behind. Never mind that new divisions were developing – that was for a future made all the more secure by the fact that nobody had the stomach for nuclear war. The rise of militant Islam, actually an ancient terror, was not yet front-page news. Wokery, with all its vicious no-platforming, was not yet the new Puritanism; it was still rather silly political correctness, focused, like most insane ideas, on America's West Coast.

In St Swithin's, Lower Quinton's church, the congregation was dwindling, as it had been all over Britain for decades. The Royal Engineers, with their long links to nearby Long Marston, had a stained-glass window dedicated to them and bought by them. The organ was moved to the west end of the vestry. Farms in the area were happy to operate under subsidies from the Common Agricultural Policy of the EU. Key people in the case of Charles Walton were dead; the Potters and most of the farmers who knew them; the policemen who had given it their all. The Warwickshire Constabulary, along with all others in the country, were now a 'service' rather than a 'force' and the enormity of the change of terminology had yet to sink in. One thing was certain; they did not make coppers like Bob Fabian and Alec Spooner any more.

In that year of 1999, a trial was held, first at Winchester Crown Court, then at Birmingham, which I believe had echoes of what happened under the shadow of Meon Hill all those years before. Christopher Thomas, described in the still old-fashioned terminology as a labourer, lived in Newport, Isle of Wight. His was an unhappy childhood and he spent much of it in a variety of children's homes. It was in these years, at the age of 11, that he was first sexually abused by Edwin Wilcox, of Ryde, described in court as 'scruffy, eccentric, a promiscuous homosexual with a criminal record.'

We do not know what happened to Thomas between the ages of 16 and 33, but by that time (January 1998) Thomas had seen his former abuser in a fish and chip shop and he lured him into his car. Presumably, Wilcox assumed that the sexual encounters would continue that evening (he was now 64); otherwise, why consent to go anywhere with Thomas? They drove to Culver Point, a headland in the east of the island with a

200ft drop to the sea. 'I dragged him to the cliff edge,' Thomas admitted to the court. 'The intention to do the deed didn't come until right at the very end.' Thomas felled Wilcox with a karate chop and jumped on his chest with both feet before 'folding' him over the fence and kicking him over the cliff's edge. His body was never found.

The first trial, at Winchester, collapsed because the volatile Thomas sacked his barrister and tried to defend himself. At one point, he lost his composure and screamed at a prosecution witness before flinging his papers across the court. 'It's my life you're messing up – you make me puke,' the *Daily Echo* reported. The judge, Mrs Justice Smith, adjourned the case and it was transferred to Birmingham before the same judge. When the jury found Thomas guilty, she said, 'You still think, still express the view that you have done society a good turn by removing Wilcox and it appears that you hold the opinion that because you were sexually abused by him you had a right to take his life.'

Thomas's new counsel, Malcolm Gibney, pointed to the failure of the system which did so little to help the Christopher Thomases of this world. The killer was sentenced to life, even though there was no body to prove murder. 'I asked him,' Thomas had said to Wilcox in those last moments, 'whether he believed in God. He said "Yes" and I told him to say a prayer. He just asked Christ to die for him and that was it.' There had been no remorse on Wilcox's part; no contrition for the other six boys he admitted to abusing. And on that wild, wet January night, Thomas drove home and 'had a good night's sleep'.

Is that, or something like it, what happened under the shadow of Meon Hill in February 1945? I believe it was. Edwin Wilcox had convictions for importuning; Charles Walton did not. Views of him varied enormously, but I was struck by the comments of an old Lower Quinton resident interviewed on an amateur website. He remembered the village as it was in the 1940s before the arrival of the new housing estates and 'wellness' centres. And he remembered the fact that children were afraid of old Charlie Walton. No one else has mentioned this. Was it merely because he was an old man who walked with a stick and talked to the birds? Or was there something altogether more sinister? Was Charles Walton indeed 'up to something queer' as Donald McCormick's police informant hinted in the 1960s? The old man kept to himself. He was never seen in the village pubs. He had lived all his life quietly under the radar. A tiny cohort of other men were described as his friends. He went walking with one of them, George Higgins, on Sundays. But what if he targeted children, boys in particular, over the time he lived in Lower Quinton? What if one of those boys was the 'Smith' that Donald McCormick wrote about and the abuse that he had endured, never confided to anybody, festering under the surface, had suddenly boiled over that day at Hillground in the unusually mild February of 1945? Christopher Thomas had seen Edwin Wilcox in a fish and chip shop and it brought back all the old memories, the old pain and the fear.

And there, alone in the middle of nowhere, was Charles Walton, 'Smith's' abuser. Was this the moment to confront him, as Thomas had done with Wilcox? To force him to apologize, to atone somehow for what he had done? And did Walton read the signs the wrong way, as I believe Wilcox had with Thomas? The Isle of Wight man got into Thomas's car because he expected sex, a continuation of what had happened before, the sole purpose of the two men's relationship. Is that why Charles Walton's trousers were undone, his flies open? Walton would have glanced around. There was no one visible on the slopes of Meon Hill and the hedge he was working on screened them from the village. What an opportunity after what may have been a gap of months or even years.

But that was not what 'Smith' had come for. He snapped, as Thomas would over fifty years later, grabbed the old man's walking stick leaning against the hedge. This was not a planned attack, not a premeditated crime, and the killer used the weapons that came to hand. He spat insults, no doubt, and bashed Walton around the head. The old man's hands came up to defend himself, leaving the wounds that Webster found, but he was no match for 'Smith'. He collapsed to the ground and 'Smith' grabbed the pitchfork. The old man was still struggling, his head bleeding and his trousers undone. 'Smith' had to hold him still, so he rammed the tines of the fork into Walton's throat, driving the steel into his jaw and neck and the ground beneath them. He wrenched the implement's rough handle down and back so that the hedge itself held Walton still. But the old man was still gurgling, still moving. Smith snatched up the billhook and hacked at the man's throat, paying him back with each frenzied stroke, exorcising the hurt, killing the demon. Then he stopped, no doubt breathing heavily, shocked and possibly appalled by what he had done. He looked down. His jacket was sprayed with Walton's blood and he could not just wander back through the village like that in broad daylight. He saw Walton's knapsack, the one that Charlotte Byway told the police he was carrying that morning and he stripped off the jacket and bundled it into the bag.

Six hundred yards away, on his way to Cacks Leys to check on his calves, Alfred Potter saw him, in his shirtsleeves now, and assumed it was Walton. Who else would be standing by the hedge but the old man who was working there? What puzzled Potter was the fact that Walton appeared to be in his shirtsleeves, whereas the old man always wore his jacket. He could not see the old man's body, lying in the shadow of the hedge, behind 'Smith's' legs.

And perhaps young Basil Hall saw 'Smith', too. If he was wrong about the time – a man on his own driving a tractor in the fields, probably without a watch – then the man he saw by a hedge, looking towards the village, might well have been Charlie Walton's killer.

But the police put their own gloss on all this. Hall had given the time as three o'clock, a full hour after Professor Webster's estimated time of death, so the man Hall saw could have no significance. In fact, according to Fabian, Hall was not even sure of the day! And as for Potter, he was sullen and taciturn, exhibiting, according to PC Lomasney, a shifty attitude; Potter was a guilty man trying to muddy the waters and deflect attention from himself. His testimony could be ignored, too.

What about Walton's finances? Several commentators on the case have followed Fabian's lead that the old man had lent money to Alfred Potter on the grounds that the farmer was not always on time with his payments. It was a quarrel over the repayment of this debt that led to Walton's death. This is to misunderstand the dynamics of village politics. Even in the 1940s, there was a strict hierarchy about such places. Alfred Potter was a landowner with status in the community. He was not exactly 'the squire' but he was not far below that. Charles Walton was an old labourer, a part-time worker from a lower class. It would be unthinkable for Potter to go cap-in-hand to such a man, however strapped he might be. Why should he, when he was part of a family business concern which owned other farms in the area, as well as the lucrative Lygon Arms in Chipping Campden? Why not go to his father or his brothers to tide him over a difficult time? And can we really believe that Charles Walton would not have mentioned this little loan to anyone? There was no hint to his cronies, nothing to Edith.

And I believe he said nothing to Edith because the disappearance of the money he had inherited from Alice, his wife, had trickled out over time in blackmail money. Somebody knew about Charles Walton and the old man was paying them to keep quiet. In terms of Alfred Potter what did it matter if he owed money? In terms of Charles Walton, if he were a predatory homosexual twenty years before the law changed to allow sex between consenting adults, that is something 'queer' that he would definitely want to keep to himself.

Who was the enigmatic 'Smith'? There are no less than twenty-five Smiths on St Swithin's tombstones, nine of them men. The register of Quinton National School, between 1883 and 1902, also has nine Smiths. Sergeant Hinksman of the Warwickshire police found fox snares along hedges near the crime scene and these were tied to three 17-year-olds, one of whom was Francis Smith. Here we have a teenager, a particularly vulnerable age-group in the context of predatory homosexuality who quite possibly had grown up in Upper or Lower Quinton and had known Charles Walton all his life. He lived at 21 Friday Street, in the road that runs behind Walton's cottage. The fox snares he had set were just yards from the murder scene. If anyone had seen young Francis walking the fields on 14 February 1945, who would have found that remotely odd? He was just checking on his snares. He had told Hinksman that he had not done so for several weeks; but we only have his word for that. And if anyone had seen him carrying a knapsack, who would have assumed it had anything in it but his snaring equipment? It is highly unlikely that this lad, the schoolboy turned electrician, is the man we are looking for. Surely, had he been abused, he would have said something to his friends Thomas Russell and Geoffrey Sheppard. Reporting Walton to the authorities may have been a step too far, but *somebody* would have known something.

Neither could Francis Smith have been the violent young man who attacked a couple at a local garage. If he had been, he would have a criminal record and all kinds of warning lights would be flashing in the minds of Sergeant Hinksman, who interviewed him and Chief Inspector Fabian, who read all the reports.

Records show that Francis Laughton Smith of Lower Quinton, died in Atherstone-on-Stour, 4 miles away, in 1945, which fits Donald McCormick's Smith who left home 'a few weeks after the Walton murder. Later his body was found. He had gassed himself and a verdict of suicide was returned.' The records imply that there is a headstone to Francis Smith in St Mary's churchyard at Atherstone, but my enquiries to the vicar produced the confusing information that there are no such headstones there now and as far as he knew, there had never been interments in the churchyard.

The 17-year-old who gave a statement to the police is listed as Francis *E.* Smith and the Atherstone records do not give us the age of the man who may, or may not, be buried there. The only other Smith mentioned in the police records is Sonny Smith, who was involved in recovering Potter's dead heifer from the Doomsday ditch on the day of the murder. If he was interviewed by the police, there is no record of the statement now and nothing is known about him.

So the 'Smith' referred to by Donald McCormick does not exist, any more than Camp 6's rat-catcher was ever a serious person of interest to the police. The 'fantasy historian' has effectively invented the belligerent young man who appears nowhere in the police files, other than Ernest Roy Smith, whom Alec Spooner rather belatedly (1948) came to believe might have some knowledge of the crime. If McCormick was fed this titbit from the records by his police informant, he may have assumed that Ernest Roy was in the frame while enquiries were actually under way in 1945.

Even allowing for the fact that he cannot identify 'Smith' and that he may have had a different name altogether, is this why the villagers of Lower and Upper Quinton were so secretive? If Charles Walton kept his proclivities hidden, very few people would know about them. The tiny handful who did, perhaps his old friend George Higgins, one or two more, would be disgusted. Higgins had had a falling out with Walton three months before he was killed; who knew what that was about? And in that climate and at that time, did those who knew close ranks? They did not want to ruin a young man's life as Charlie Walton had tried to do. They would say nothing, especially when the police came calling. Look back at Laurie Lee's take on this in this book's Introduction.

Some people reading this book will no doubt find my conclusion distasteful. How can I accuse Charles Walton of a crime and 'Smith' of another one when I have no evidence against them? Bob Fabian had no evidence against Alfred Potter either, but that did not stop him from hounding the man and naming him in internal police papers. I believe he came within a whisker of being charged. Neither is there the remotest evidence that Walton had any connection whatsoever with witchcraft; but that has not stopped thousands of people worldwide pointing the finger and stating openly that he had. In fact, *every single* account of the Meon Hill murder has this at its core.

Look at the internet today and you will find dozens of websites devoted to the case. Mysterious Universe, Mikestillalive, White Dragon, Horror History, Mysteries of Mercia, Reasoned Crime Chronicle, Controversial.Com, Reddit, Coolingintereststuff, Vivaldo, C.R. Berry, Fullybooked, Paranormal, Blurryphotos, The Aged P, Morbidology, Horus Behdety, Unexplained Mysteries, Me Time For the Mind, Histverse, Fortean Times, Hellogiggles … at that point, I ran screaming out of the room! One or two of these try to adopt a rational approach, as I hope I have in this book, but they are quickly swamped by the nonsensical and the absurd.

The coppers involved in the case would not have recognized much of this. At best, they would have shaken their heads and tutted at the myriad mistakes and assumptions online.

Alfred Potter, the only man in Fabian's frame, had died in 1961. Neither he nor his wife, Lilian, have marked graves. If he *was* a killer, he effectively got away with murder, not the first or last example of that. Two years after Charles Walton died, Alec Spooner solved a case in Radford Semele, near Leamington Spa, easily the bloodiest in the village's history. It was, to be fair, open and shut, in which a mild-mannered man, Fred Ashby, finally snapped after years of physical abuse from his son, then home on leave from the RAF. 'I did it,' Ashby told PC Harris, the first bobby on the scene, 'I shot him.' Ashby pleaded guilty to manslaughter and served ten years.

Two years after that, Spooner had another straightforward case on his hands. On Tuesday, 25 January 1949, 19-year-old Gordon Towle walked into Leamington Spa Police Station, then in the High Street and handed over a Sten gun. 'I have shot a man,' he said. 'I am ill.' He had been taunted by a colleague for not having served in the war – 'my head went funny and I shot him.' Towle was found to be insane and Spooner's involvement in the case was straightforward. The only unanswered question this time was – where did the Sten gun come from?

In the meantime, Spooner had arrested a gang of car thieves so large that a special assize court had to be held in Warwick.

'Super Spooner' was transferred to Nuneaton in 1959 as divisional superintendent. He retired five years later and worked in security, as many ex-coppers did, for the National Coal Board. He died in December 1970. His obituaries in local papers called him 'the CID's witchcraft hunt man', but five years later, the *Coventry Evening Telegraph* reported a local who said about the Walton case – 'it's time they closed the book.'

Albert Webb, as we have seen, was made inspector in the weeks after the Met bowed out of the Walton case. Undoubtedly, his most high-profile success came four years later when he secured the conviction of one of Britain's most notorious killers, John George Haigh, the acid bath murderer. A narcissistic sociopath brought up by Plymouth Brethren parents, Haigh morphed from angelic choirboy to petty thief, fraudster and finally killer.

By the time Webb was working on the Walton case, Haigh had already claimed his first victim, caving in the skull of William McSwan before dumping his body in a 40-gallon drum of sulphuric acid. Six months after Meon Hill, he disposed of McSwan's parents in the same way. Other victims followed, but it was the murder of Olive Durand-Deacon in February 1949 that led to his undoing. He was well educated, but had the mistaken belief that *corpus delicti* meant a missing body and if that was the case (his victims dissolved in acid) then he had no case to answer. In fact, Mrs Durand-Deacon's teeth survived the sulphuric acid and Webb charged Haigh with murder.

'Tell me frankly,' the killer said to Webb, 'what are the chances of anybody being released from Broadmoor?' Haigh claimed to be a vampire killer, drinking his victim's blood from a wine glass, in an attempt to cheat the hangman. It did not work. The jury took fifteen minutes to find him guilty and he was hanged by Albert Pierrepoint at Wandsworth prison in August 1949.

But it was Robert Fabian who outshone them all. It must have rankled that Charles Walton's killer was never caught by him or anyone else. That did not deter him, however, from finding a fame that was possibly unique. Apart from his three books, in which he wanders further from the truth as time goes on, he is usually credited with being the country's first television detective. Actually, he was the country's *only* television detective and it may be that someone in the corridors of power decided that introducing *actual* policemen to the screen, large or small, was perhaps not a good idea. He waited until he retired from the Met as superintendent, in 1949, before he took to writing. Based on *Fabian of the Yard*, a television series aired between 1954 and 1956, as the obsession with the witchcraft angle of Meon Hill erupted. It began on a Saturday-night slot and starred actor Bruce Seton as the trilby-hatted, trench-coated detective who had routinely cracked cases using 'detail, science and tenacity'. Fabian was no actor but he appeared for two minutes at the end of each half-hour episode, talking to camera. The programme sold to America, where it was subtitled 'Patrol Car'. Fabian went on to become quizmaster in the radio show *The $64,000 Question* and once appeared, as a sort of national treasure, on *Desert Island Discs*, explaining his favourite music.

It may be that the Fabian series was a deliberate antidote to *Scotland Yard*, narrated by the crime expert Edgar Lustgarten, although these were first shown in cinemas, not television. That series purported to cover real crimes in which the Met was involved, but few of them bore any relation to the real thing, using aliases and fictional policemen. Fabian died in Epsom in 1978, no nearer solving Charles Walton's murder than he had been in the spring of 1945.

The problem for Fabian had always been Quinton's wall of silence. 'Cottage doors were shut in our faces and even the most innocent witnesses seemed unable to meet our eyes.' In one instance, when the police had been waiting all day to interview a local, he turned up and Fabian introduced himself – 'I'm enquiring about the late Charles Walton …' but the witness interrupted him, 'He's been dead and buried a month now – what are you worrying about?' and he shut the door.

Perhaps old Charlie Walton, and certainly today's inhabitants of Lower and Upper Quinton, deserve better.

Bibliography

Begg, Paul and Skinner, Keith, *The Scotland Yard Files,* Headline, 1992

Bloom, Rev. J. Harvey, *Folk Lore, Old Customs and Superstitions in Shakespeare Land,* Mitchell Hughes and Clarke, 1929

Calder, Angus, *The People's War*, Pimlico, 1969

Domesday Book, Alecto Historical Editions (Penguin) 2003

Dunwich, Gerina, *A–Z of Wicca,* Boxtree, 1998

Eddleston, John J., *The Encyclopaedia of Executions,* John Blake, 2002

Fabian, Robert, *Fabian of the Yard,* Heirloom Modern World Library, 1955

Fabian, Robert, *London After Dark,* The Naldrett Press, 1954

Fabian, Robert, *The Anatomy of Crime,* Pelham Books, 1970

Fairlie, Gerard, *The Reluctant Cop,* Hodder and Stoughton, 1958

Fido, Martin and Skinner, Keith, *The Official Encyclopaedia of Scotland Yard,* Virgin, 1999

Goodall, Felicity, *Voices from the Home Front,* David and Charles, 2006

Hatherill, George, *A Detective's Story,* Andre Deutsch, 1971

Holland, Clive, *Warwickshire,* Adam and Charles Black, 1912

Lazarus, Richard, *Unnatural Causes,* Futura, 1991

Leamington and Shakespeare's Warwickshire, Ward Lock, 1941

Lee, Laurie, *Cider With Rosie,* Bracken Books, 1984/1959

Linnane, Fergus, *London's Underworld,* Robson Books, 2003

Manual of Police Training (West Yorks Constabulary) 1938

McDermid, Val, *Forensics: The Anatomy of Crime,* Profile Books, 2015

Morley, George, *Warwick and Leamington,* Blackie and Sons

Murder Casebook (Vol 71), Marshall Cavendish, 1991

Murray, Margaret, *My First Hundred Years,* William Kimber, 1963

Murray, Margaret, *The God of the Witches,* Faber and Faber, 1931

Murray, Margaret, *The Witch-Cult in Western Europe,* Clarendon Press, 1921

Newman, Paul, *Under the Shadow of Meon Hill,* Abraxas ad DGR, 2009

Parish Church of St Swithin, Quinton

Picknett, Lynn, *The Encyclopaedia of the Paranormal,* Guild Publishing, 1990

Science Against Crime, Marshall Cavendish, 1982

Summers, Montague, *History of Witchcraft and Demonology,* Kegan Paul, 1926

Taylor, Bernard and Knight, Stephen, *Perfect Murder,* Grafton, 1987

Various, *Folklore Myths and Legends of Britain,* Reader's Digest, 1973

Wilson, Colin, *Murder in the 1940s,* Carroll and Graf, 1993

Winder, Robert, *Bloody Foreigners,* Abacus Books, 2004

Index